THE SACRED LANDMARKS SERIES

Michael J. Tevesz, Editor

Revelations: Photographs of Cleveland's African American Churches

MICHAEL STEPHEN LEVY

The Sacred Landmarks Series includes both works of scholarship and general interest titles that preserve the history and increase understanding of religious sites, structures, and organizations in northeast Ohio, the United States, and around the world.

REVELATIONS

Photographs of Cleveland's African American Churches

Michael Stephen Levy

Published in cooperation with Cleveland State University's Maxine Goodman Levin College of Urban Affairs' Center for Sacred Landmarks

THE KENT STATE UNIVERSITY PRESS   KENT, OHIO

Cleveland State University
Maxine Goodman Levin College of Urban Affairs
Center for Sacred Landmarks

Published in cooperation with Cleveland State University's Maxine Goodman Levin College of Urban Affairs' Center for Sacred Landmarks

Library of Congress Catalog Card Number 2008001520
ISBN 978-0-87338-937-2
Manufactured in China

The following photographs were taken for a photo assignment for the *Cleveland Plain Dealer: Funeral for Mervyn Jones Sr.* (2003), *The Bird Flies* (left; 2003), *Two Funerals* (2005, 2006), *The Baptism of the Glenville High School Football Team* (2005), *Rogue Service* (2004), *The Reverend Dr. Otis Moss Jr.* (2004), *Overall* (left; 2004), *Not Alone* (2005), *Too Close to Home* (left; 2005), *The Touching of a Young Man's Heart* (left; 2005), *The Reverend Huey Harris* (center; 2005).

LIBRARY OF CONGRESS CATALOGING-IN-PUBLICATION DATA
Levy, Michael S., 1960–
Revelations : photographs of Cleveland's African American churches / Michael Stephen Levy.
p. cm. — (Sacred landmarks series)
ISBN 978-0-87338-937-2 (hardcover : alk. paper) ∞
1. African American churches—Ohio—Cleveland—Pictorial works.
2. Sacred space—Ohio—Cleveland—Pictorial works.
3. Cleveland (Ohio)—Religious life and customs—Pictorial works.
I. Title.
BR563.N4L485 2008
277.71'3208308996073—dc22 2008001520

British Library Cataloging-in-Publication data are available.

12 11 10 09 08 5 4 3 2 1

I dedicate this book to my father, WILLIAM V. LEVY

CONTENTS

FOREWORD

The Honorable Stephanie Tubbs Jones
U.S. Congress (OH-11)

Lift up your heads, O you gates; be lifted up, you ancient doors, that the King of glory may come in.
—Psalms 24:7

Like many African Americans in this country, I grew up in the church. For me, it is a constant in a world that is ever changing. When things in my life are troubled, when my heart is heavy, when I want to thank the Lord for his grace and mercy, I go to church, and there I renew my faith and recharge my spirit.

My family's spiritual life was strong and steady. My parents impressed on me and my sisters the importance of church attendance, and regardless of how late we stayed out the night before, we would attend church in the morning. I recall well waking up and putting on my "Sunday best" and going, as a family, to worship. I remember the feeling of entering the Lord's house and being greeted by the ushers in their black suits, with fans in tow, and hearing the deacons gently humming in the front row and seeing the nurses in their crisp white dresses, the choir in colorful robes, and the pastor at the pulpit. Together we would recite the Lord's Prayer, and together we would sing "Ride on, King Jesus / No man cannot hinder thee!"

The church has long served as a rite of passage for many African Americans, the most significant moment being baptism. So many of us have stood, dressed in white, in the baptismal pool as our church families looked on with love and encouragement and then felt the sudden rush as the pastor submerged us and the water flowed over us. We share the recollection of emerging from those waters forever changed.

. . .

In *Revelations,* Mike Levy turns his camera toward Cleveland's black churches. His extraordinary photographs celebrate the people of Cleveland's African American houses of worship, which have weathered some of our country's most turbulent times, including the Great Depression, the civil rights movement, and times of civil unrest, including the Hough riots of the 1960s, and served as places of refuge and beacons of hope.

These pictures are intimate, deeply personal, capturing men and women in prayer and praise, in moments of great joy and intense grief. One photo included here was taken at the funeral of my beloved husband, Mervyn L. Jones Sr. Not only did Mr. Levy capture so achingly well our loss, but he managed to convey at the same time the sincere outpouring of love and respect for Mervyn and our family. When I see this picture I do not mourn. I reflect, instead, on how the church is one place where you know you are constantly surrounded by support, love, and prayer. No matter where the church is located, no matter what ornate fixtures adorn the church or how big or small, God is always present—and, as we were taught and as we know, God is love.

Through his lens, Mr. Levy captures the joy, sadness, soul, and spirit of the black church and moves us with photographs of quiet reflection, exuberant praise, and abiding fellowship. He enables *all* of us to see the strength of our elders and the power and promise of our young people—all gathered together in worship.

Those unfamiliar with the black church will gain insight into these pillars of the African American community. Those of us who grew up in the church will recognize, remember, reflect. Every reader will be moved.

God bless!

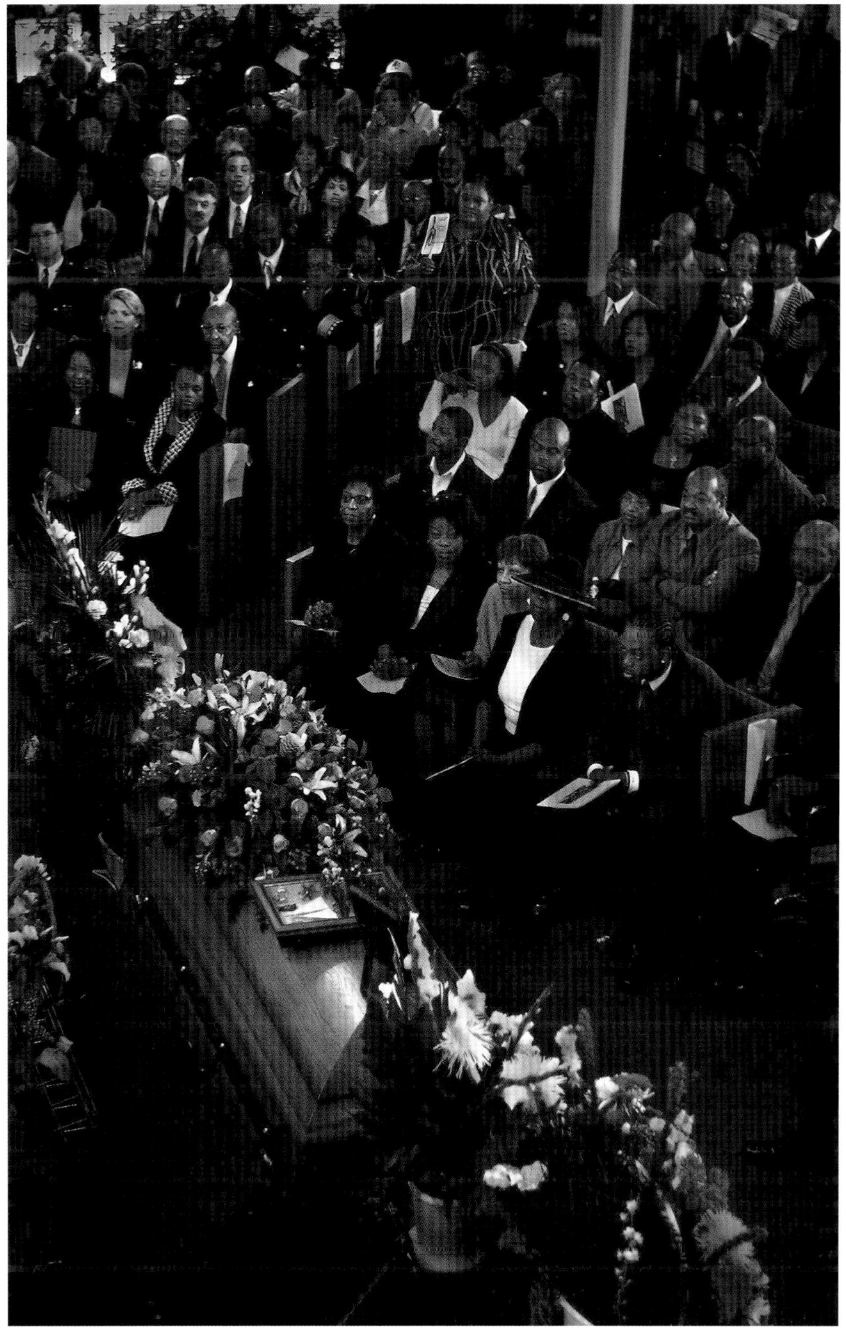

FUNERAL FOR
MERVYN L. JONES SR.
Bethany Baptist Church,
October 7, 2003

PREFACE

The black church project—my name for this body of work—began somewhat coincidentally when, in 2002, *Plain Dealer* photo assignment editor Richard Conway handed me a piece of paper and said, "See what you can do with this." The assignment read "photograph Manna House, 8201 Cedar Ave., Cleveland, for an Olivera Perkins story."

At the time I was a newspaper photojournalist and, mostly, shot for single images that told a story. Also during that time I was newly divorced from a twenty-year marriage (not to mention the college courtship) and was becoming painfully aware of an evolving and consuming mental illness. I had become isolated from the children I love more than anything in this world and was about to plummet into a depression that would result in psychiatric hospitalizations.

So I was in a state of distress when I took on this assignment. My thoughts were only of me, of my situation. I shot my first pictures at Manna House before and during a morning twelve-step meeting attended by a group of men, some of whom were homeless, some dealing with addiction, some newly released from the penal system. All of them were black. Yet there I was—Jewish, white male, suburban bred, college educated, professional, and owner of a three-car-garage home (and a mortgage to prove it). And I did not feel out of place. Before I had stepped into Manna House, I thought I was different from the men I was there to photograph. But when I left that morning, I knew I was no different. As Manna House pastor Frank Smith has told me many times, "If you come for help with your authentic self, not your projected idealized image, you have a place that will accept and help."

The following Sunday I attended a worship service, which was preceded by a warm breakfast of scrambled eggs, grits, biscuits, sausage, orange juice, and coffee, all lovingly prepared in their homey kitchen. After breakfast we all climbed the stairs to the small room that was the sanctuary of the Church of Recovery. Music was expertly produced on a small electronic keyboard and drum set. There was powerful sermonizing by Pastor Smith. People cried as they prayed. I was moved to tears. I witnessed and felt relief and hope.

I am Jewish, and I found healing at an African American church service. So, when people ask me, "Why did you choose African American churches as a concentration?" I say,

"Because they accepted me." These congregations and individuals allowed me to enter through their doors and photograph what I could see. And those opportunities at that time helped me to rediscover and nurture my own identity. Before I began each session, I silently prayed that as a documentarian I may be used as an instrument of the Lord of all Lords to do "His" work. I asked to be shown what I was meant to see. Then I stepped into the churches, the halls, the meeting rooms, the choir lofts and made photographs that were satisfying to me.

Over the course of this project, I was inside more than forty African American Christian churches in and around Cleveland, some large and prominent and others small and modest. I witnessed through my camera all means of worship by black Christians. Although I strove to be invisible when photographing, I interacted with the pastors and congregants before and after the services. At all times I was respectful of my surroundings and my subjects; I took pictures of church interiors only when permitted and obtained, whenever possible, individuals' permission to photograph them and include their images in this book.

I recognize that I have attempted the impossible—to photograph the intangible quality of faith—but in so doing have captured humans in the intimate act of trying to communicate with God.

I have been guided in my photography of black churches by the belief that there is a correlation between the African American experience and the Gospel of Jesus Christ, that suffering and hardship are inherent to the process of spiritual growth. The question that I will continue to ask myself until I understand the answer is "How can people affected by hardship continue to have faith?" What I have learned through this project—by watching, witnessing—is that faith enables people to persevere, endure. Privileged through this experience, I worked to capture an image of Cleveland's inner city, its African American community, that contrasts sharply with the bleak scenes, physical and economic, of so many Cleveland neighborhoods.

During this project I left newspaper journalism and began to look at my work, and hear my own voice, in a different way. I see now that although these images represent Christianity in the African American community, they also are evidence of my inner dialogue over the last five years. I was profoundly moved and fundamentally changed by this experience, artistically and spiritually. And I'm deeply grateful for the doors opened to me, the opportunities afforded me.

A NOTE ON THE PHOTOGRAPHS

To tell the story of the black churches, instead of using narrative text, I juxtaposed photographs, bleeding them together in order to create a "new," single image out of two separate pieces. In some instances it's the contrasts between two photographs that make for a revealing new image; in other cases it's recurrent images, themes, faces, colors, patterns. I was inspired to do this after reading psychology based on dialectic philosophy, which posits that if you really want to understand the truth of a matter, you must consider all facts, not just the ones you find convenient or comfortable; you must examine and accept the existence of both sides of the coin.

To make my pictures, I used a 35mm digital camera. And in order to not disturb the worship services, I did not use any supplemental lighting (like lamps or a flash).

The Gospel train's a-coming,
I hear it just at hand.
I hear the car wheels moving,
And rumbling through the land.

Get on board, little children,
Get on board, little children,
Get on board, little children,
There's room for many a more.

The fare is cheap and all can go,
The rich and poor are there,
No second class aboard this train,
No difference in the fare.

Get on board, little children,
Get on board, little children,
Get on board, little children,
There's room for many a more.

—Traditional

OPEN WINDOW

Eaglewing Missionary Baptist
Church, May 28, 2006

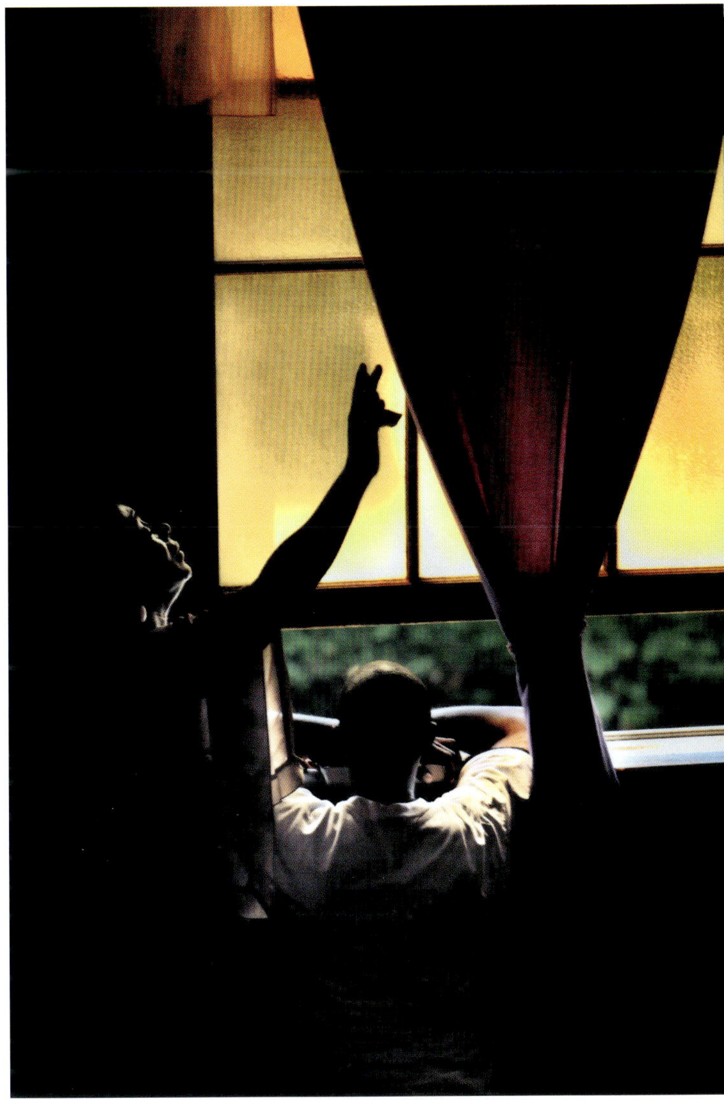
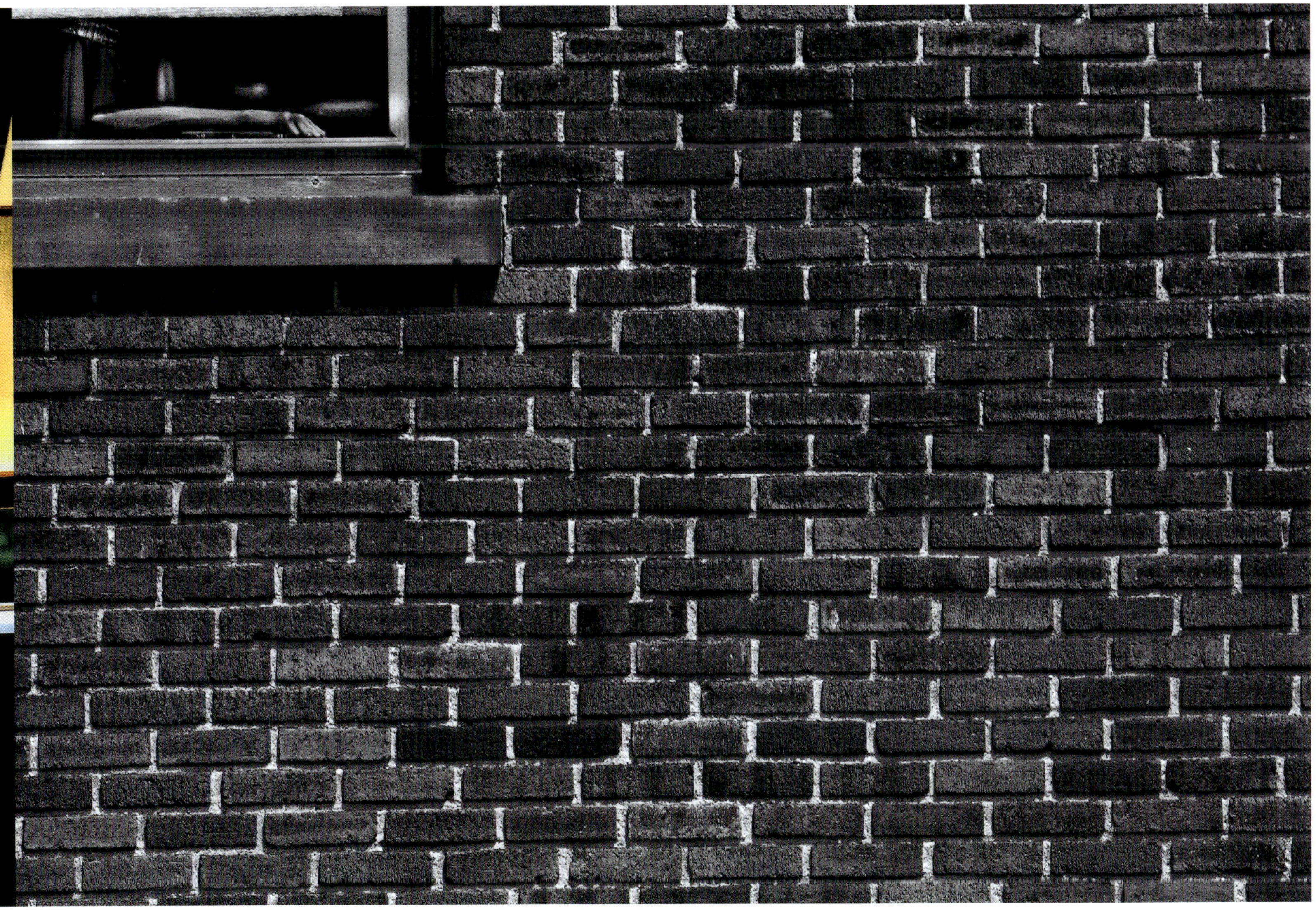

TRINITY

(Left) Noon Day Deliverance Nondenominational Church, Central Avenue, September 16, 2003. (Middle) Greater Mt. Tabor Missionary Baptist Church, October 10, 2003. (Right) Gospel Temple of Apostolic Church of God, October 27, 2003

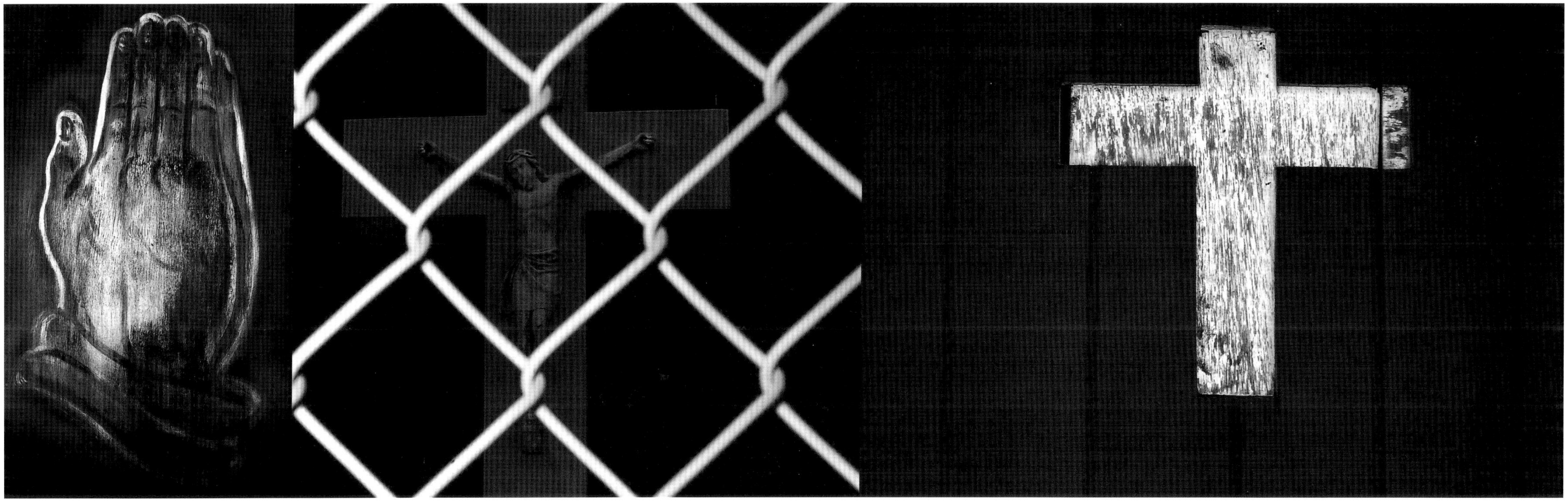

TOO CLOSE TO HOME, OR WHY WE PRAY

(Left) Playground at Outhwaite housing project, the scene of the fatal shooting of a boy, April 4, 2005. (Right) Friendship Baptist Church and Outhwaite housing project, February 5, 2006.

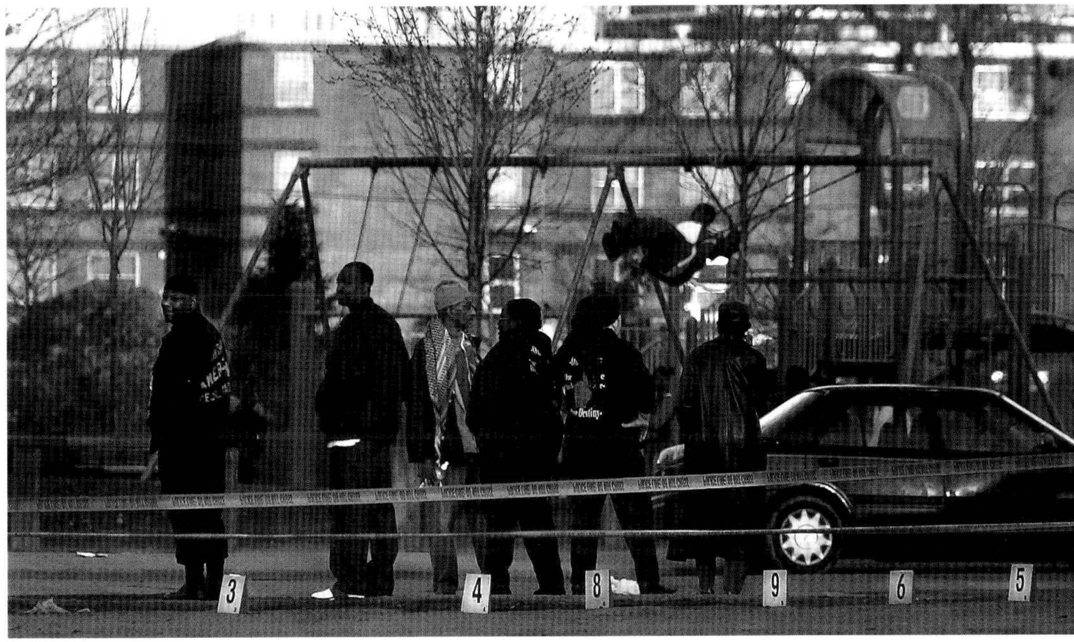
3
4
8
9
6
5

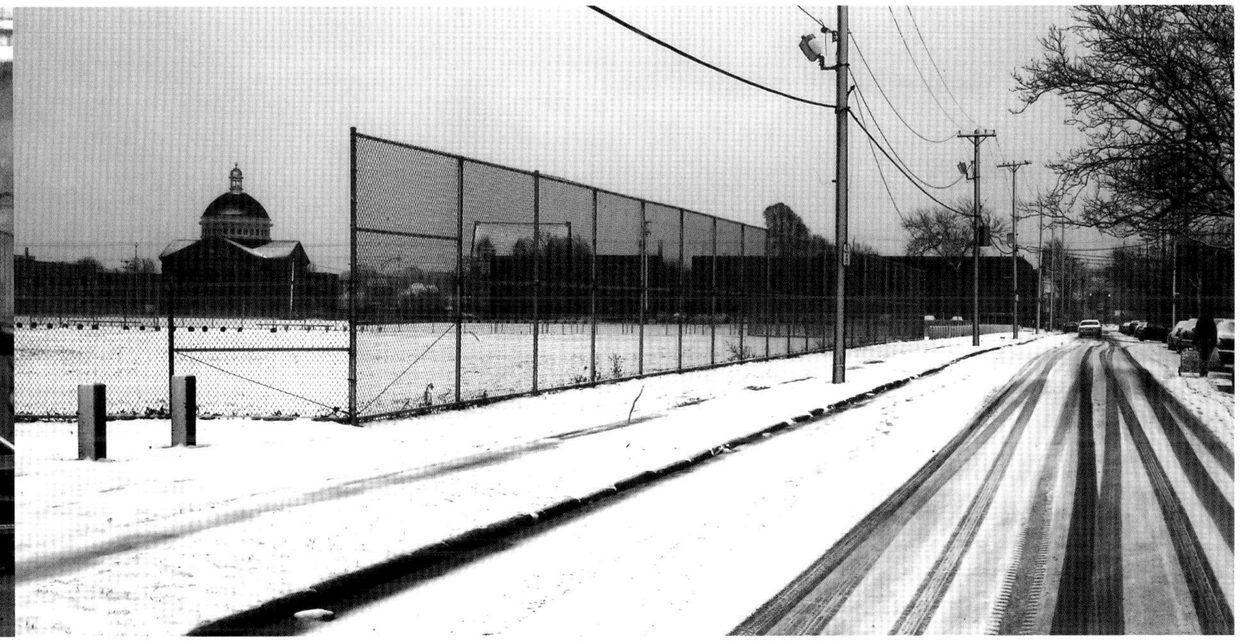

CHURCH

Antioch Baptist Church, July 22, 2006

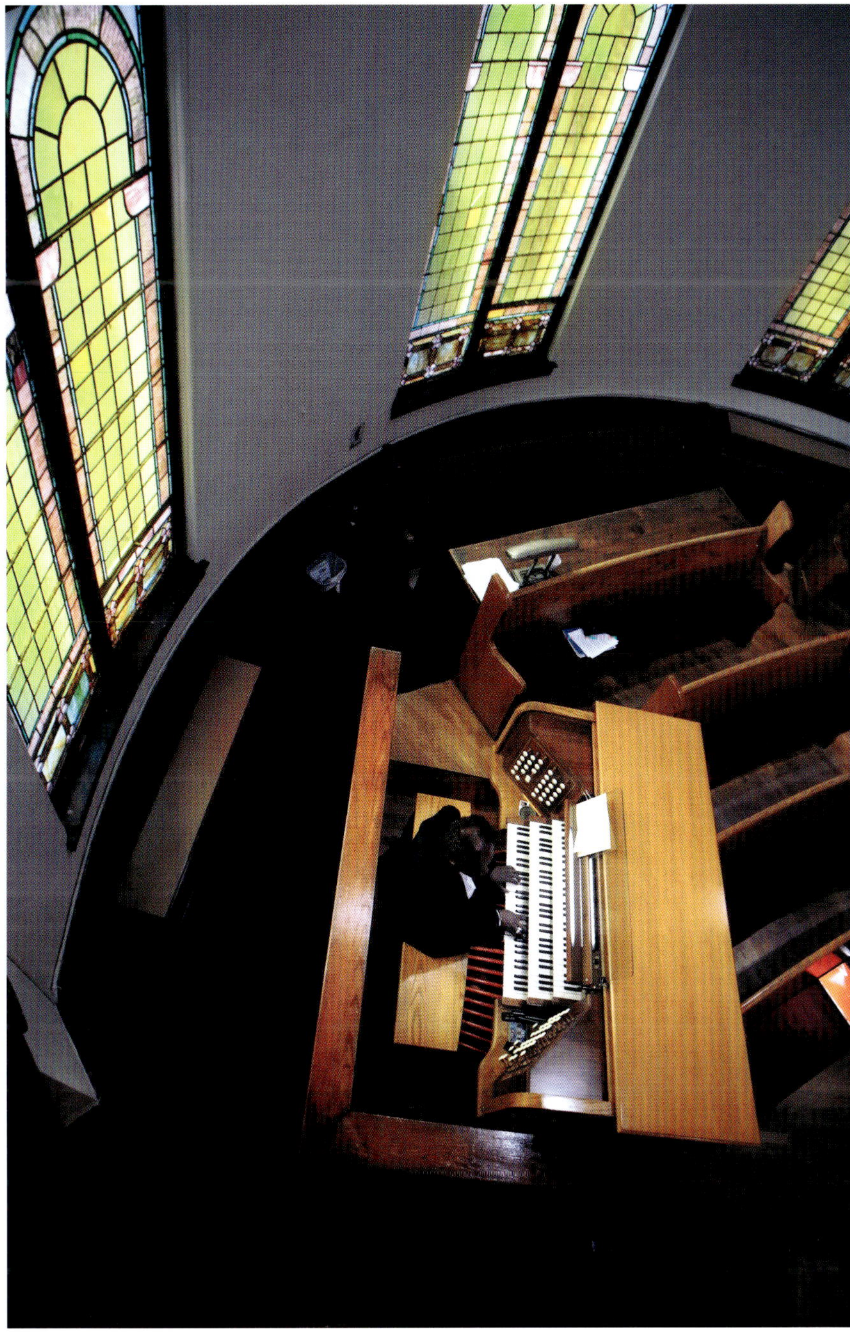

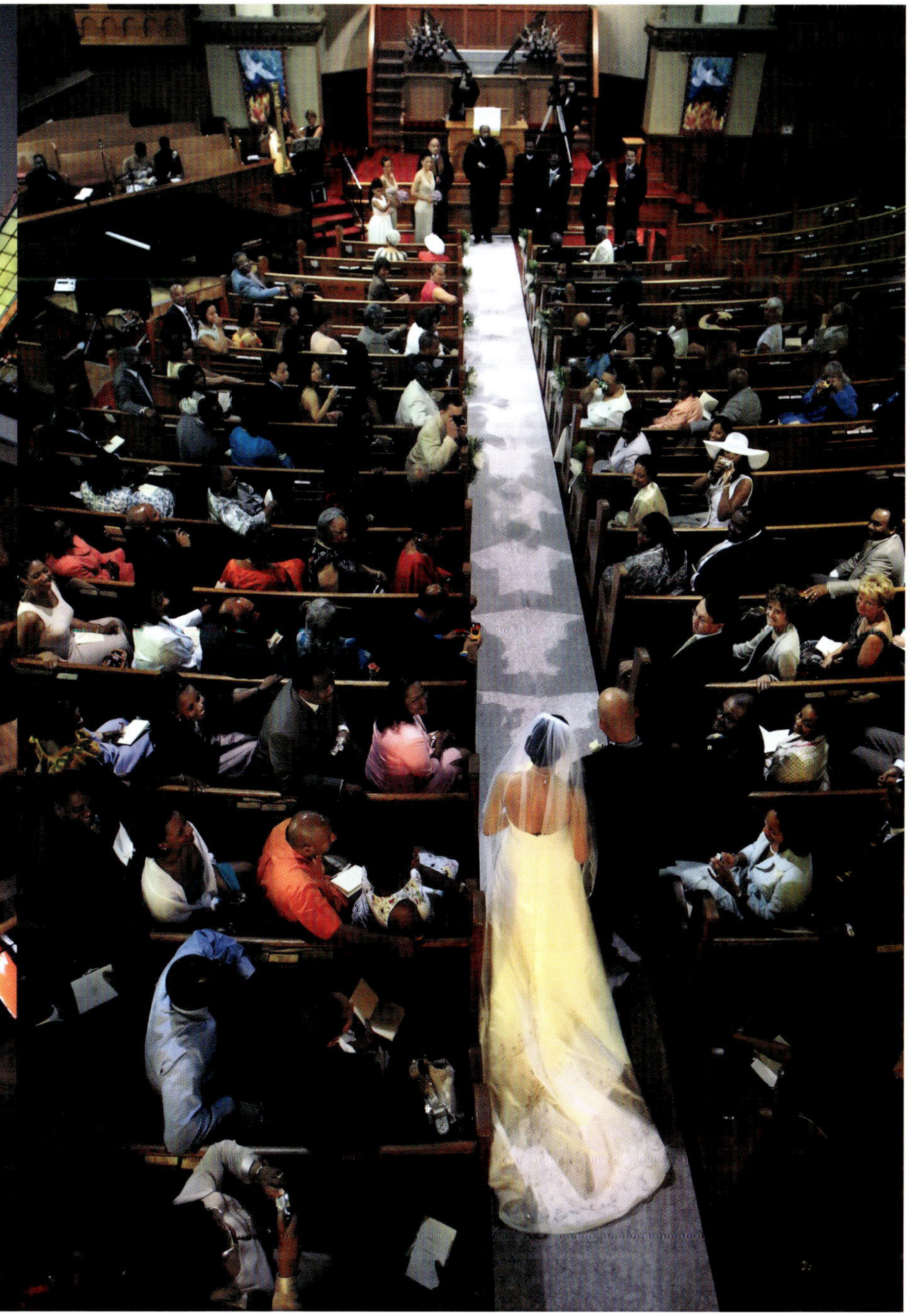

THE TOUCHING OF A YOUNG MAN'S HEART

(Left) Shiloh Baptist Church, January 25, 2005. (Right) Mt. Sinai Baptist Church, January 25, 2005

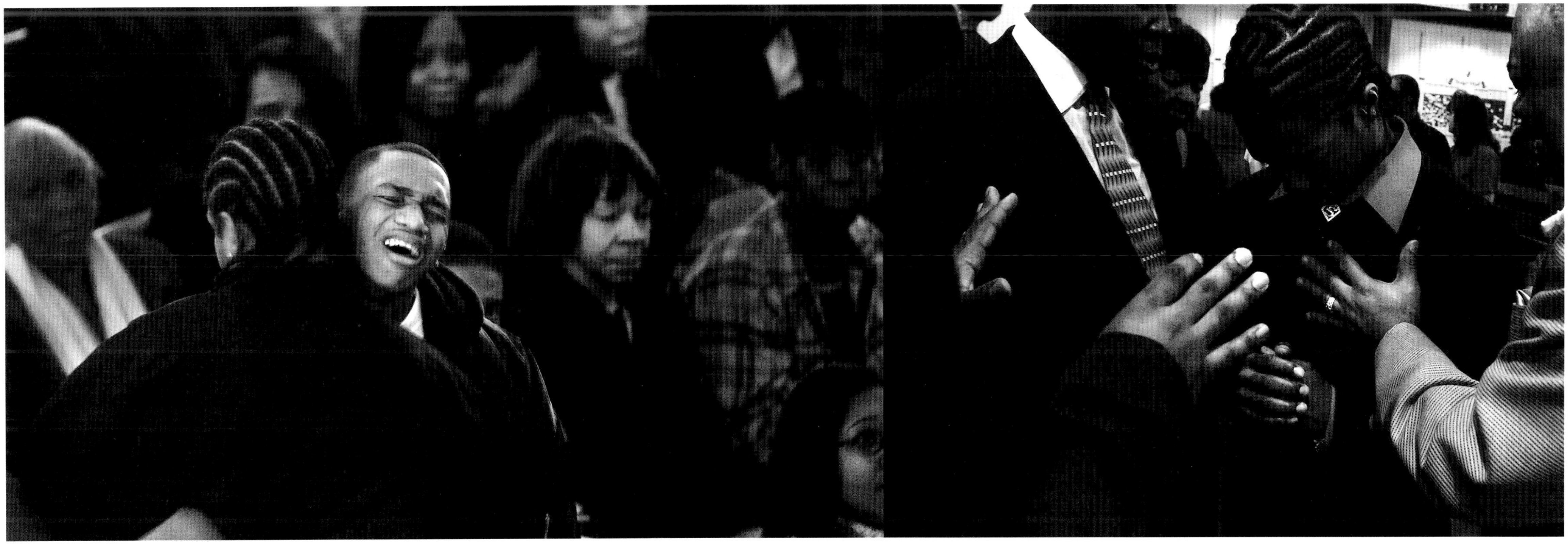

FOSTER

Windermere United Methodist Church, June 4, 2006

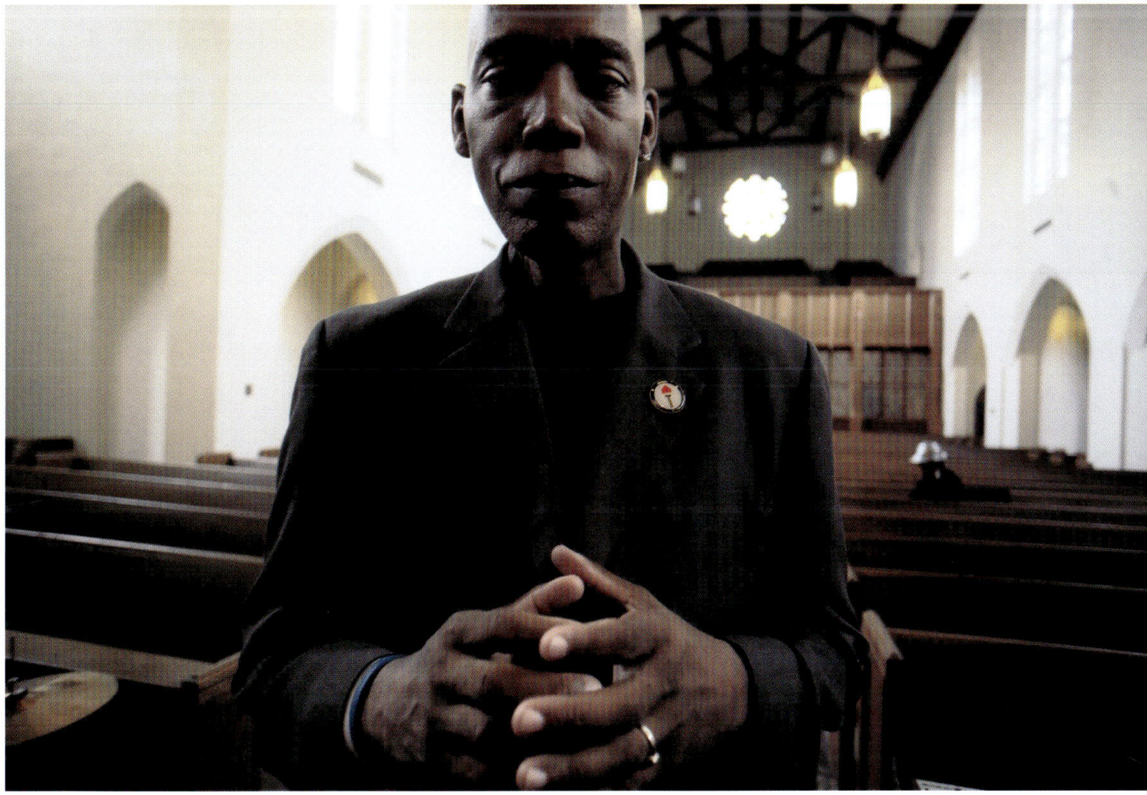
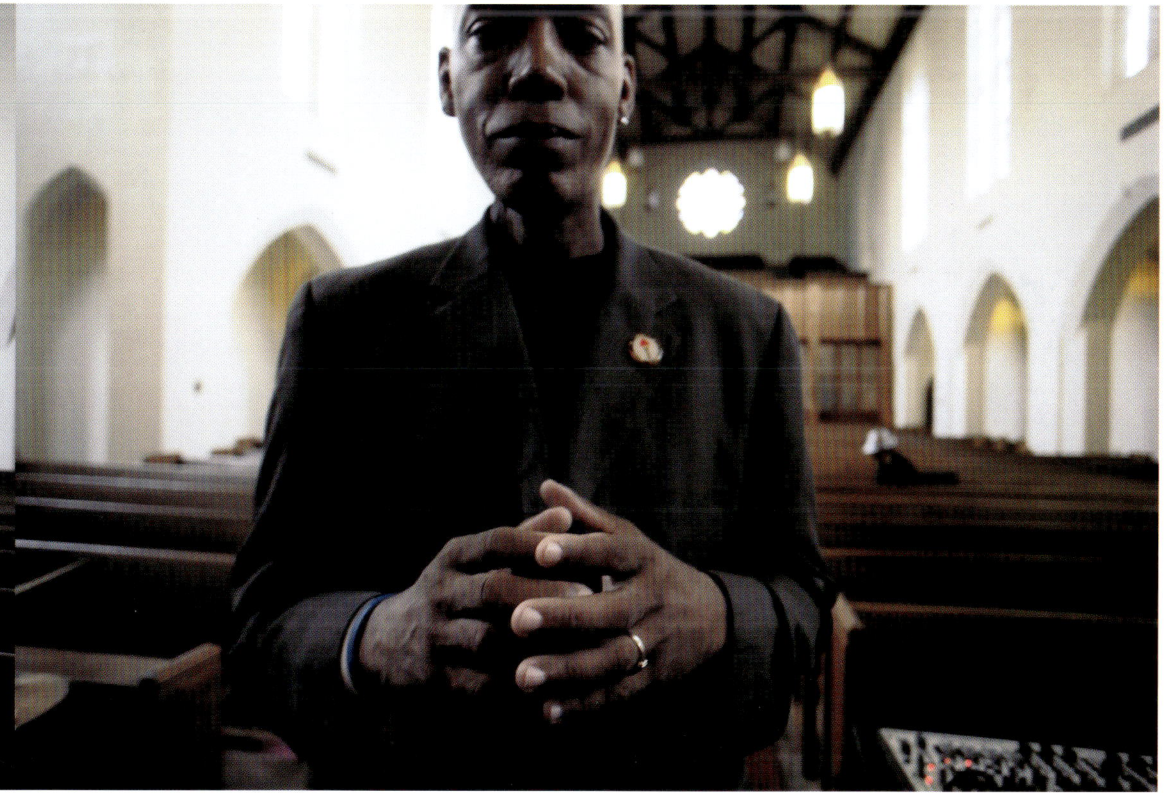

TWO CROSSES

(Left) Ebenezer Assembly of Christ, January 25, 2004. (Right) Eaglewing Missionary Baptist Church, May 28, 2006

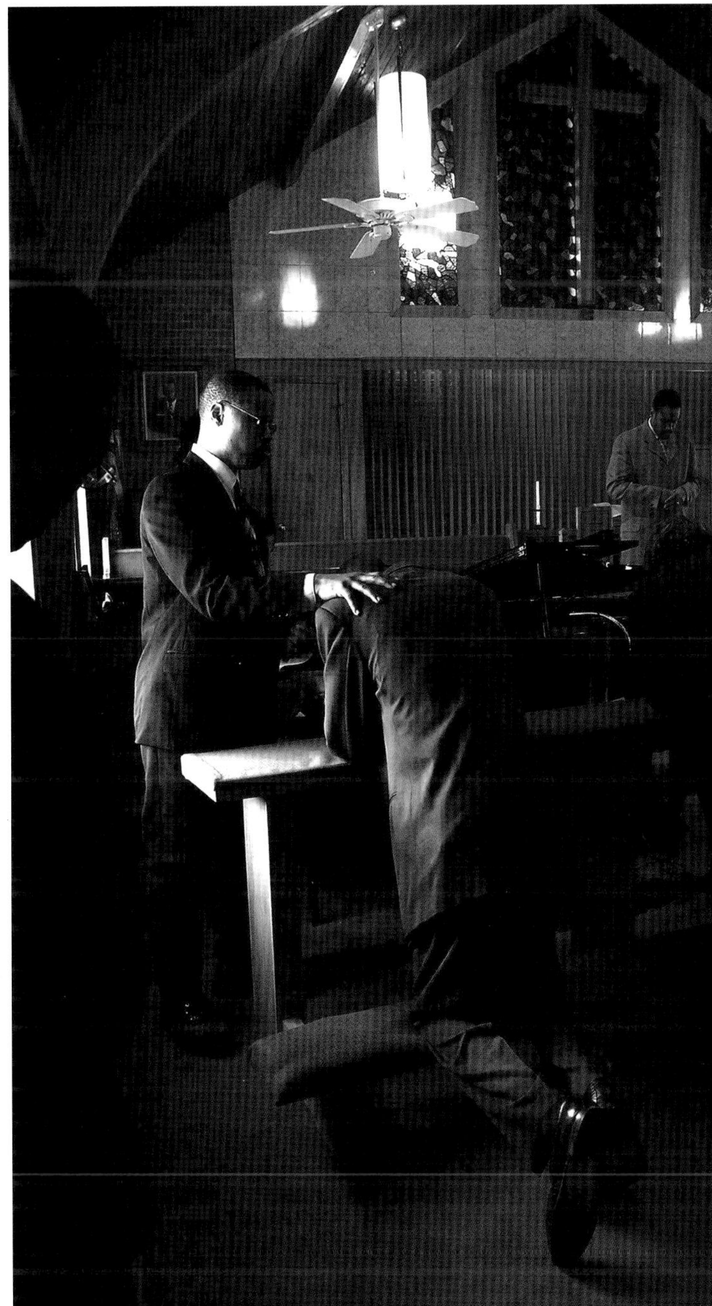
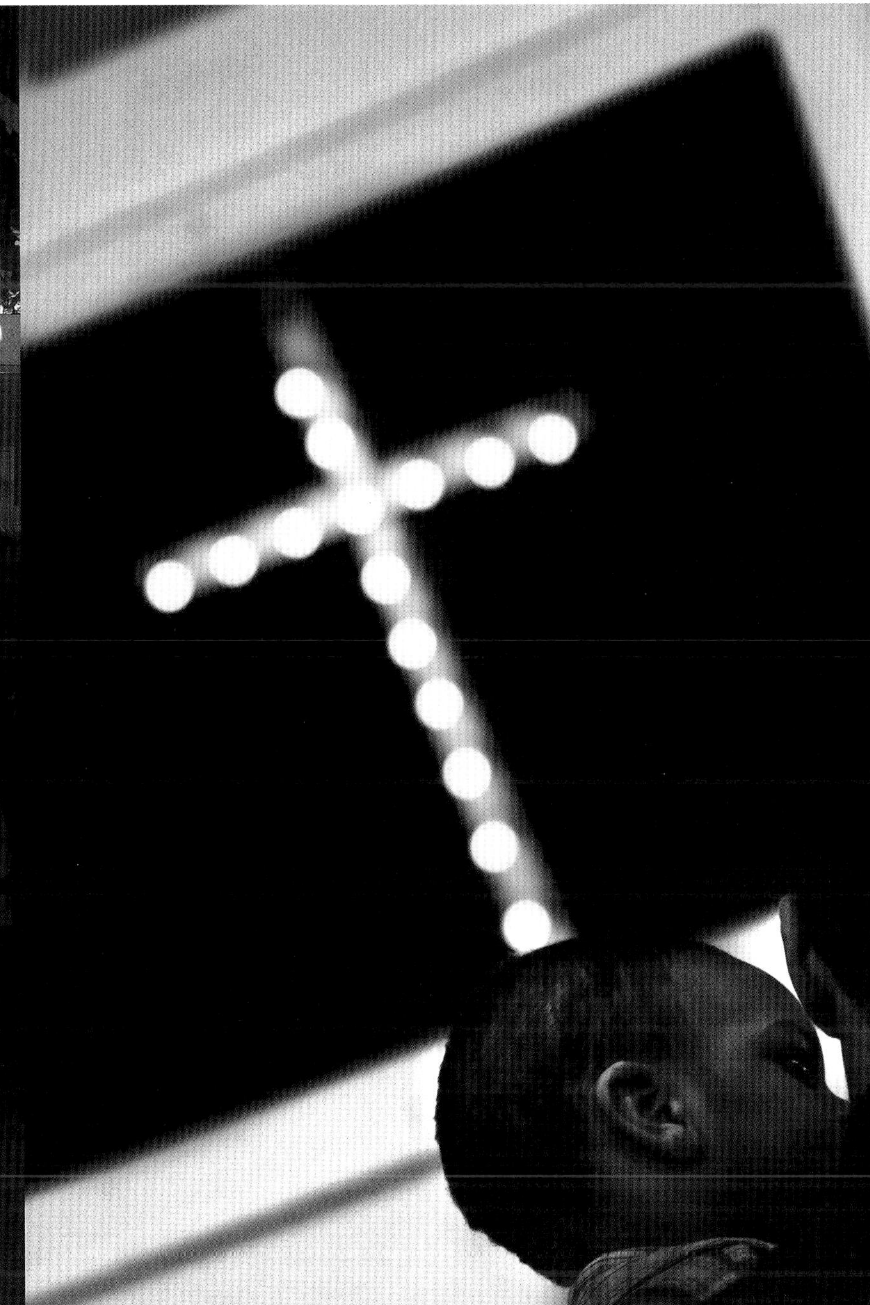

WHAT IS WORSHIP?

The Reverend Marvin A. McMickle

From the earliest days of the New Testament church in Jerusalem, worship has been the common thread that binds the believers together. Even though the people were different in terms of language, culture, religious background, and life experience, they became a community of faith when they joined together in several distinctive acts of worship that marked them as followers of Jesus Christ.

The first distinctive act is the regular observance of the Lord's Day: "Do not forsake the assembling of yourselves together" (Hebrews 10:25). Central to the life of a Christian is the weekly observance of the worship of God on the first day of the week in honor of the resurrection of Jesus from the dead. Weekly worship with other members of the believing community is the beginning of the Christian life; without that regular time of communal worship, the church cannot accomplish its evangelistic purpose.

The meaning of worship evolves out of the regular gathering of believers that was rooted in Old Testament Judaism. If you look at the synagogue service as described in Luke 4:16–21, you see a series of events that took place on a regular basis. It should not be surprising, therefore, that the order of worship in most Christian churches looks very much like the order of worship that was common in the synagogues of the first century A.D. There is a certain community (a congregation of believers) that meets on a certain day (Sunday and other times as needed) in a certain place (a sanctuary or other designated meeting place) to read from and study a certain book (the Bible) and to hear a sermon or lessons from a certain person (a preacher or designated leader). As with the synagogue, this standard weekly formula for worship is augmented by prayers, rituals, and hymns.

It is absolutely essential that every Christian be a part of this weekly time of spiritual renewal and focus. There are a great many distractions and temptations in the world that can challenge and undermine the faith of even the strongest and most devoted Christian. What helps to keep us focused and faithful during the week when we are *not* together are those times and acts of worship when we *are* together on the Lord's Day. In addition to reading and studying the Bible, which is the most important thing we can do as Christians, the other acts of worship that all Christians should observe include praying a variety of prayers, praising God in song, celebrating the Lord's Supper, performing the ordinance of baptism, and giving tithes and other offerings.

Worship should not be viewed primarily as a "how" question with the focus on the ways in which a particular person or a particular congregation goes about expressing themselves in the presence of God. Too many Christians waste too much time debating whether or not worship requires a certain amount of emotion or exuberance or whether they should employ a certain kind of music or whether the worship service should last for a precise period of time. All of these things are matters of formula that serve to regulate what happens when believers come together. But worship is not first and foremost a matter of formula; worship is a matter of faith. Therefore, the first question should never be "how" but "why"—Why should we worship, and why should we gear our lives around that weekly schedule of practices? Once a Christian has come face to face with the "why" of worship, the issue of "how" will take care of itself.

facing page
GOING TO CHURCH
Live Ministries/Church of Recovery, July 12, 2003

Christians worship God for two basic reasons: creation and redemption. We worship God as the architect and mainstay of the created order: "The earth is the Lord's and the fullness thereof; the world and they that dwell therein" (Psalm 24:1). We confess that everything that exists is the result of the handiwork of the God who reveals himself in the pages of the Bible, reminding ourselves that "without him nothing was made that has been made" (John 1:3). The great Christian hymn puts it well when it says

> O, Lord my God, when I in awesome wonder,
> Consider all the worlds they hands have made.
> I see the stars; I hear the rolling thunder;
> Thy power throughout the universe displayed.
> Then sings my soul, my savior, God to thee,
> How great thou art!

And as Christians we worship in response to God's work of redemption in Jesus Christ. We worship God because, as Philippians 2:5–11 reminds us, God's love for us caused him to take on human form in Jesus of Nazareth and take upon himself the penalty for all the sins of the whole world, sins that would have otherwise kept us from enjoying fellowship with God. On the cross at Calvary, Jesus freely offered up his life as an act of atonement (at-one-ment) so that anyone who puts their faith in him can find forgiveness for their sins, new fellowship with God, abundant life in this world, and eternal life with God beyond death. That is the marvelous message of John 3:16: "God so loved the world that he gave his one and only Son that whoever believes in him shall not perish, but has everlasting life."

For this we give praise and thanksgiving. For this we gather to worship.

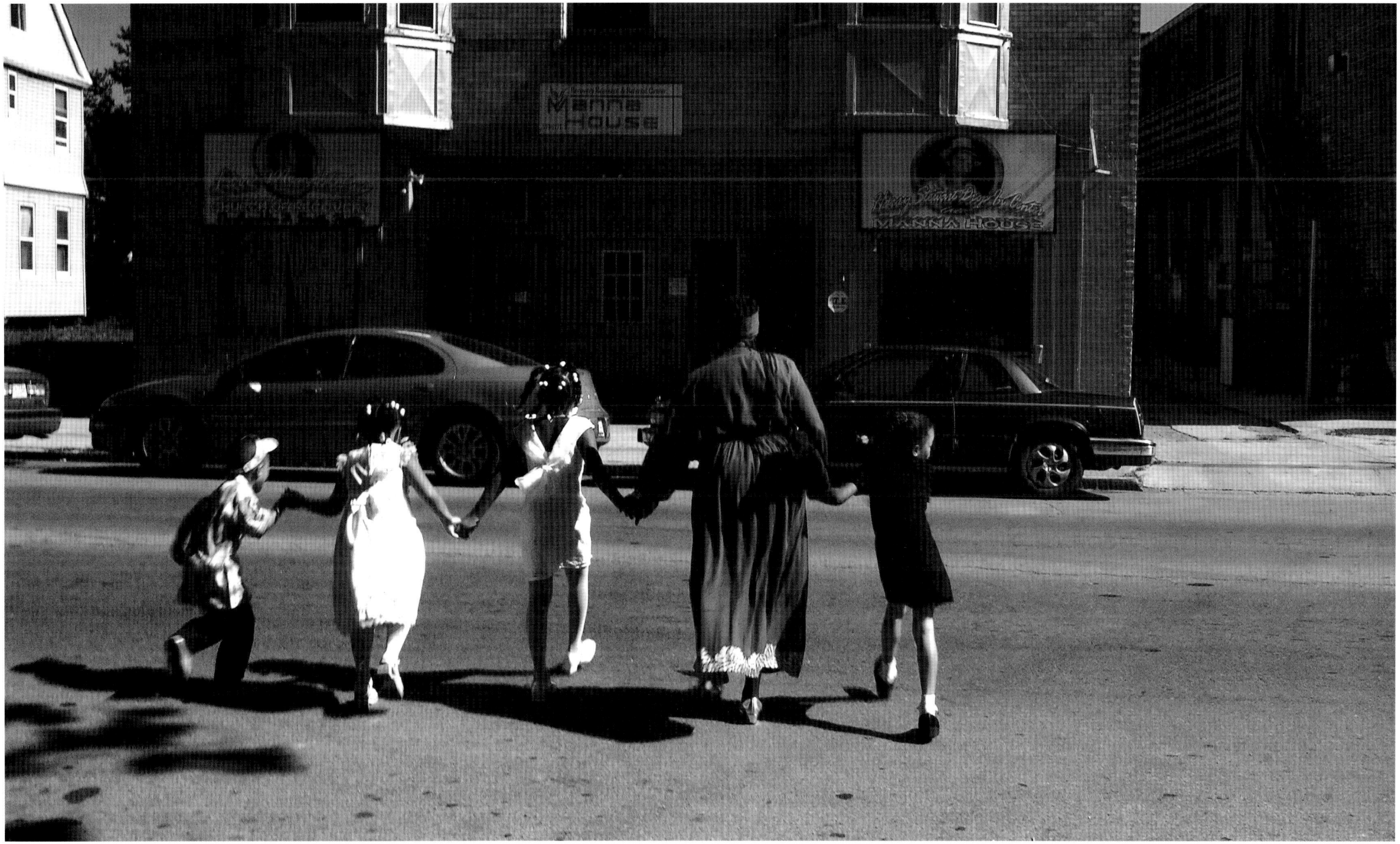
Manna House
MANNA HOUSE

WOMEN IN CHURCH

(Left) Cleveland Church of Christ, June 20, 2004. (Right) Mt. Haven Baptist Church, November 7, 2003

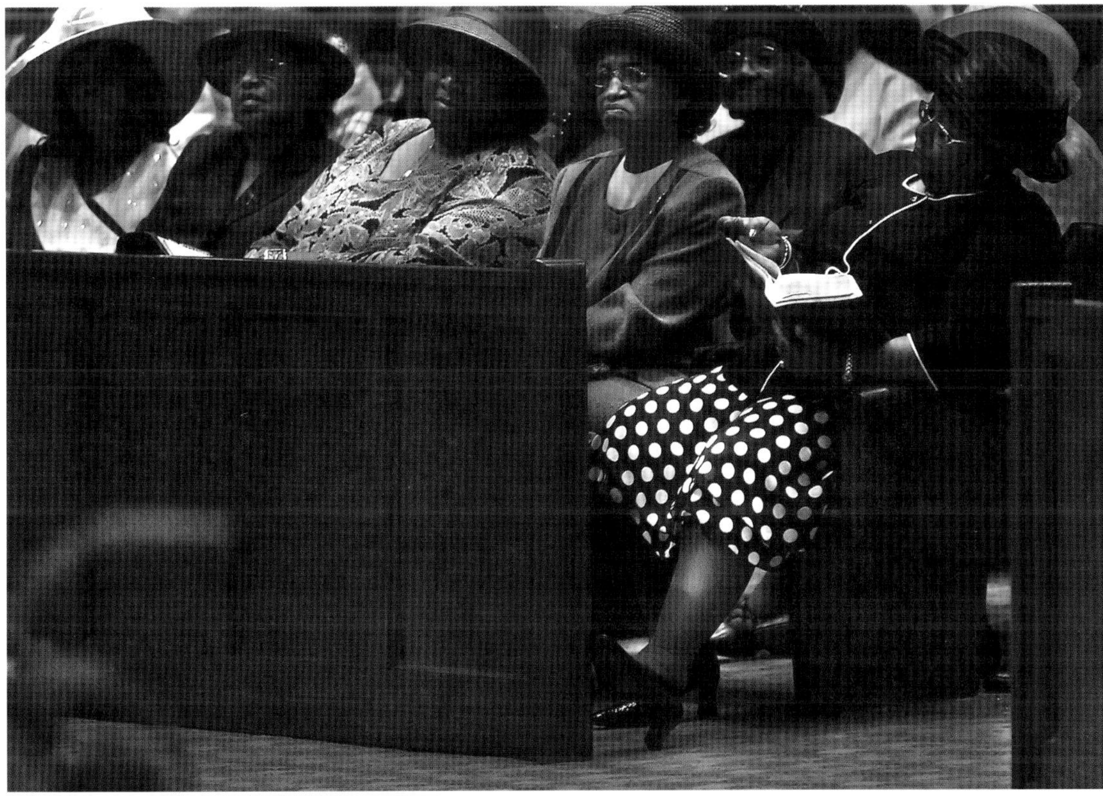

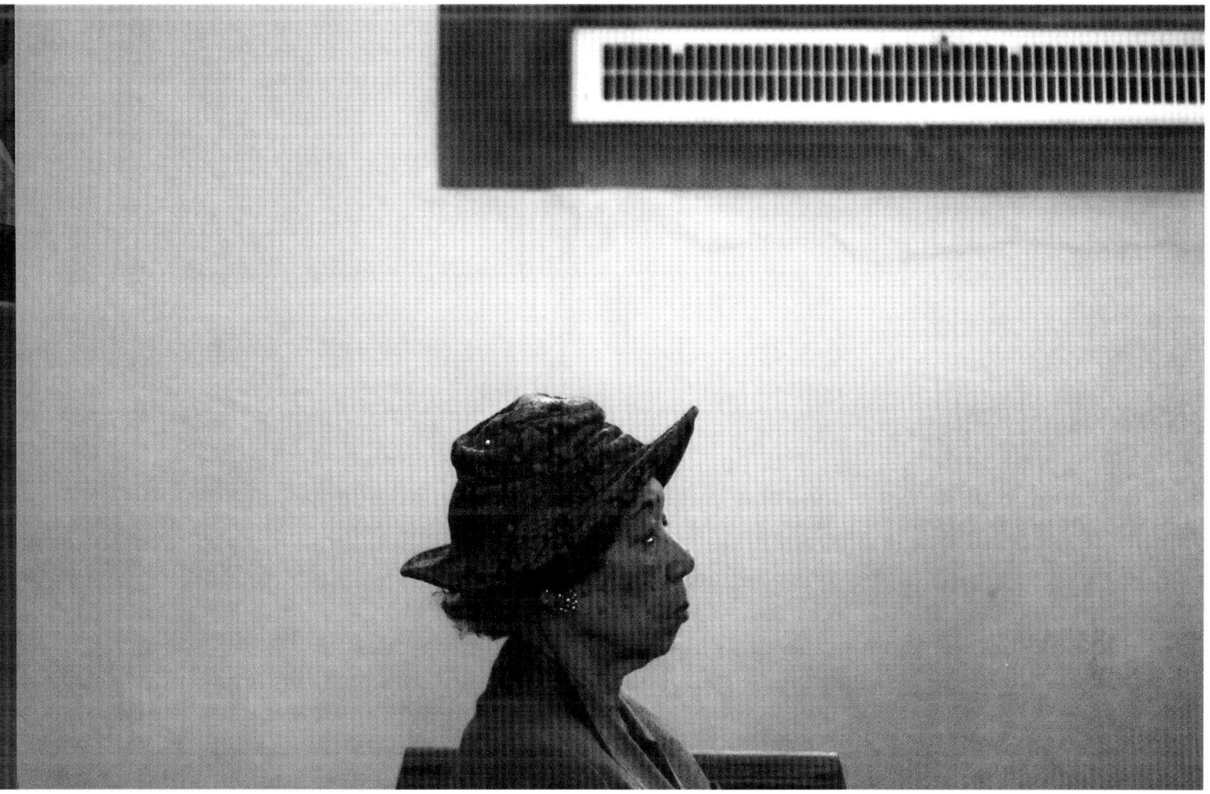

this page

THREE HATS

(Top) Olivet Institutional Baptist Church, April, 11, 2004. (Bottom) The Greater Abyssinia Baptist Church, May 1, 2004

facing page

SEATED

(Left) Antioch Baptist Church, May 5, 2004. (Right) Holy Trinity Baptist Church, April 11, 2004

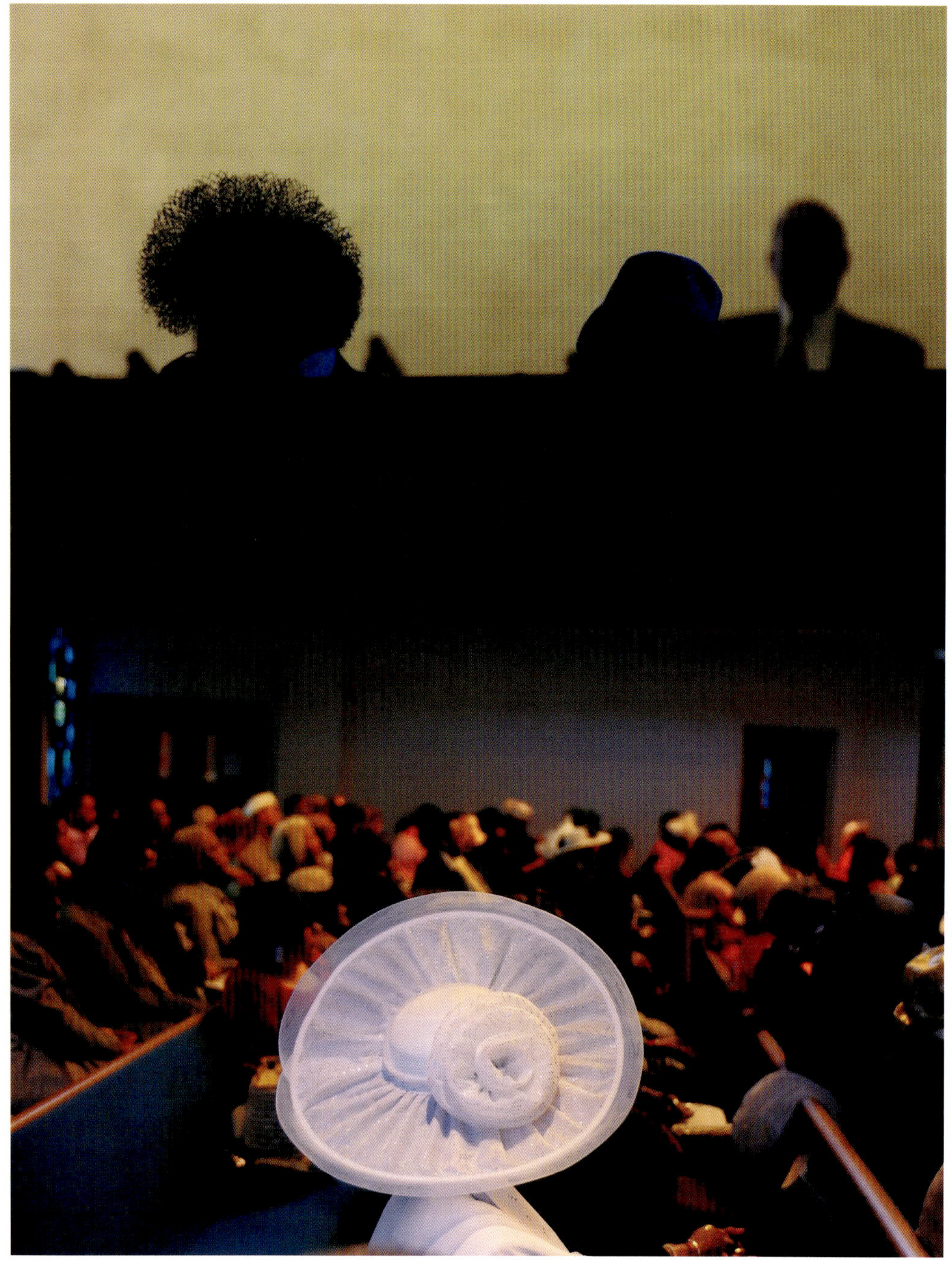

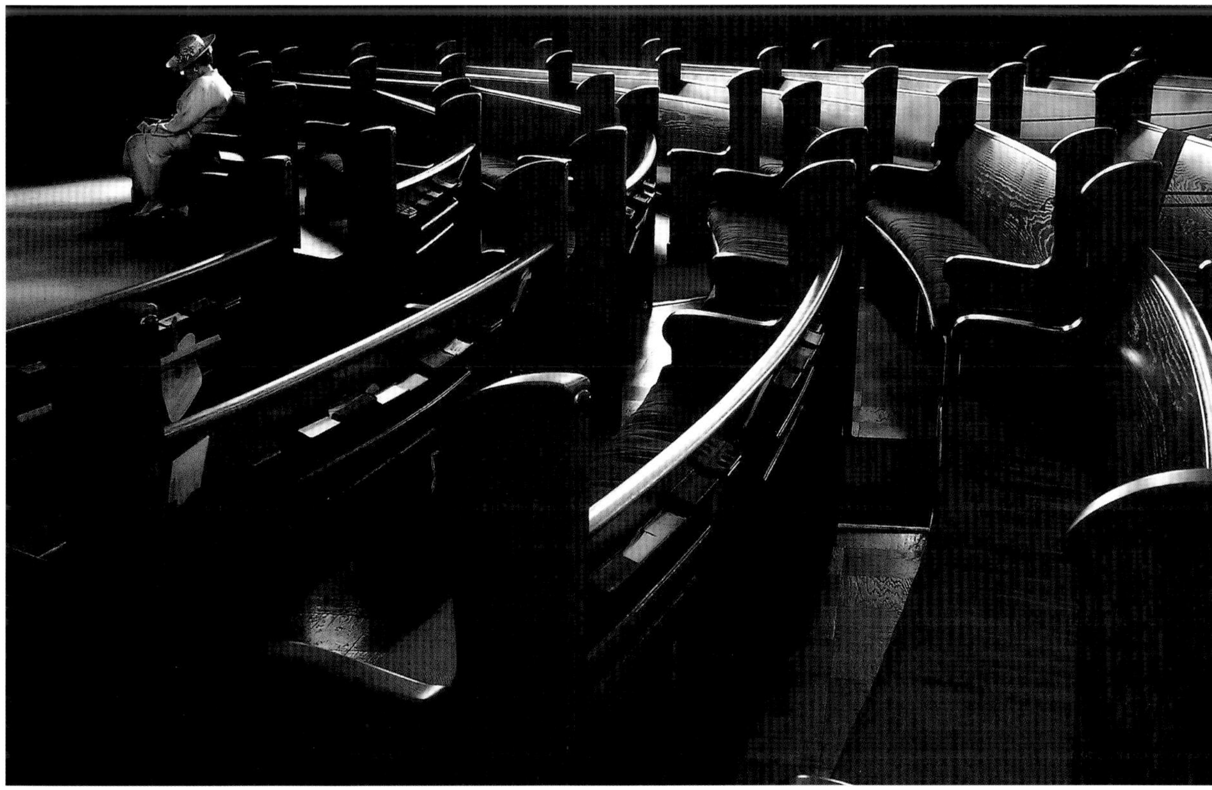

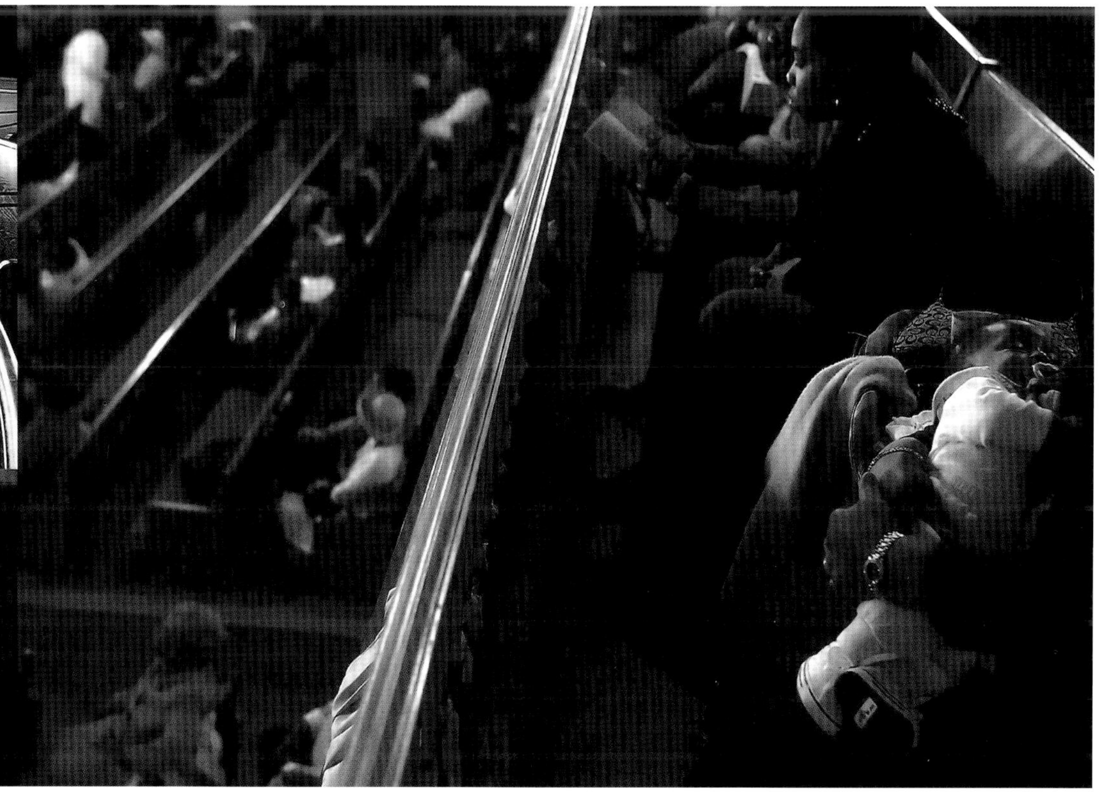

NOT ALONE

St. John AME Church, October 2, 2005

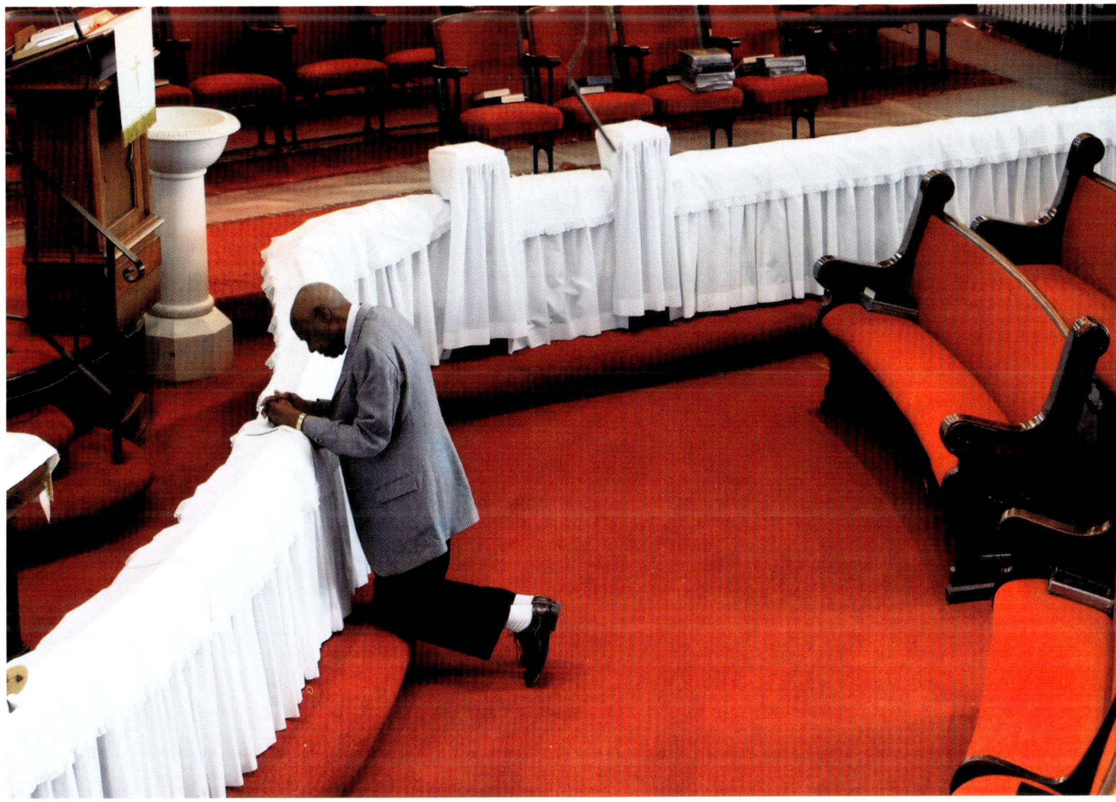

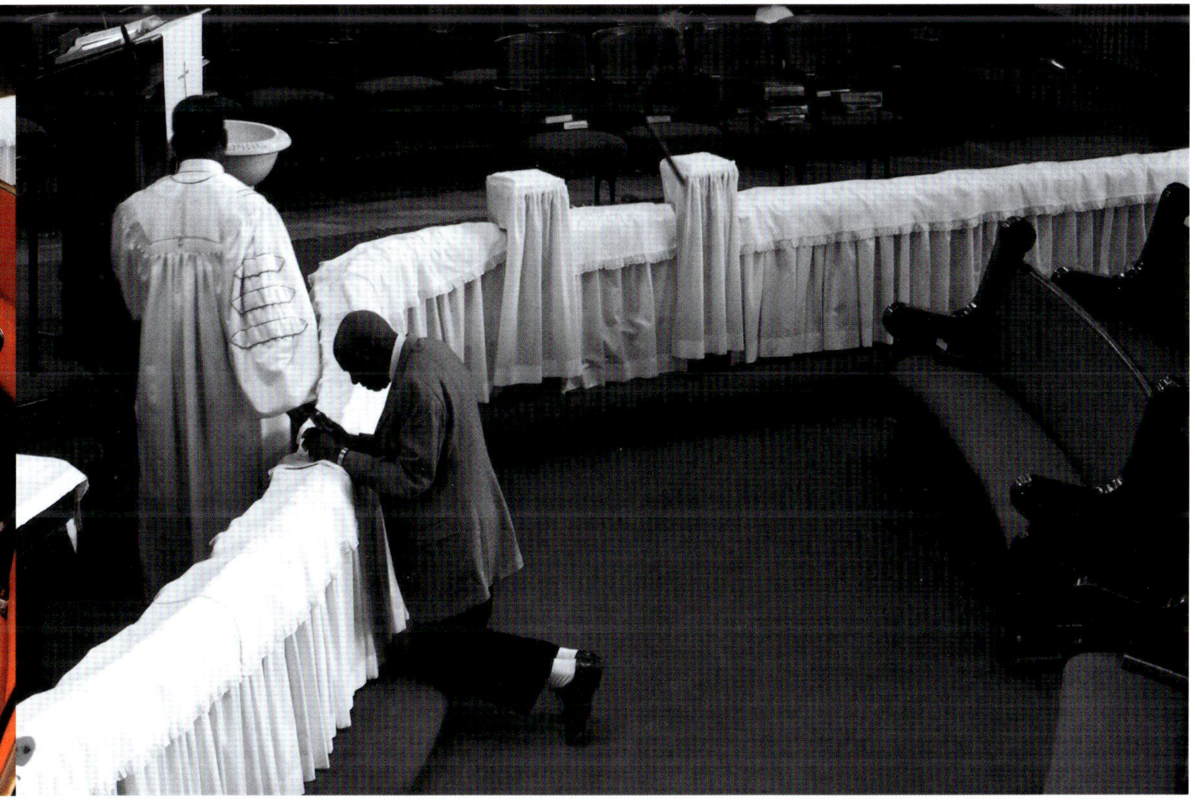

REST IN PEACE

(Left) Triedstone Baptist Church, April 13, 2005. (Right) Windermere United Methodist Church, June 4, 2006.

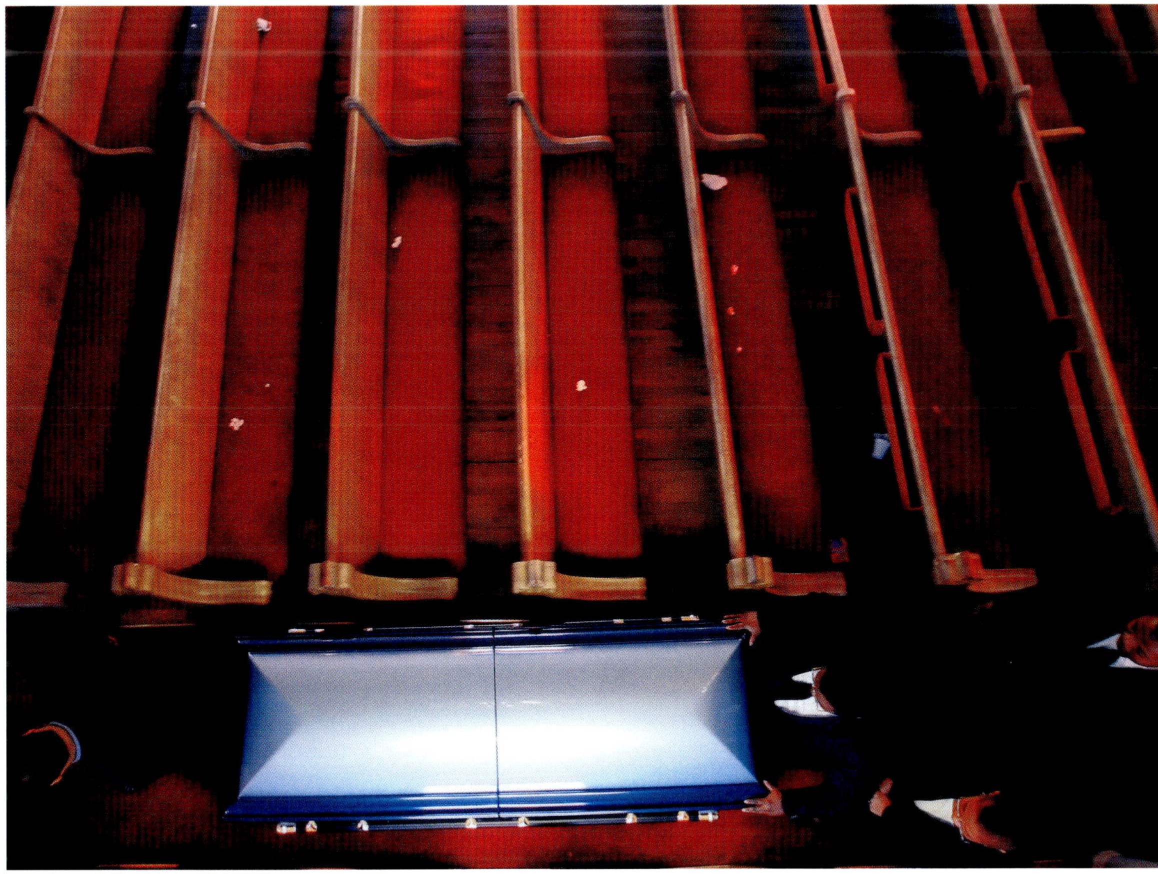

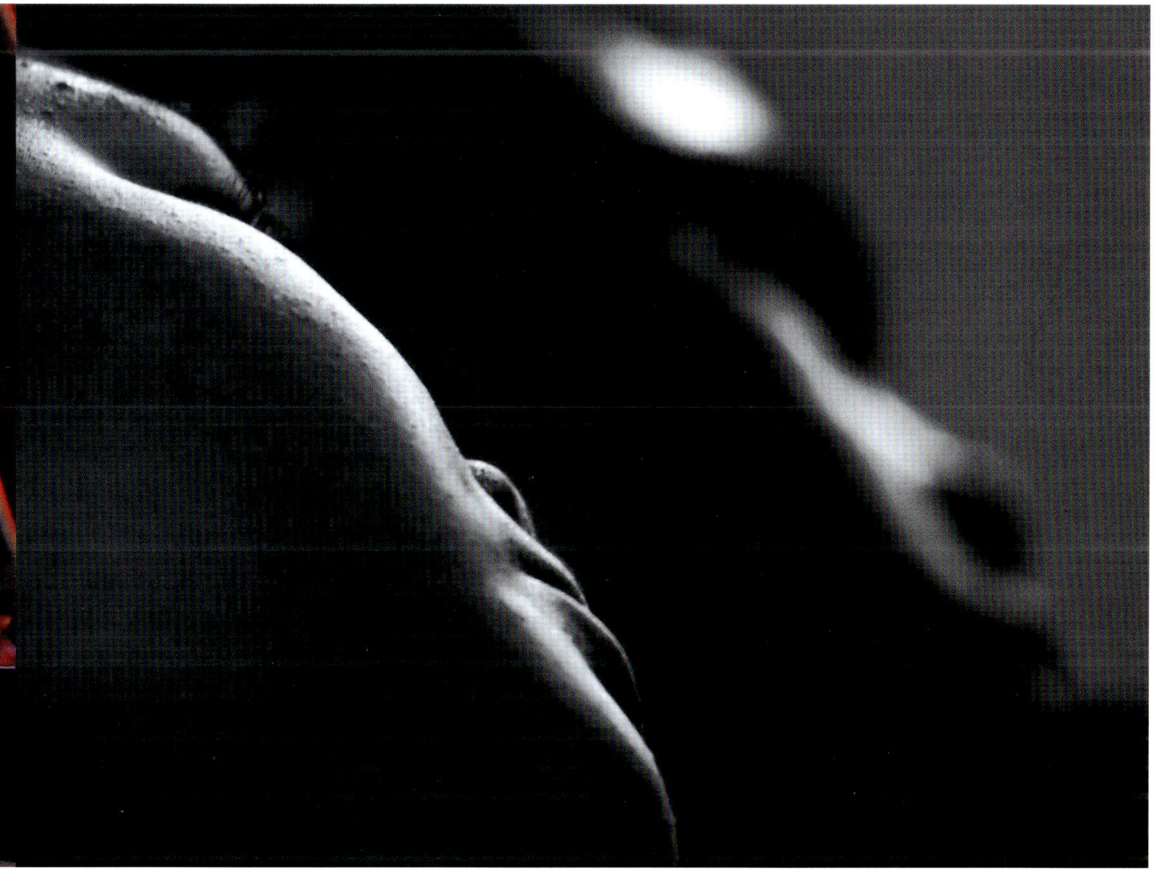

OVERALL

The Greater Abyssinia Baptist Church, May 1, 2004

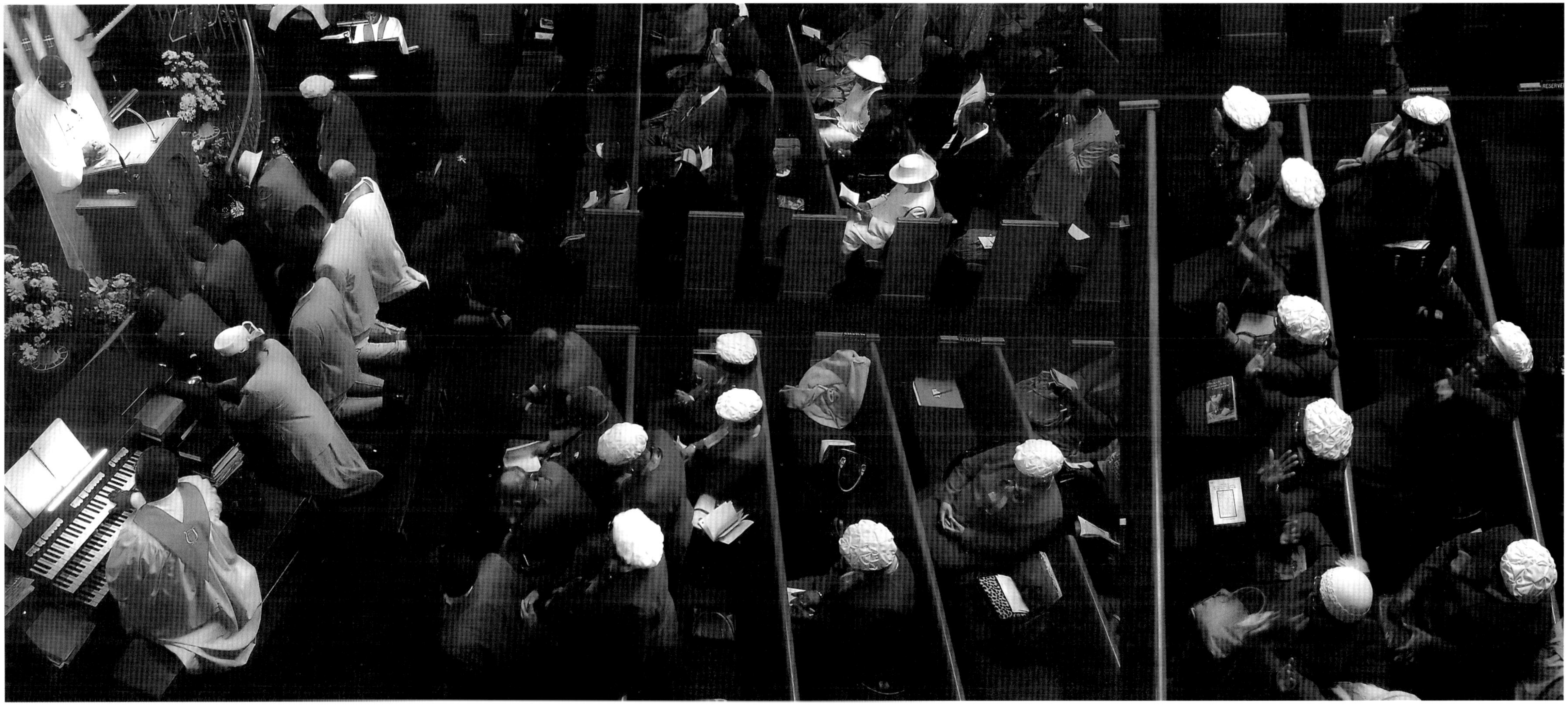

OUT OF DARKNESS

Pentecostal Church of Christ,

February 8, 2004

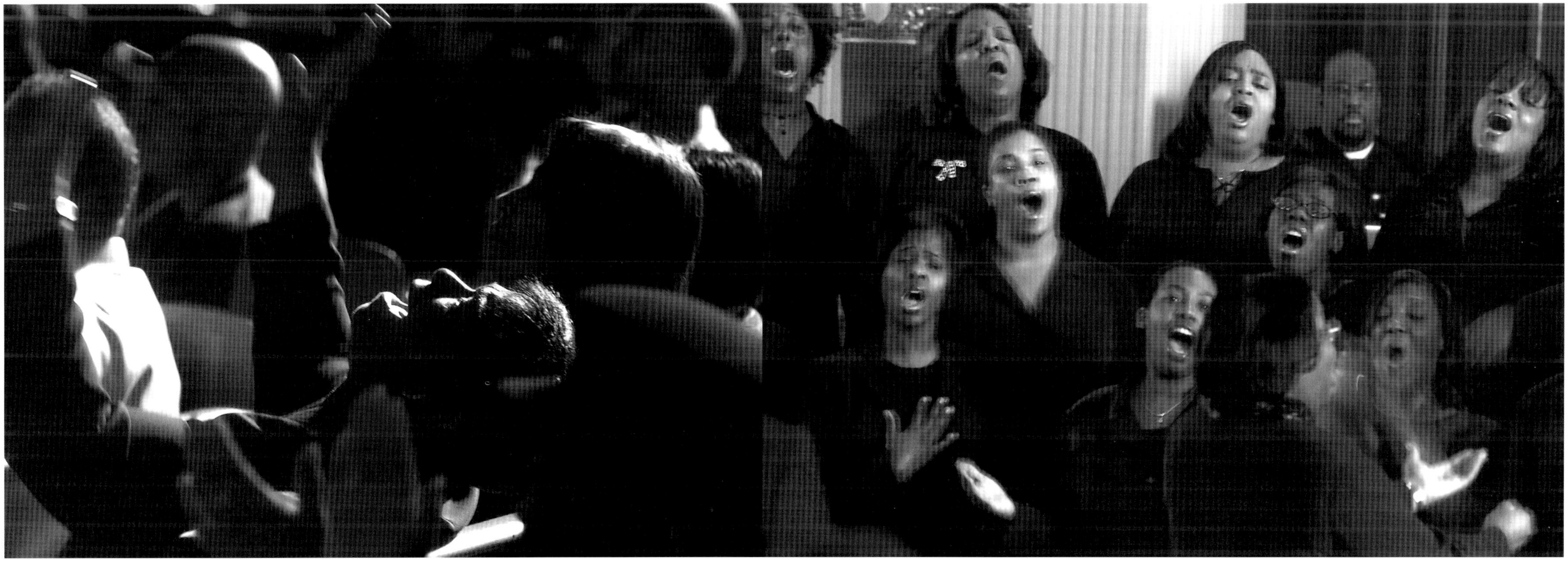

REVELATION
Cleveland Church of Christ,
June 19, 2004

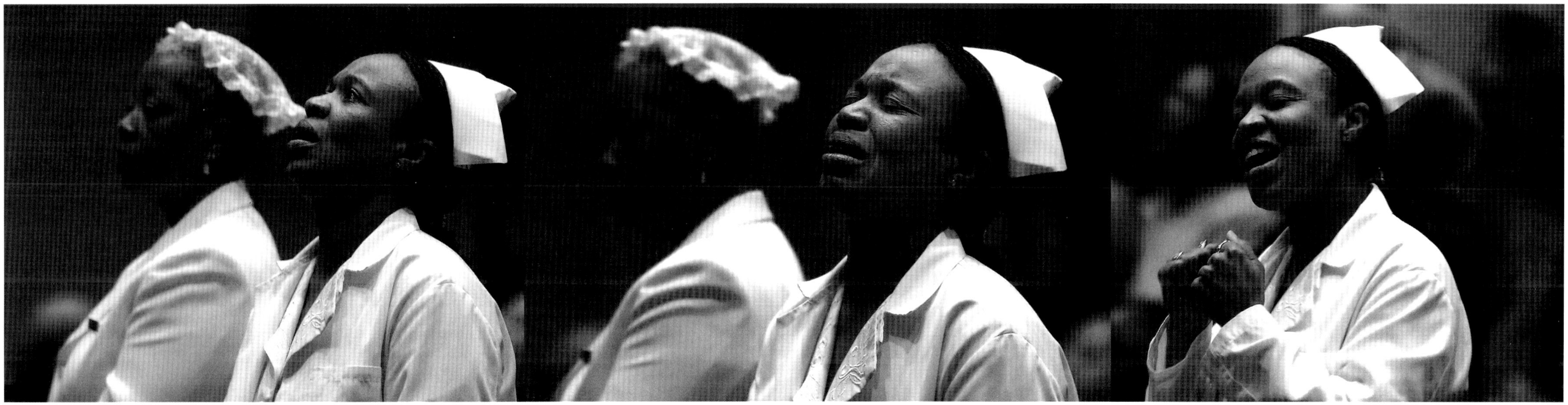

TENT OF FIRE REVIVAL
God's House of Prayer and Deliverance Holy Church, July 15, 2004

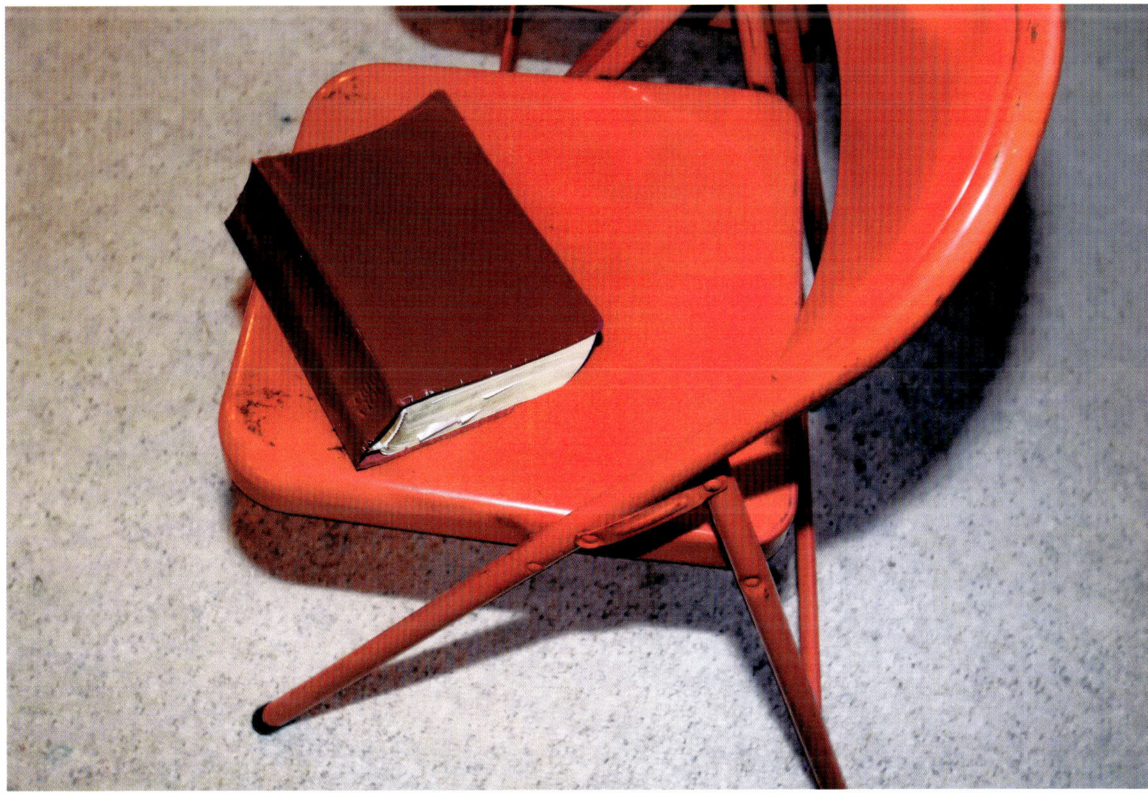

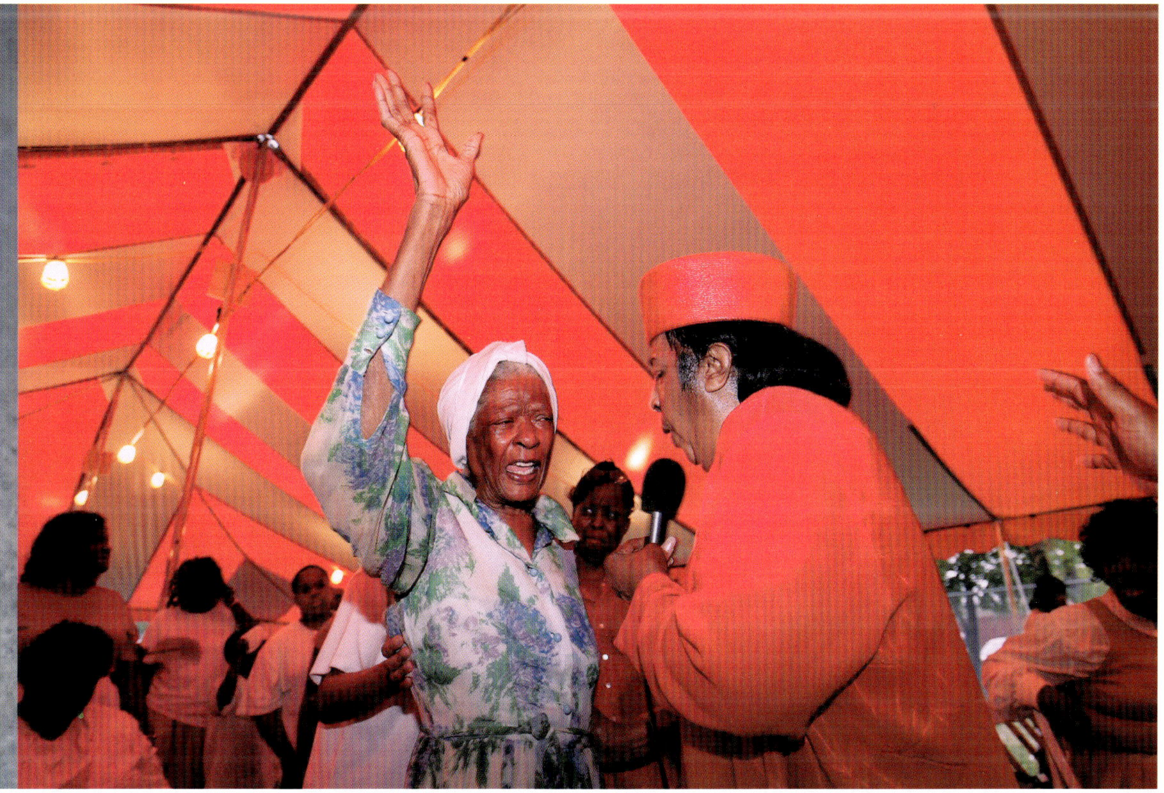

WE LOVE OUR CHILDREN

(Left) A Muslim man and his child attend the funeral of Shakira Johnson, Mt. Sinai Baptist Church, October 25, 2003. (Right) Balm in Gilead Missionary Baptist Church, January 31, 2004

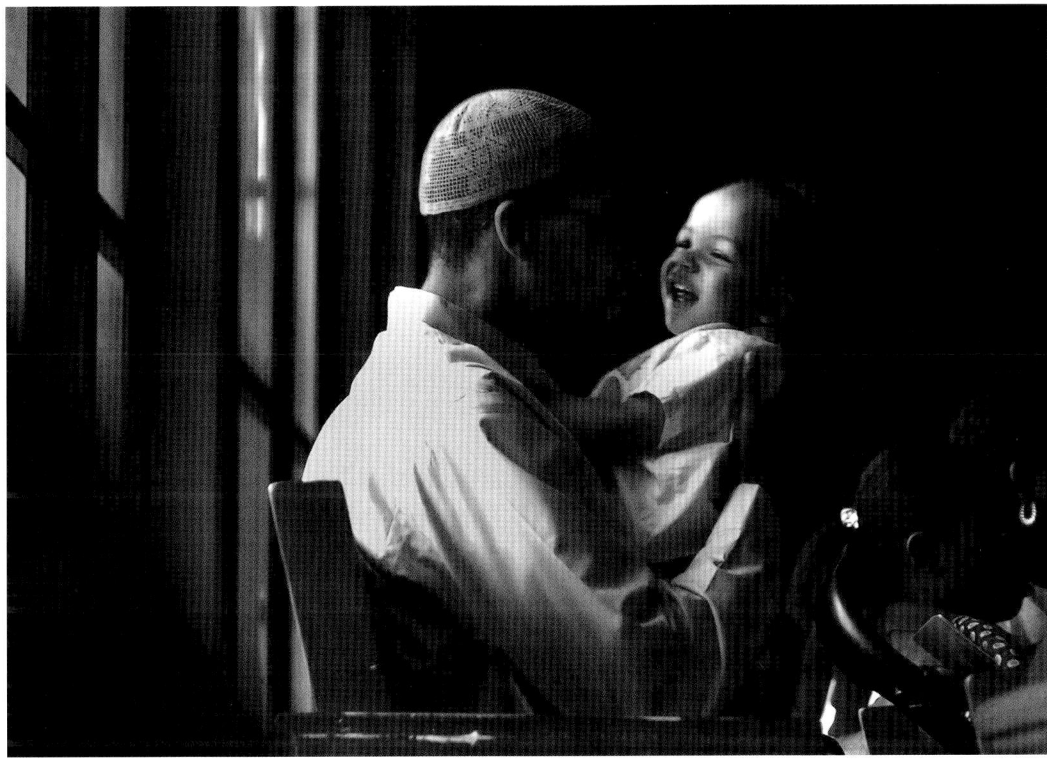
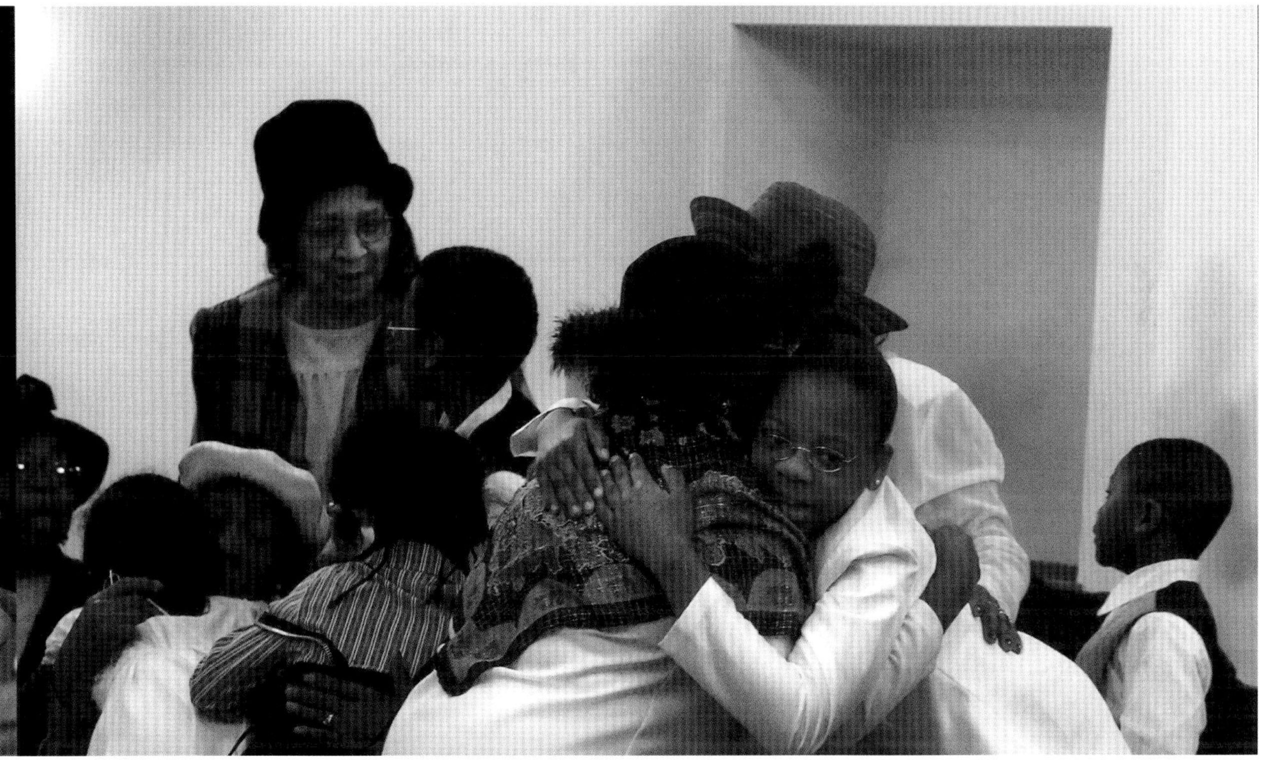

RED HAT

Glenville Seventh-Day Adventist
Church, July 15, 2006

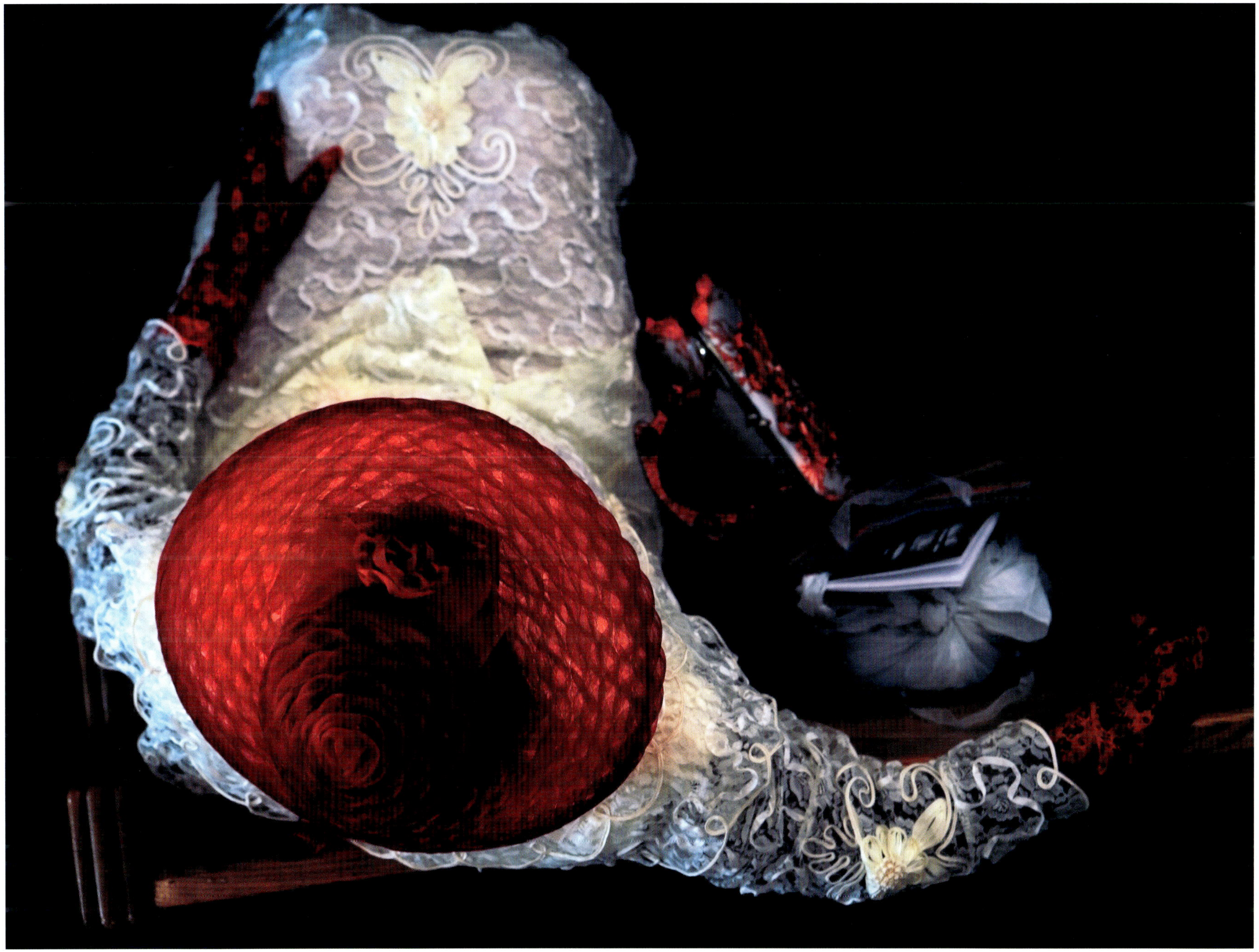

YOUNG AND OLD

Mt. Sinai Baptist Church,

August 8, 2004

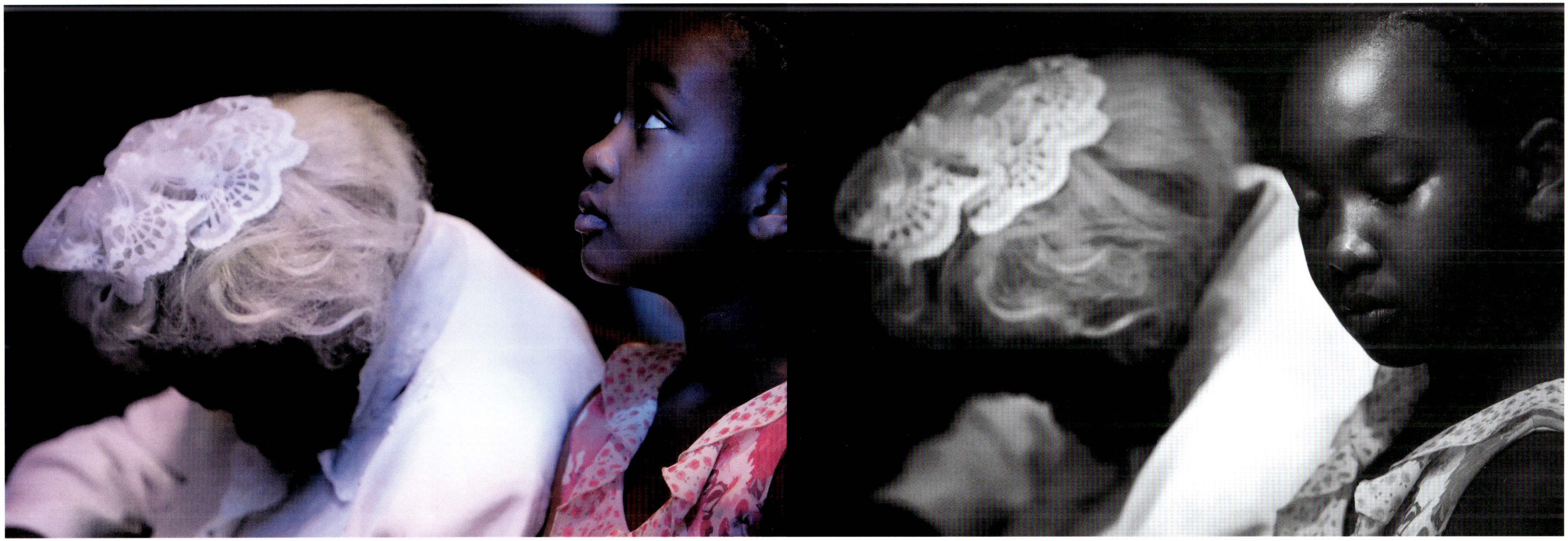

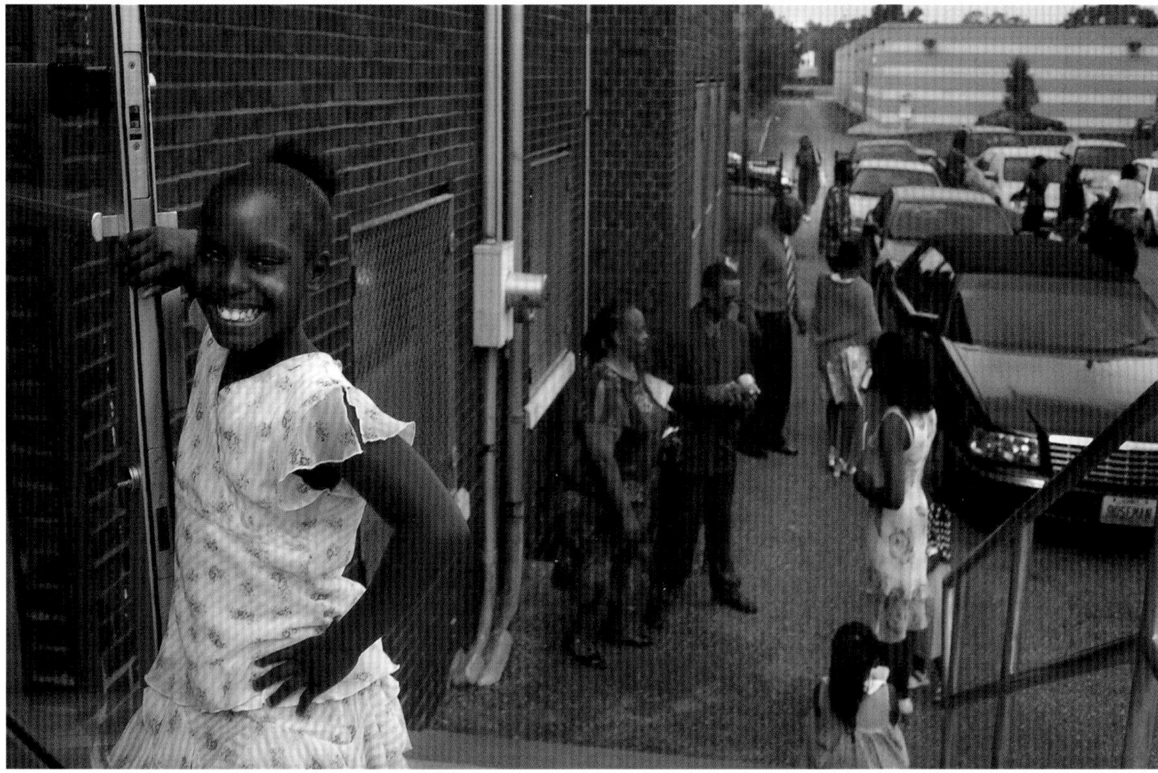
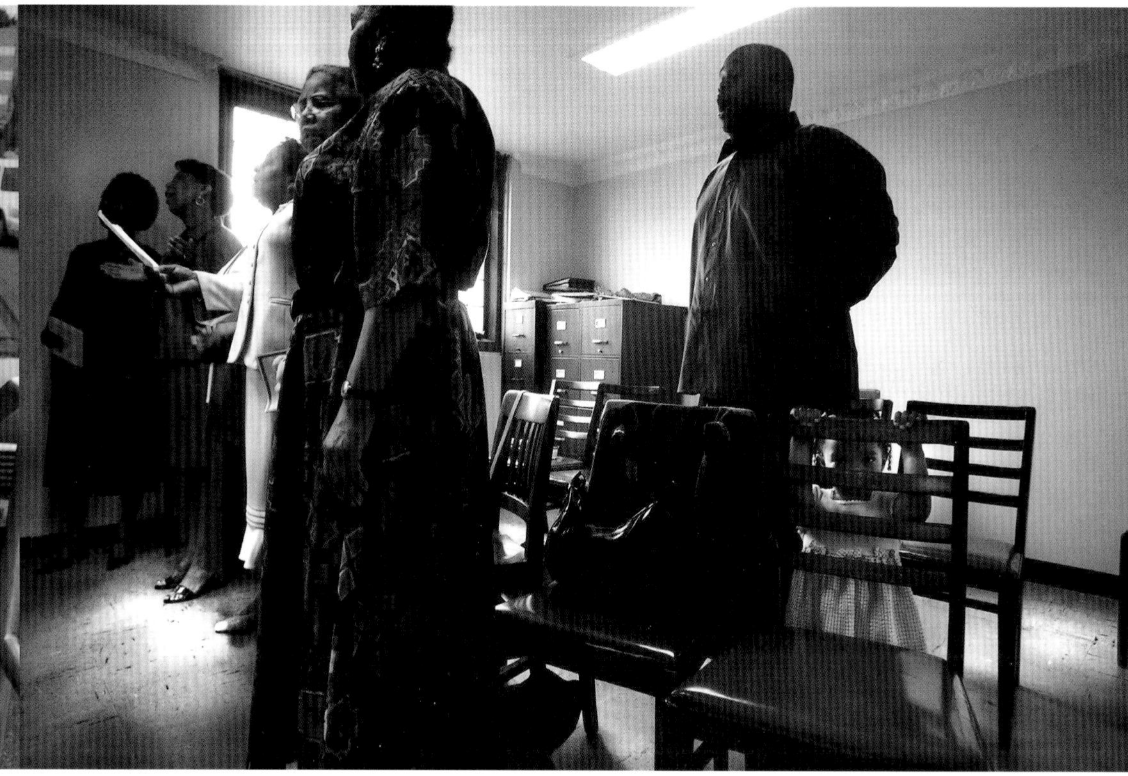

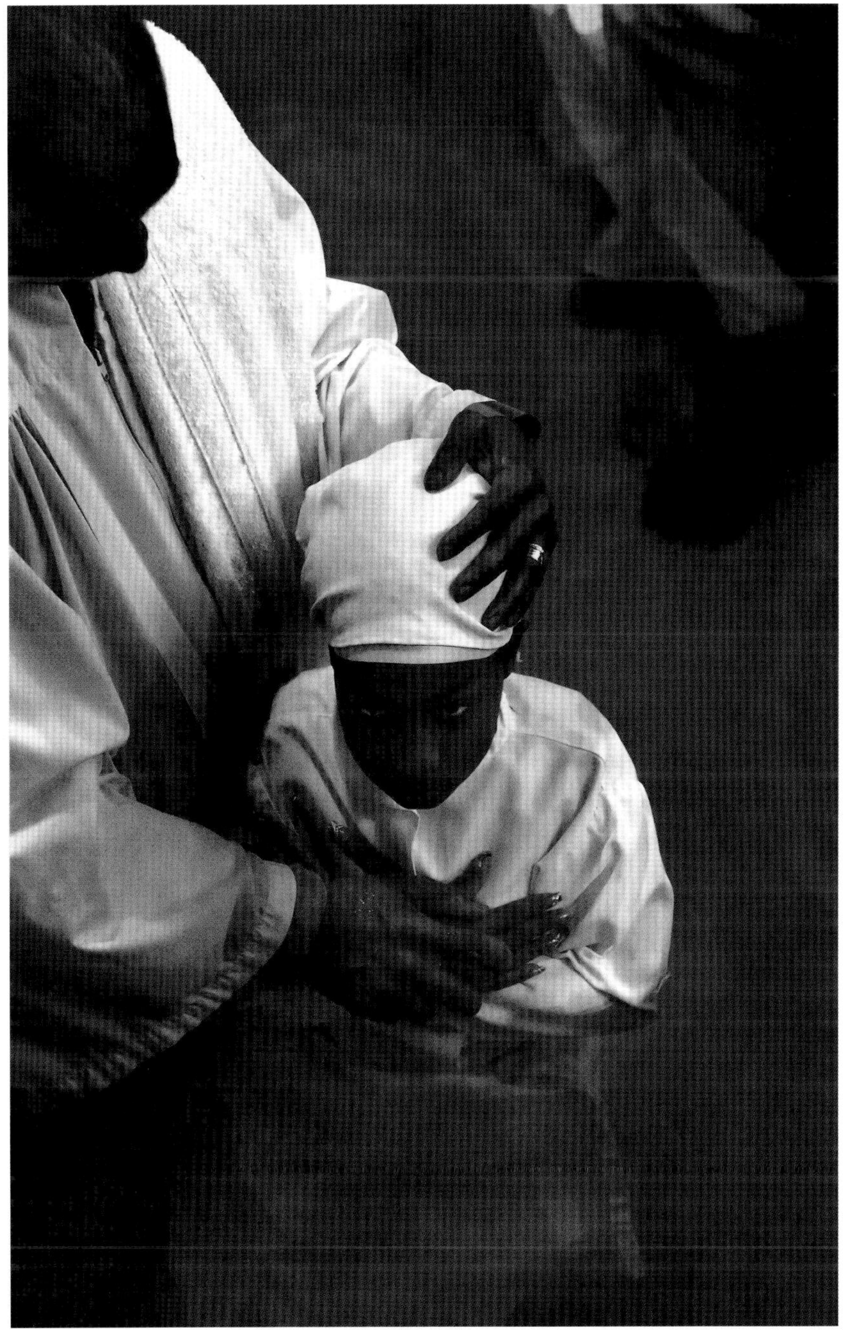

facing page

TWO GIRLS IN DRESSES

(Left) Glenville Seventh-Day Adventist Church, July 15, 2006. (Right) Windermere United Methodist Church, June 4, 2006

this page

THE REVEREND DR. OTIS MOSS JR.

Olivet Institutional Baptist Church, April 11, 2004

TWO BAPTISMS

(Left) Mt. Zion Church, August 6, 2006. (Right) Olivet Institutional Baptist Church, April 11, 2004

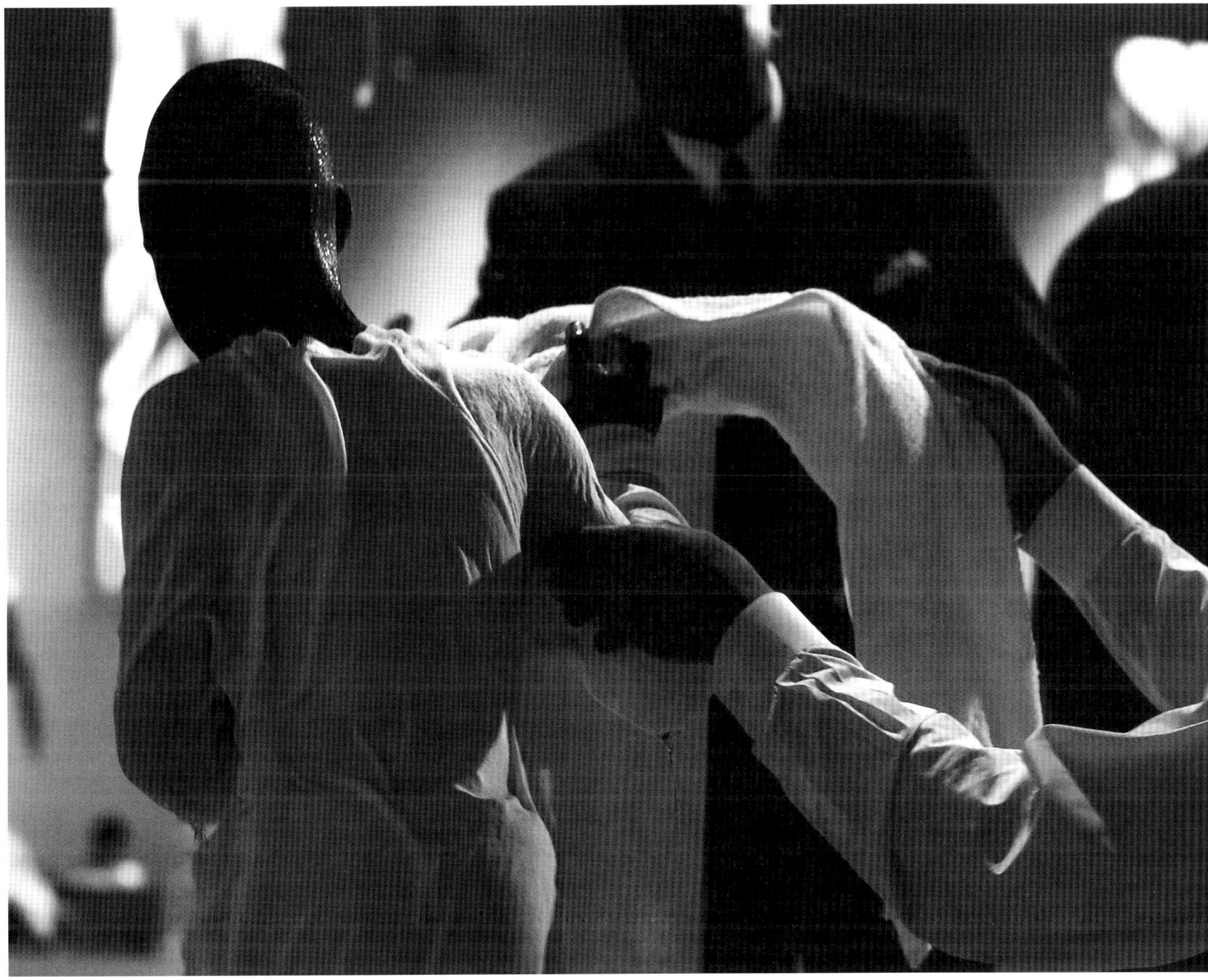
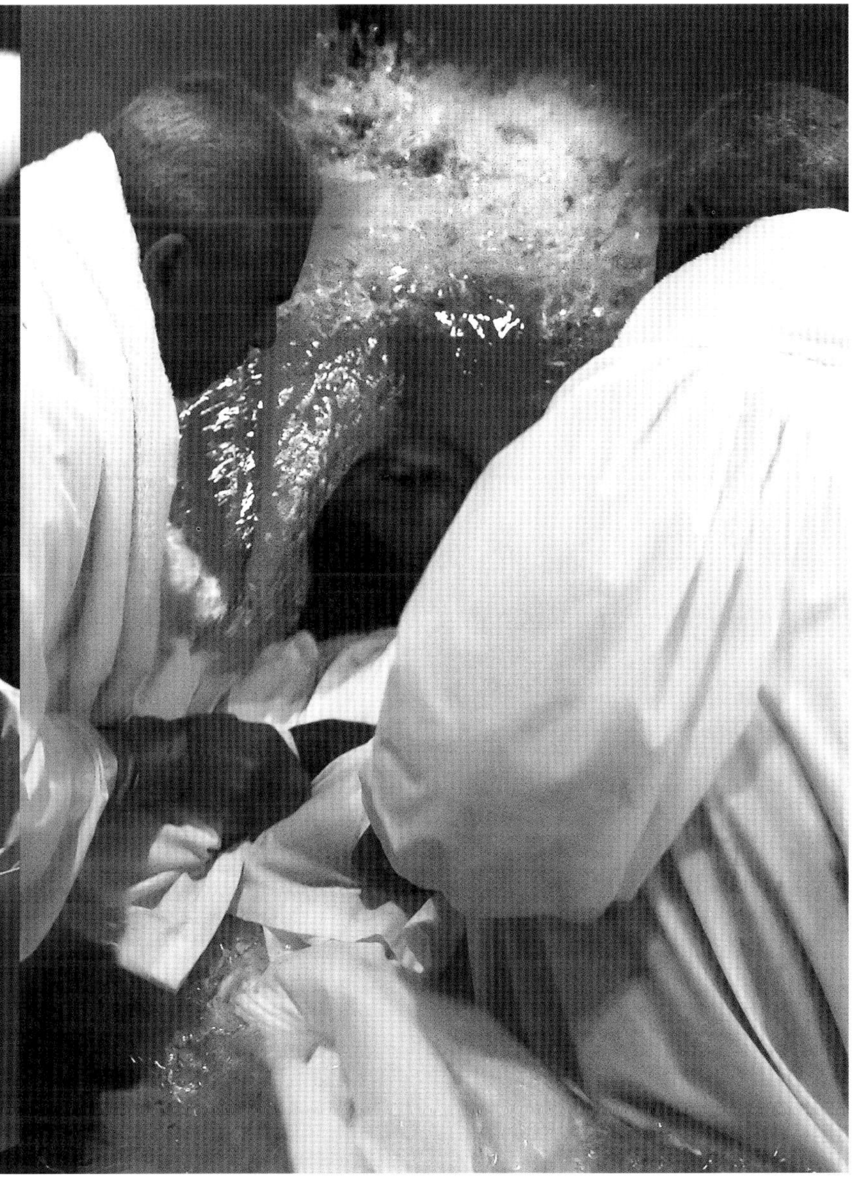

HIGH AND LOW

A prayer rally at Quicken Loans Arena, Cleveland, February 13, 2006

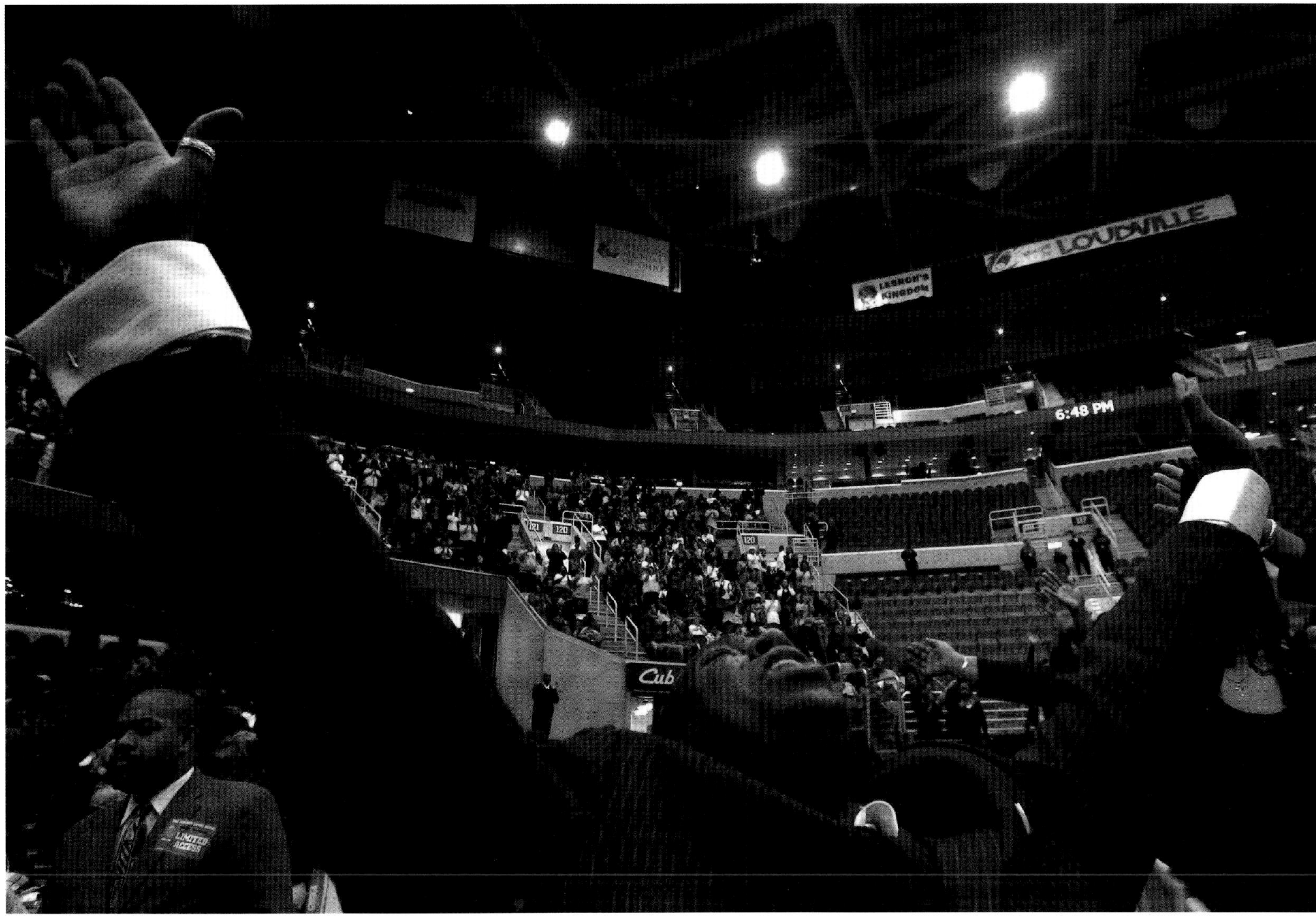
LOUDVILLE
6:48 PM

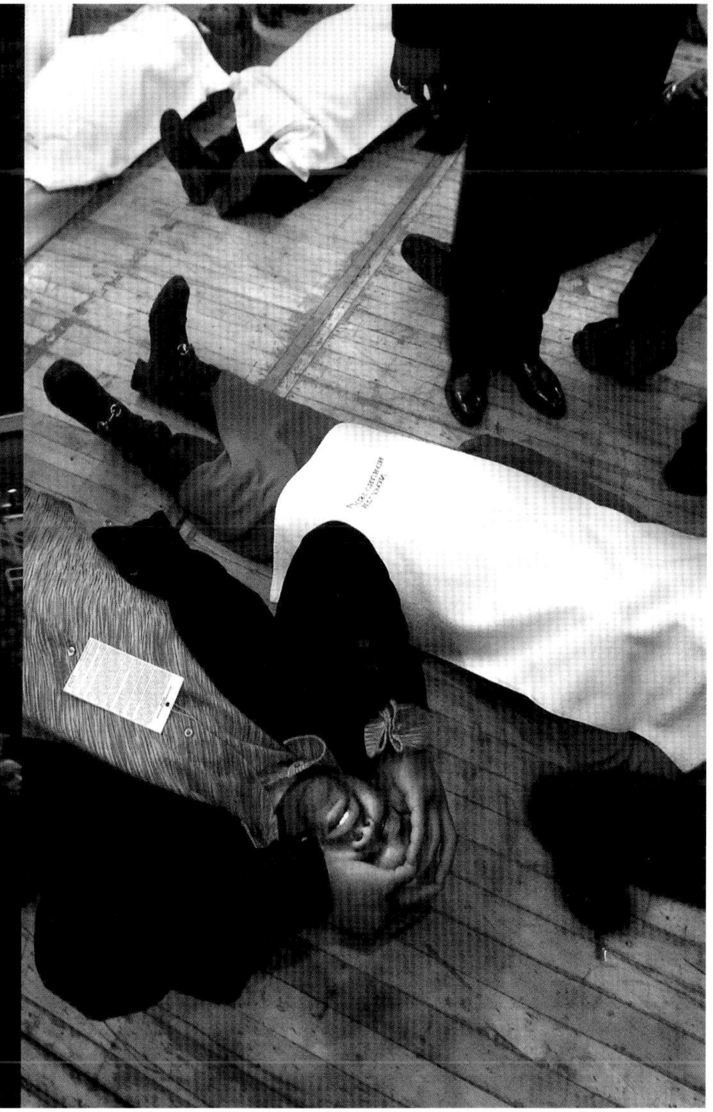

THE FLOCK

(Left) Live Ministries/Church of Recovery, January 13, 2003. (Right) New Jerusalem Church of God in Christ, April 3, 2006

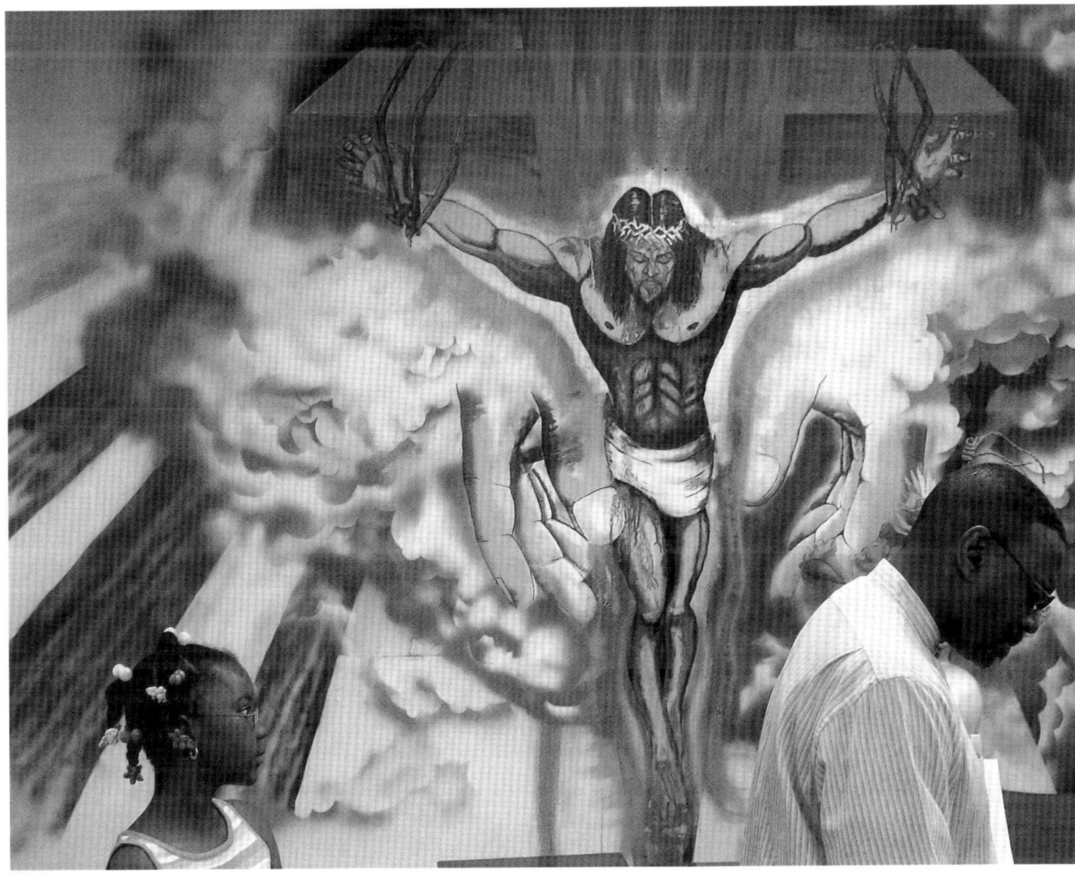

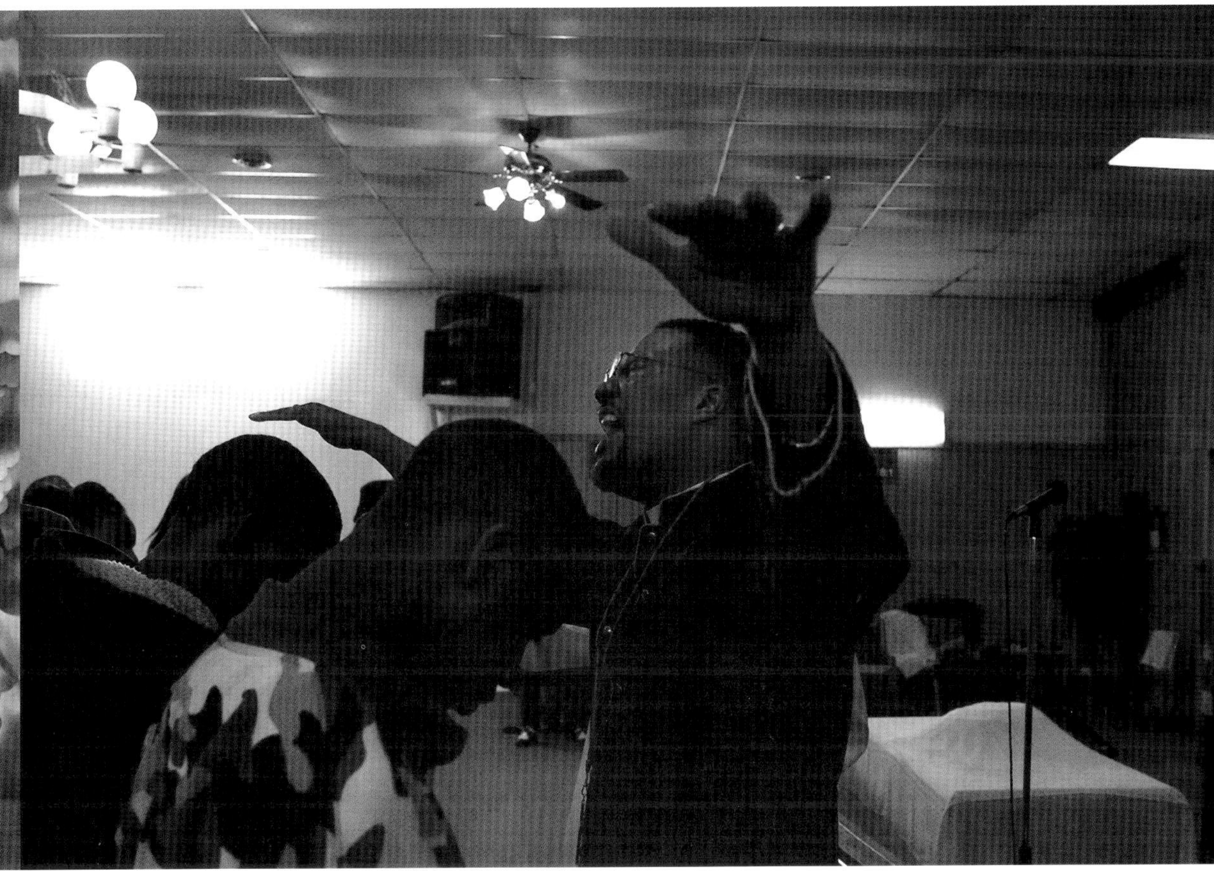

There is a balm in Gilead
To make the wounded whole,
There is a balm in Gilead
To heal the sin-sick soul.

—Traditional

THE REVEREND HUEY HARRIS

(Left) A Sunday church service at an apartment in Elyria, June 6, 2005. (Center and right) A Bible study held in a backyard in Maple Heights, June 12, 2005

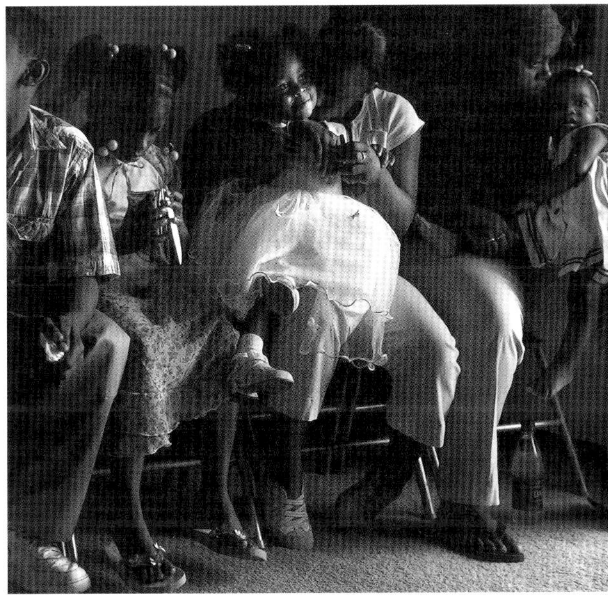
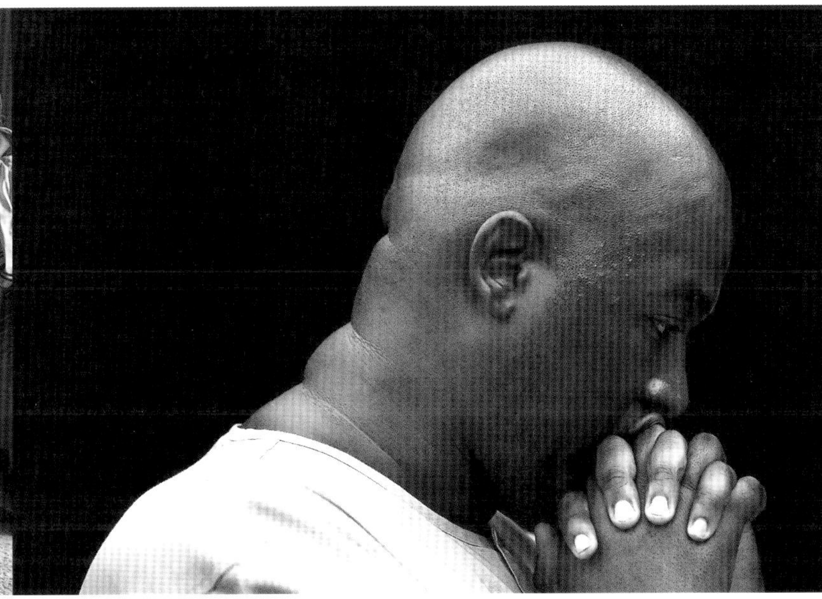
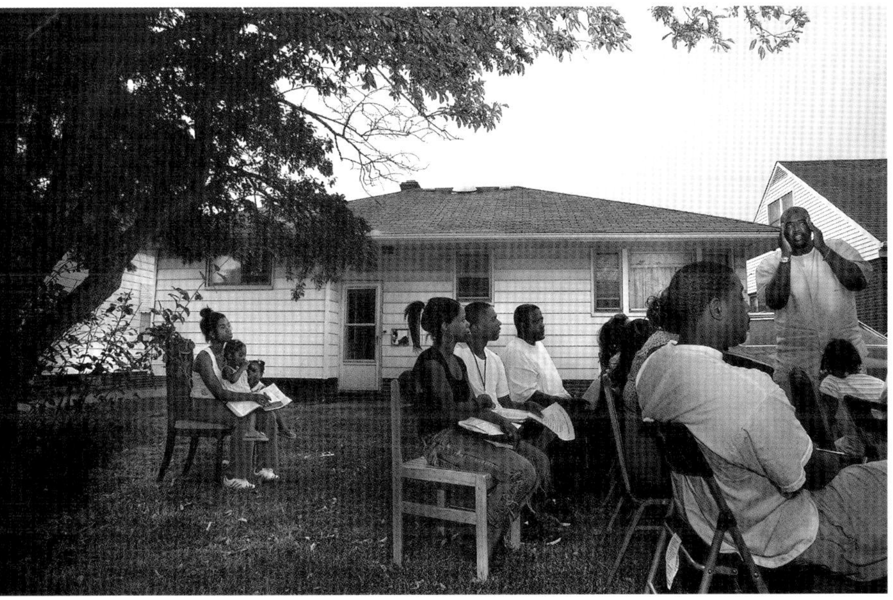

MEN AT PRAYER
(Left) Mt. Sinai Baptist Church, October 8, 2004. (Right) St. Paul AME Zion Church, January 17, 2004

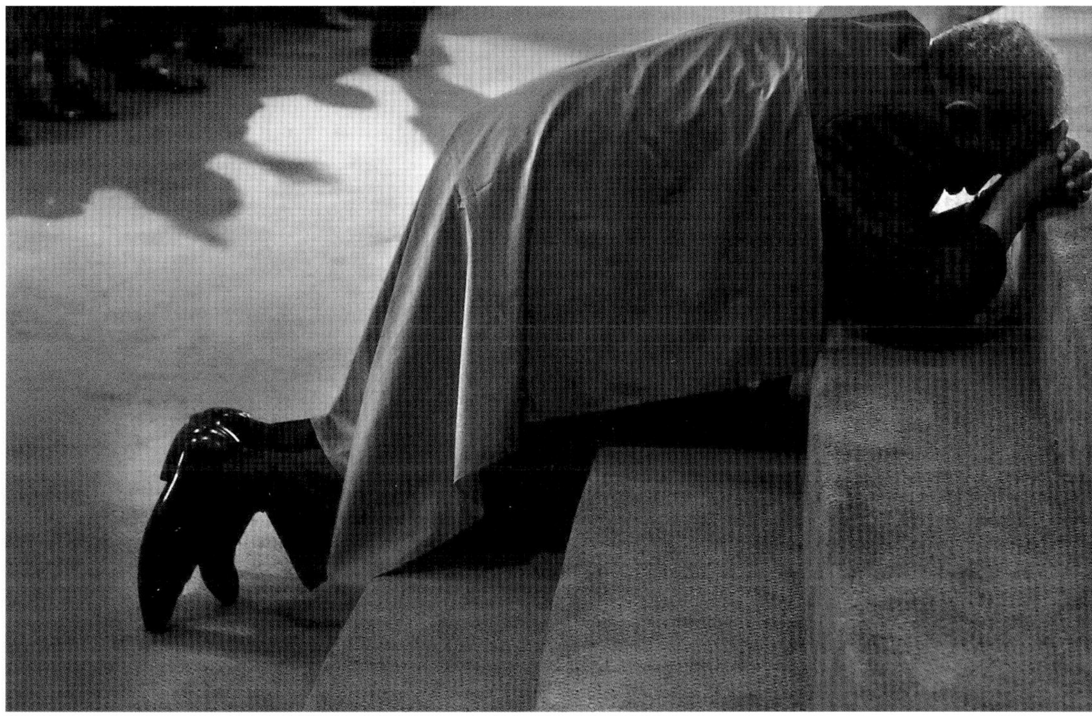

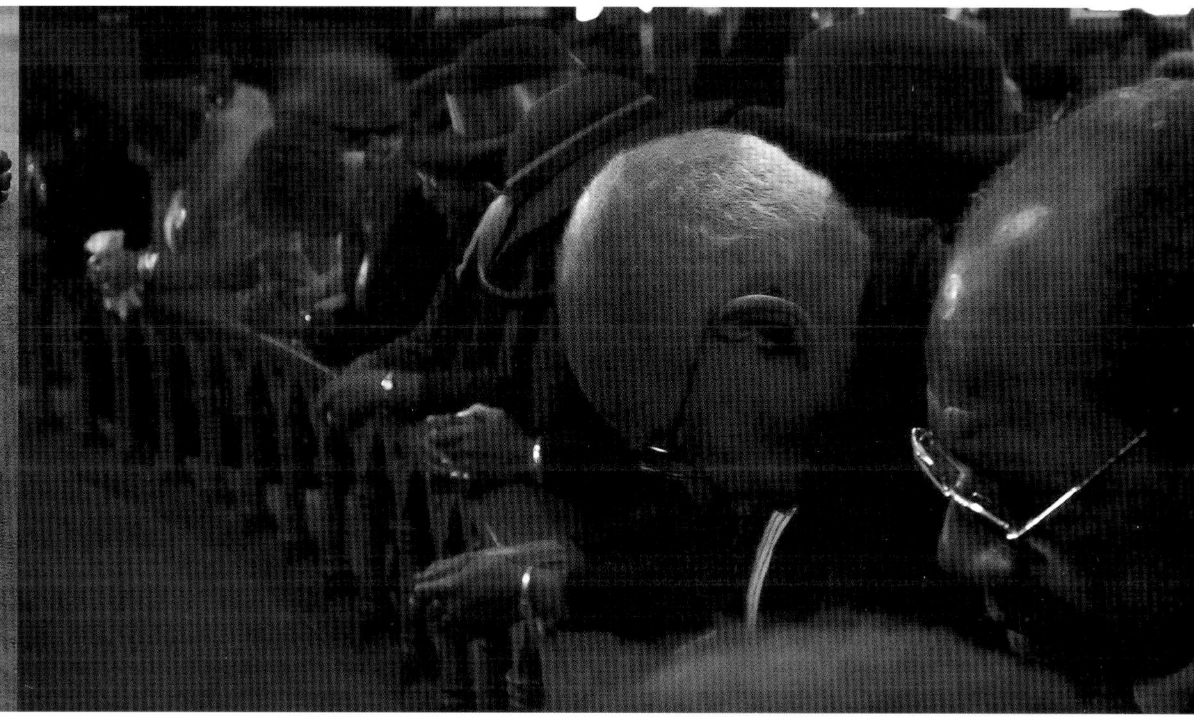

IMAGES

(Left) St. Adalbert Roman Catholic Church, December 24, 2006.
(Right) Detail of a mural in Live Ministries/Church of Recovery, July 13, 2003

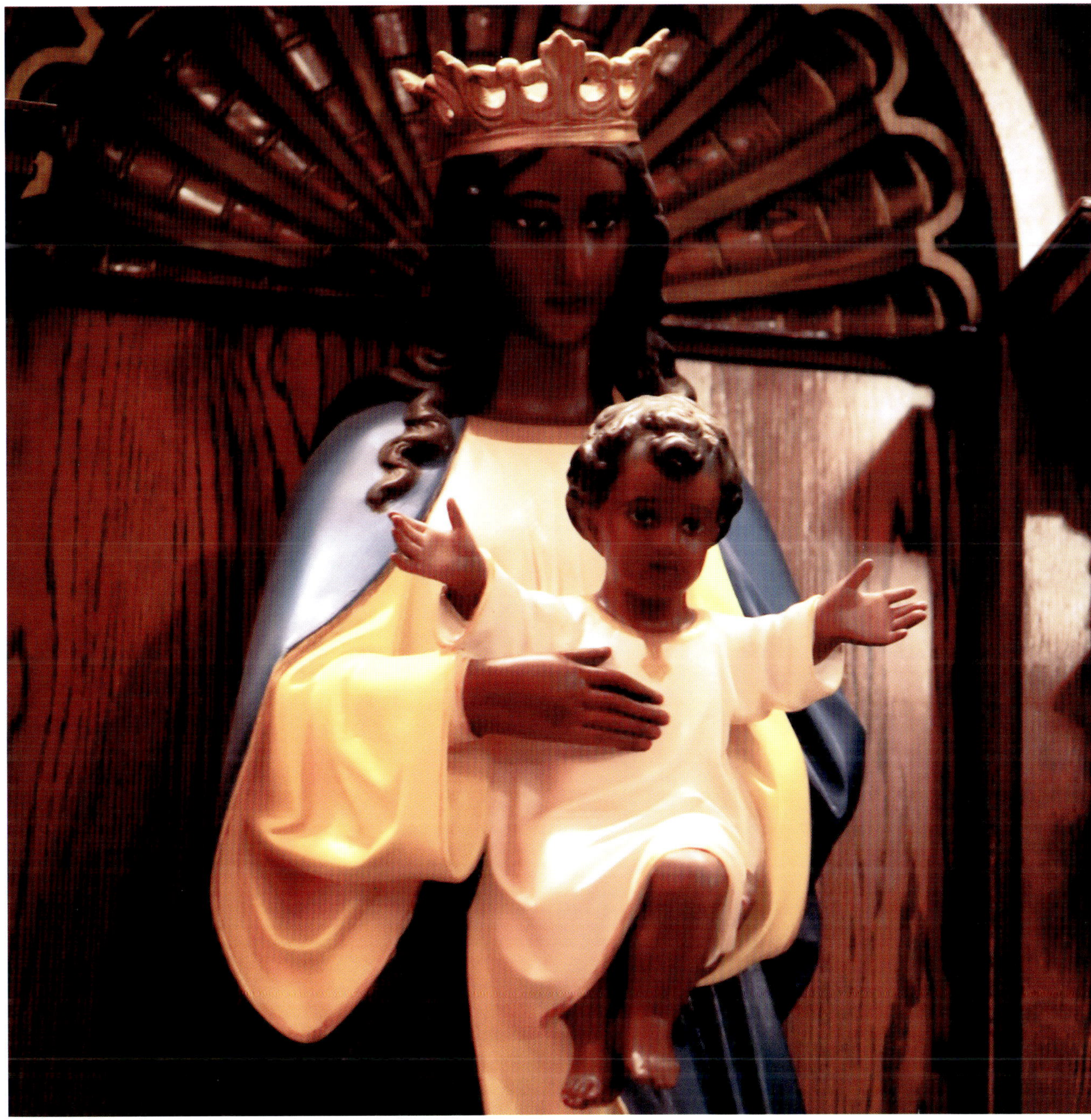

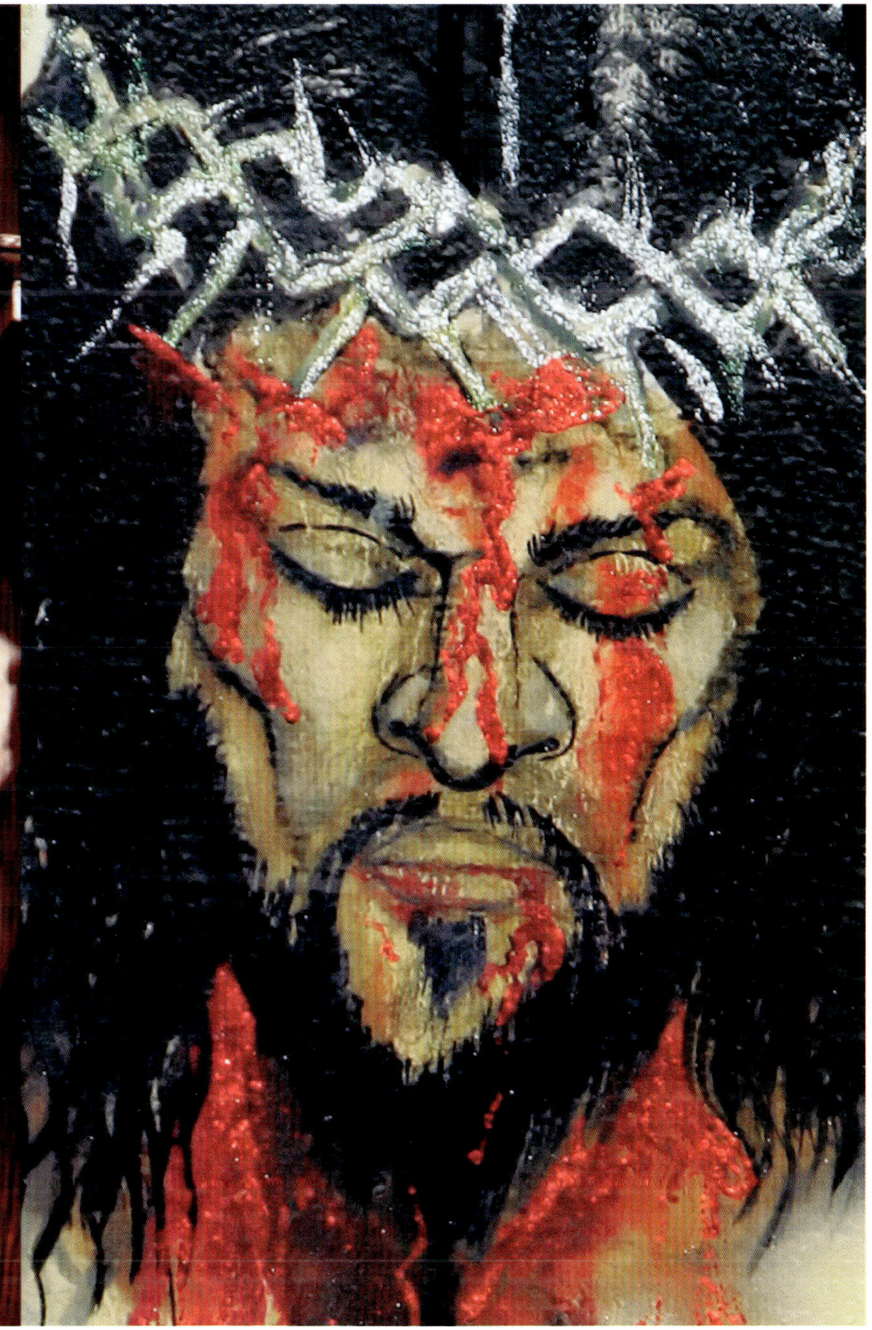

THE MUSIC DIRECTOR

Mt. Zion Church, August 6, 2006

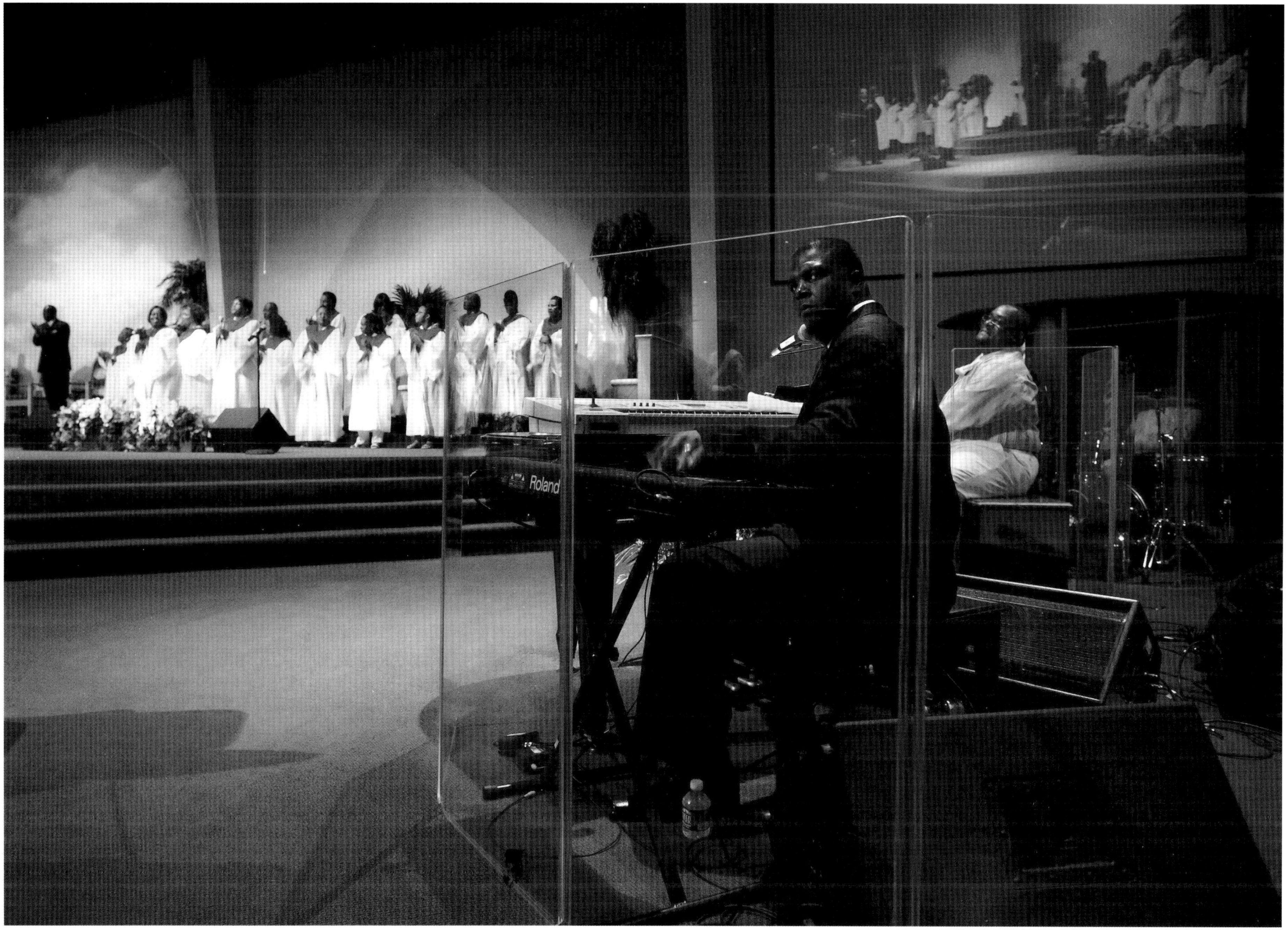
Roland

THE BALCONY

The Greater Abyssinia Baptist Church, May 1, 2004

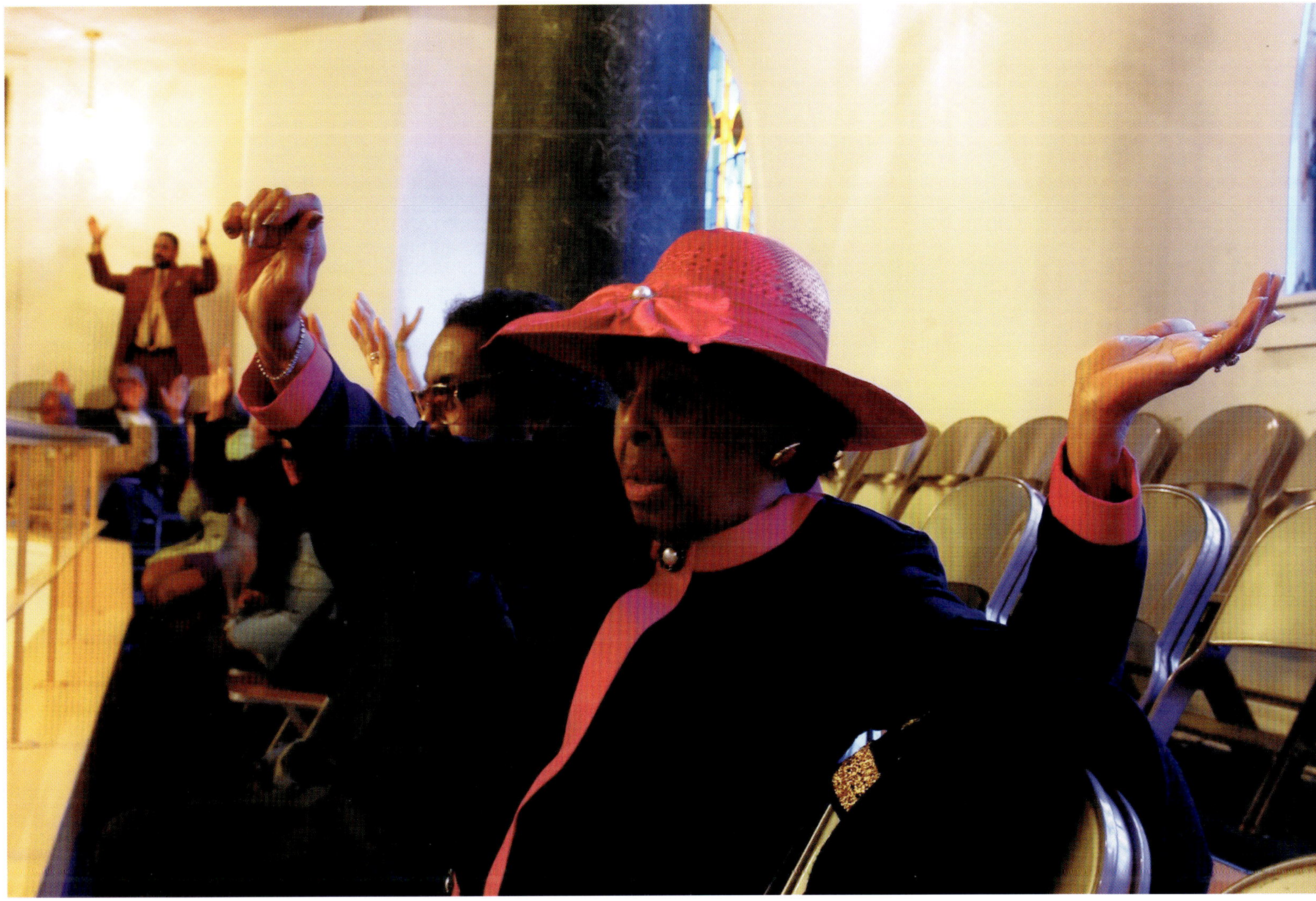

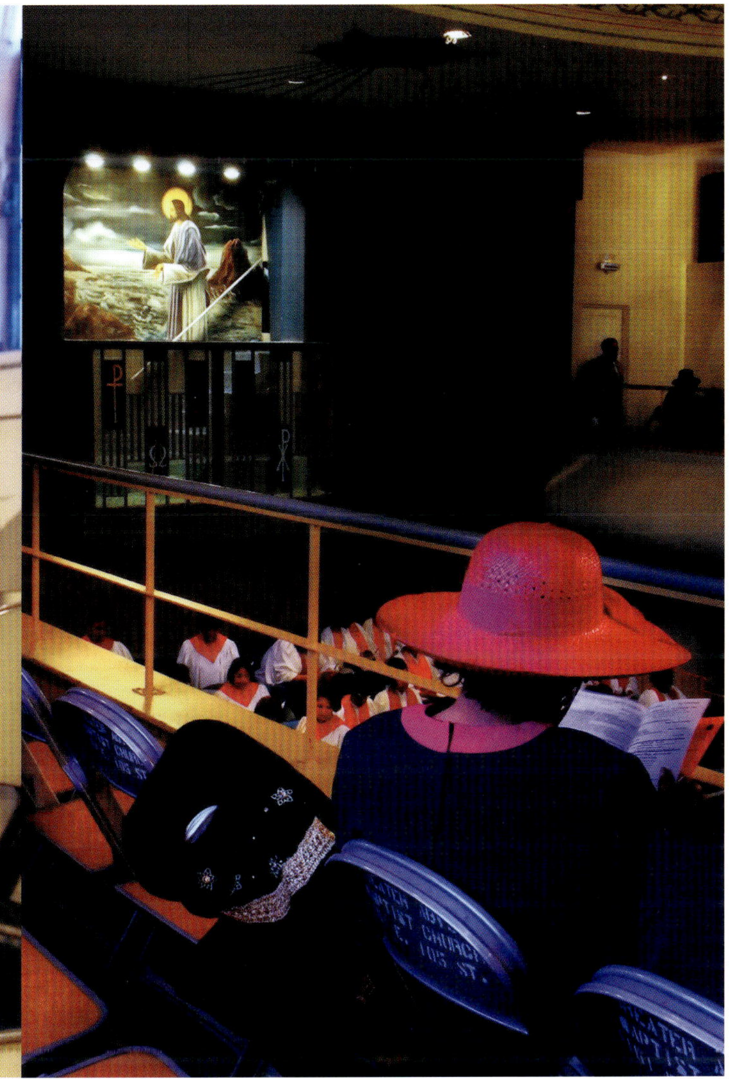

PATTERNS

St. John AME Church, October 2, 2005

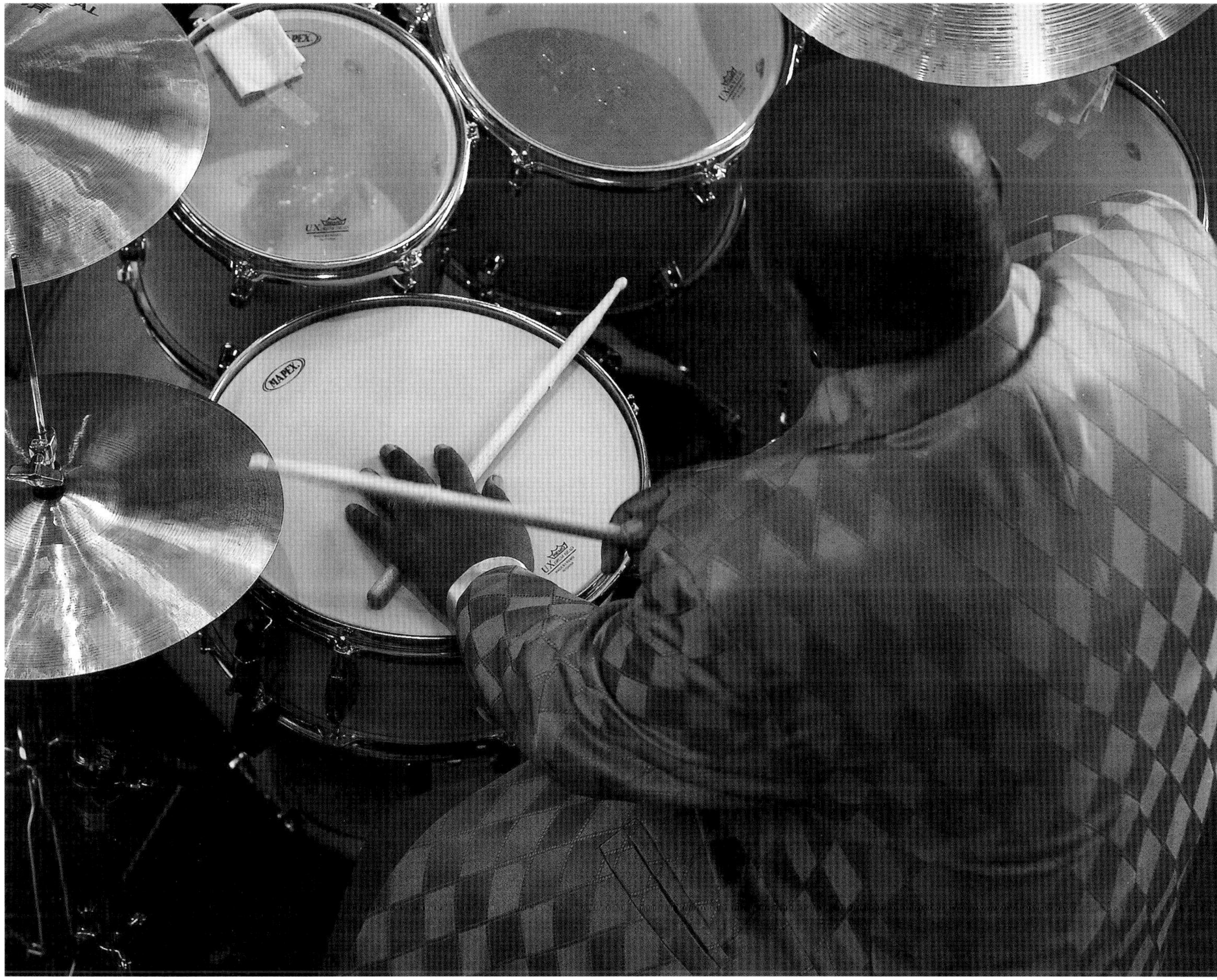
MAPEX

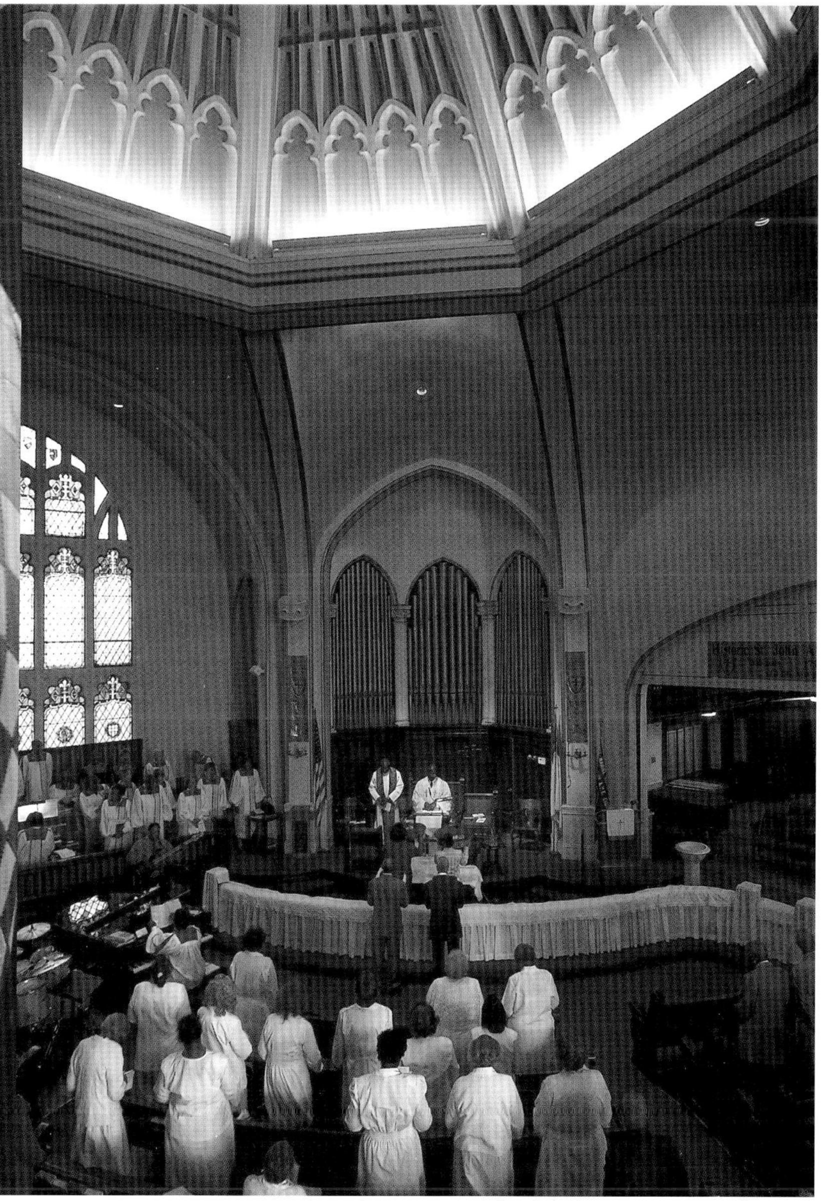

THE BAPTISM OF THE GLENVILLE HIGH SCHOOL FOOTBALL TEAM

Members of the Glenville High School football team await baptism, Calvary Hill Missionary Baptist Church, November 6, 2005

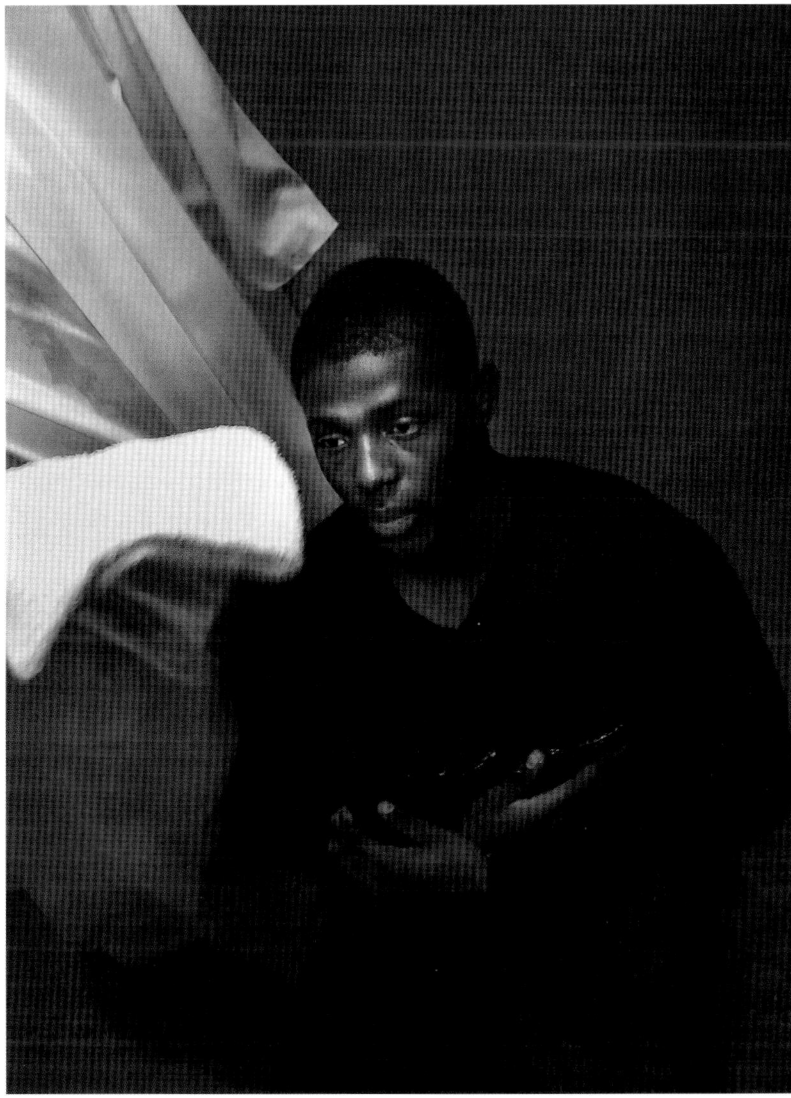

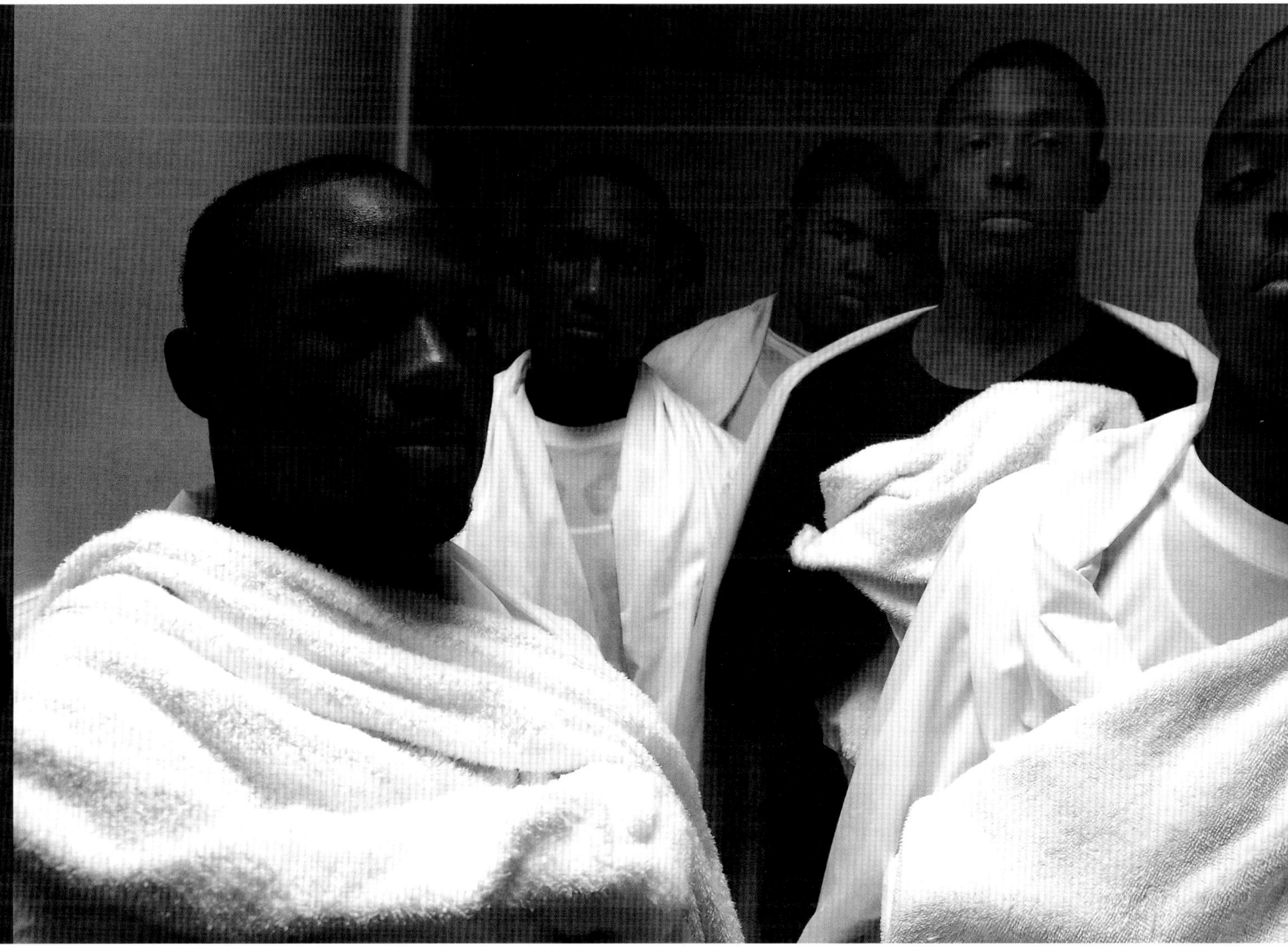

TENT REVIVAL
21st Annual Overland Tent
Crusade, Luke Easter Park,
Cleveland, July 7, 2004

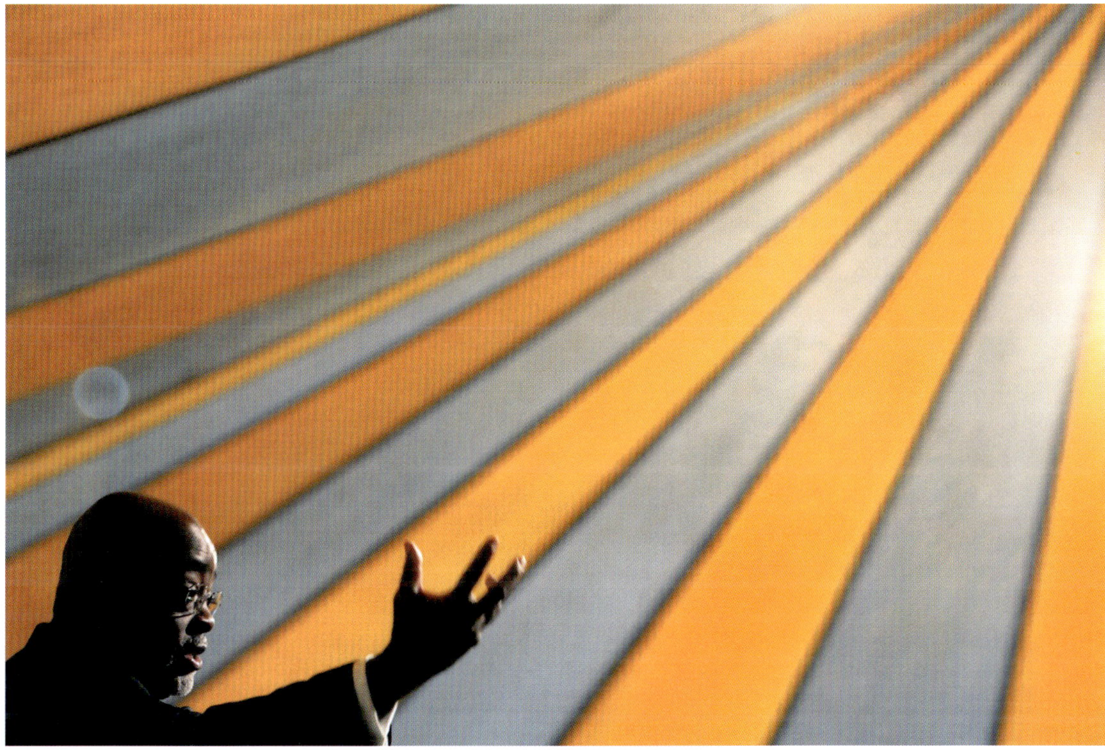

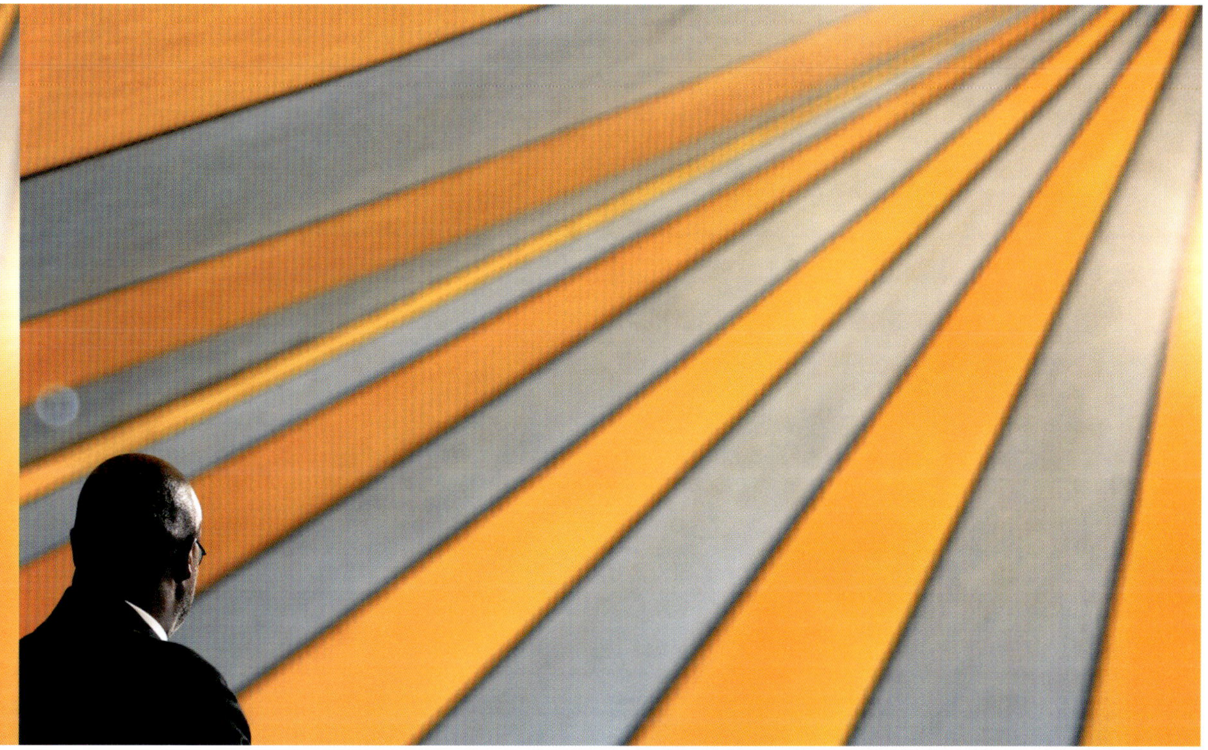

THE PASTOR'S PRAYER FOR YOUTH

The Reverend Otis Moss Jr.

Eternal God, Creator, Redeemer, Liberator, and Giver of all things beautiful, we praise you and thank you for your everlasting love.

We pray for wise minds, great health, and creative lives. Keep us to your glory and teach us in all conditions and circumstances to do your will.

Protect us in mind, body, and spirit from the hatred, violence, and disrespect of this world and the communities where we reside. Dear God, if we should become targets of hate and violence, help us never to become bearers and producers of hate and violence.

Equip us, we pray, to be ambassadors of hope. Equip us to be rappers of reason, respect, responsibility, reverence, and excellence.

"O Lord, our Lord, how excellent is thy name in all the earth."

In the name of Jesus. Amen.

PATHFINDERS
Glenville Seventh-Day Adventist Church, June 10, 2006.

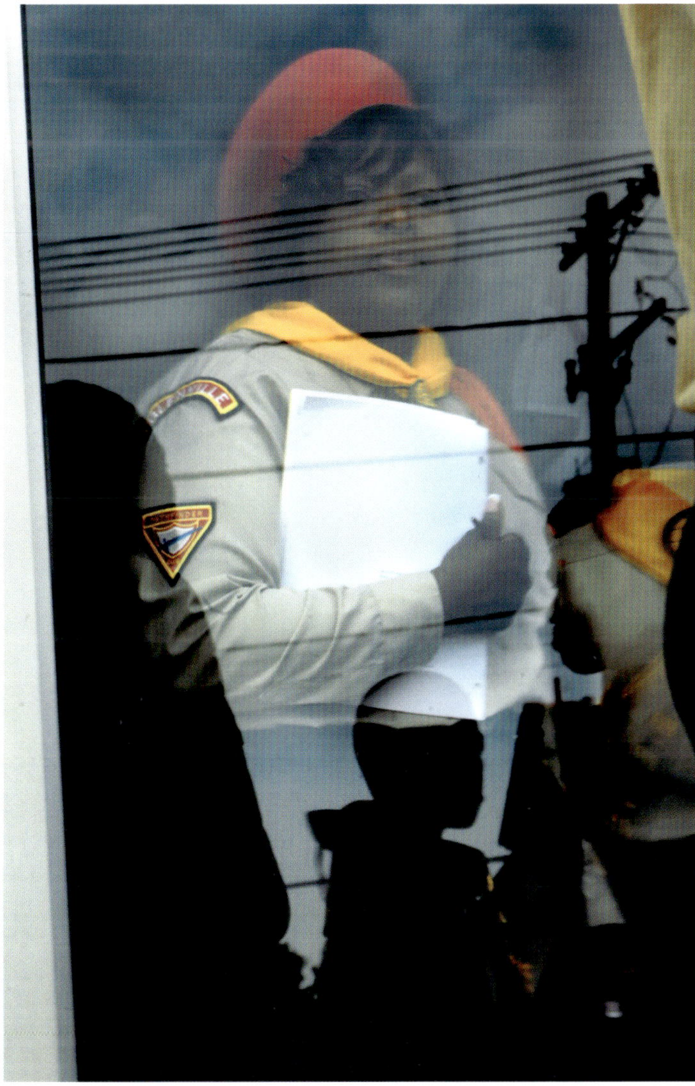

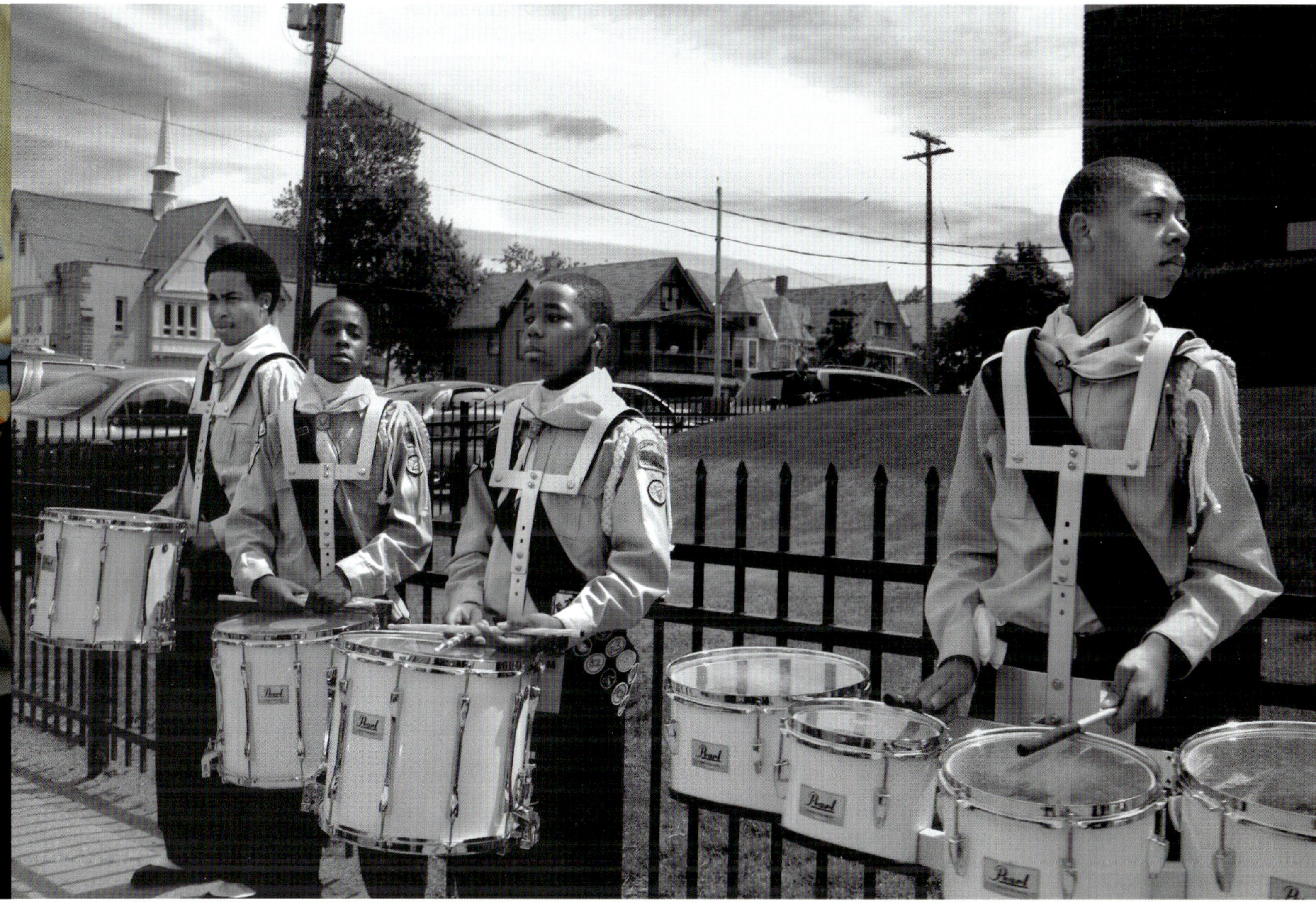
Pearl

this page

CARRY ON

St. Andrews Episcopal Church, March 21, 2004

facing page

STREET SCENES

(Left) New Revelation Baptist Church, June 20, 2004. (Right) An abandoned church on East 79th Street, October 29, 2000

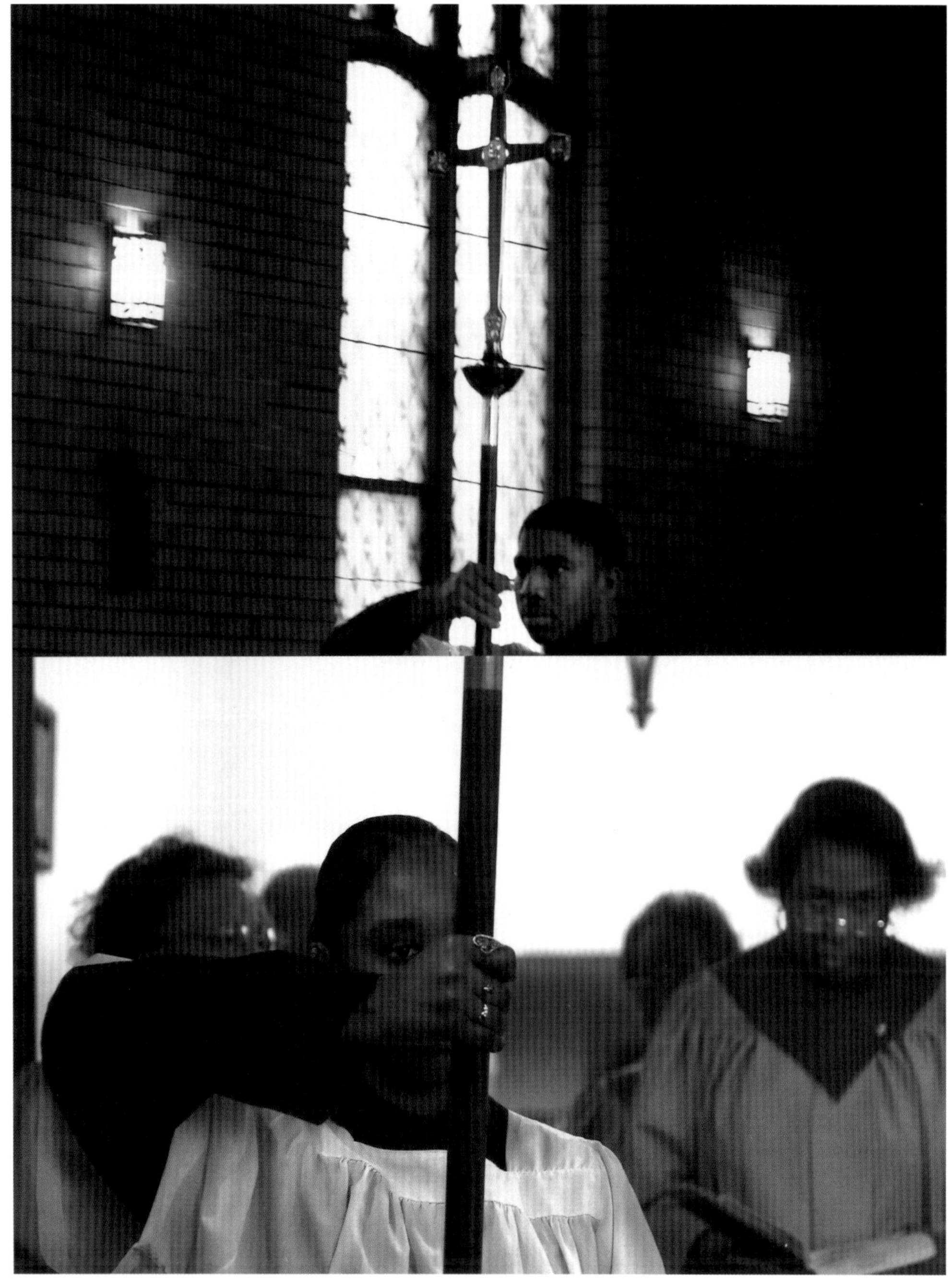

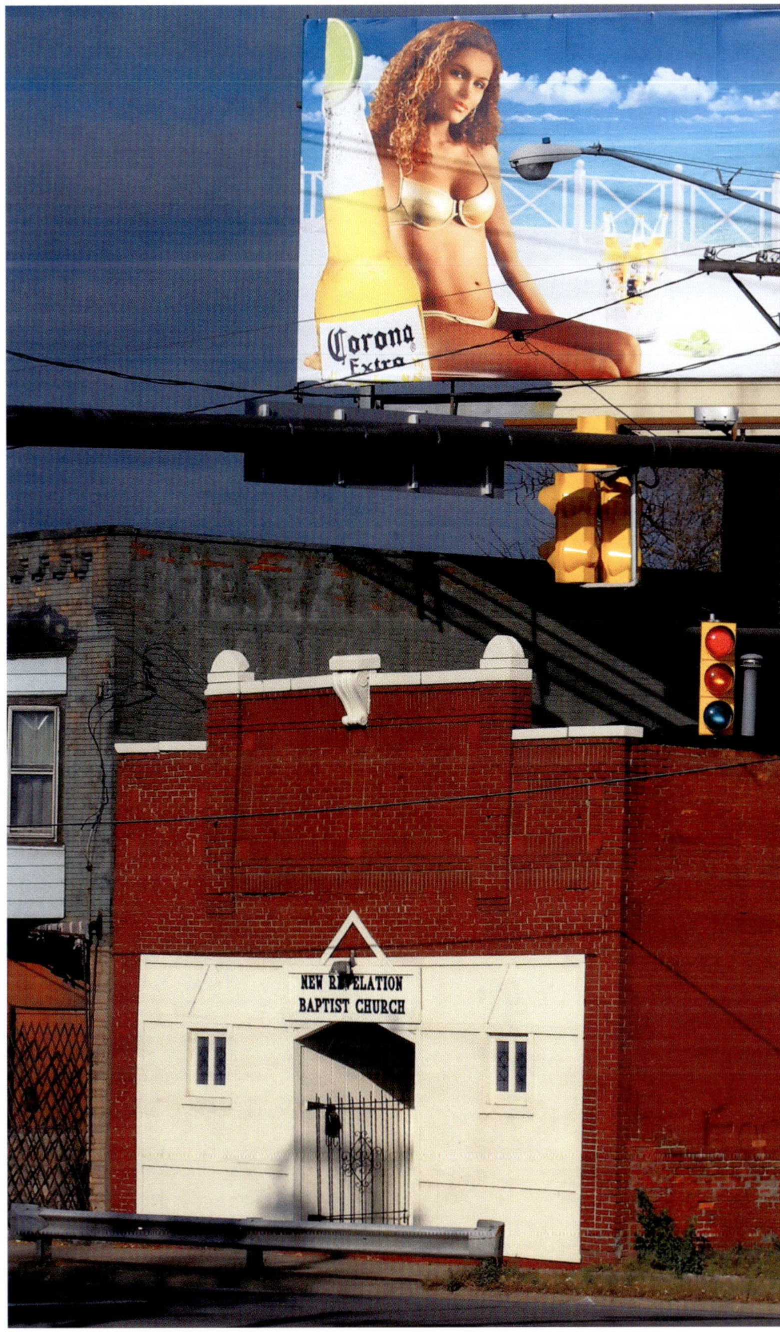
Corona
Extra
BAPTIST CHURCH

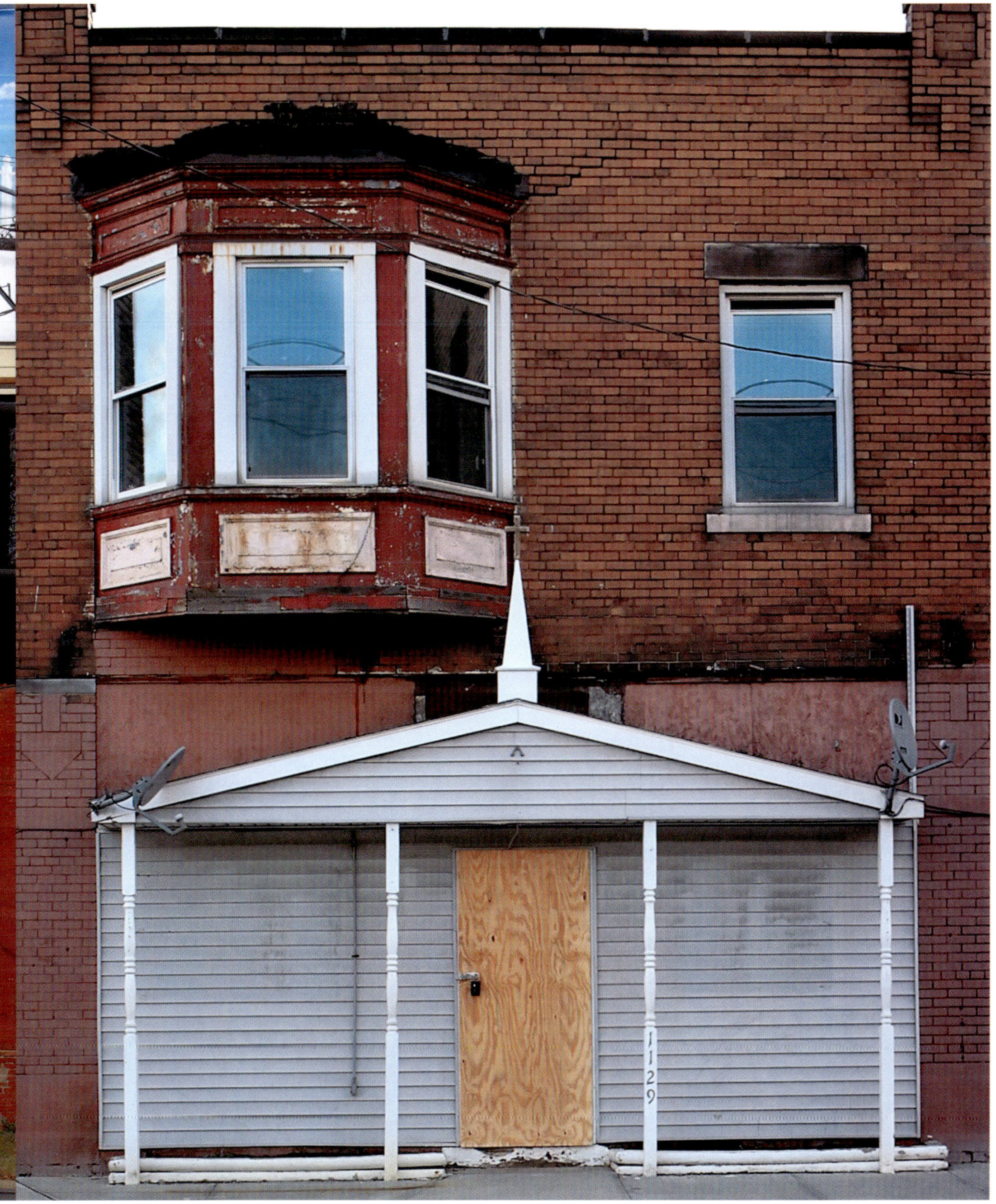
1129

HANDS

(Left) Antioch Baptist Church, October 26, 2003. (Right) Live Ministries/Church of Recovery, August 31, 2003

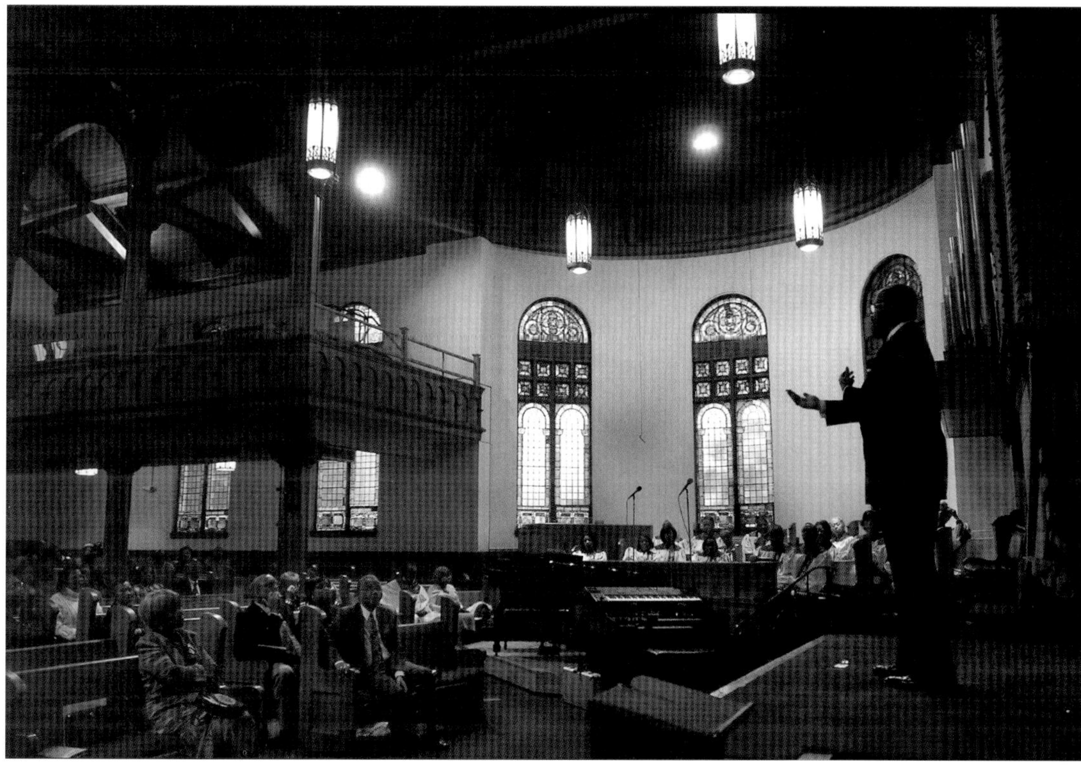

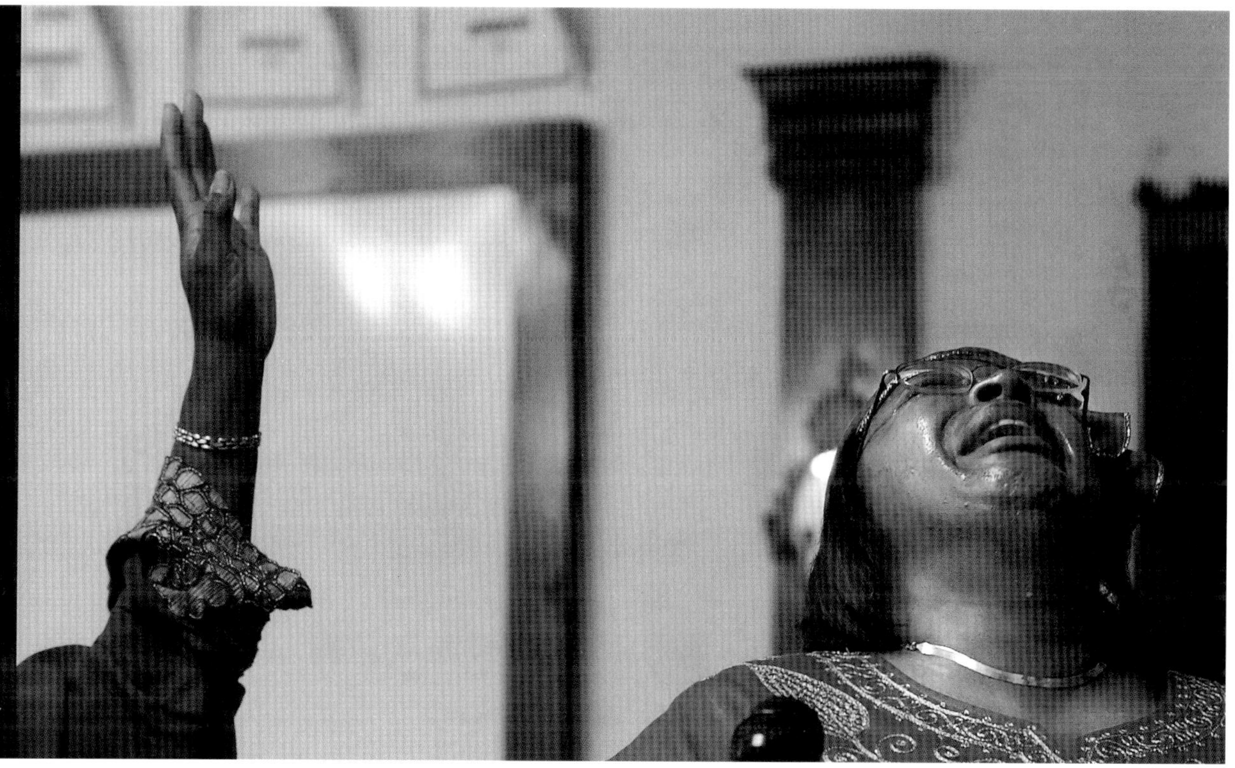

ONE

(Left) New Jerusalem Church of God in Christ, April 2, 2006. (Right) Tent of Fire Revival, July 15, 2004

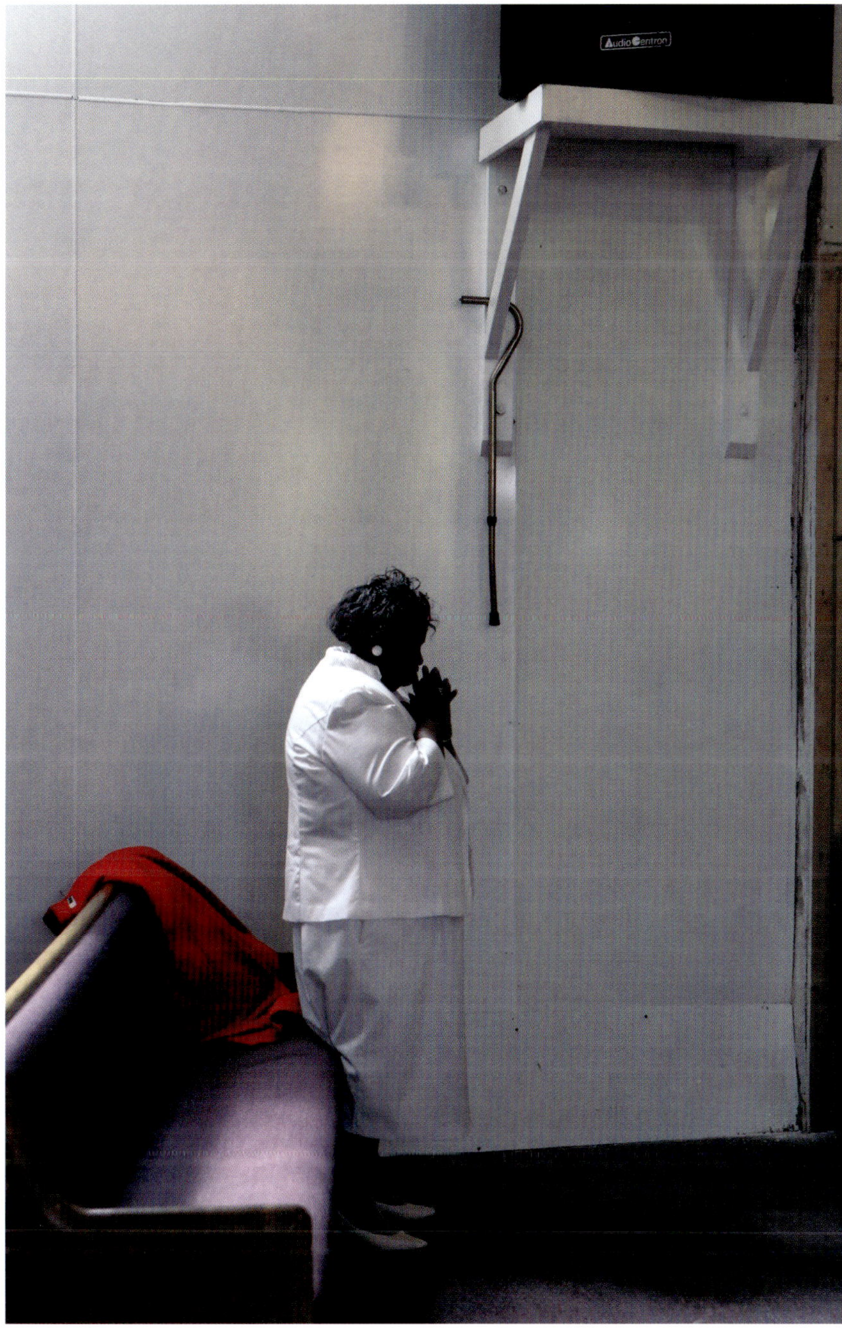

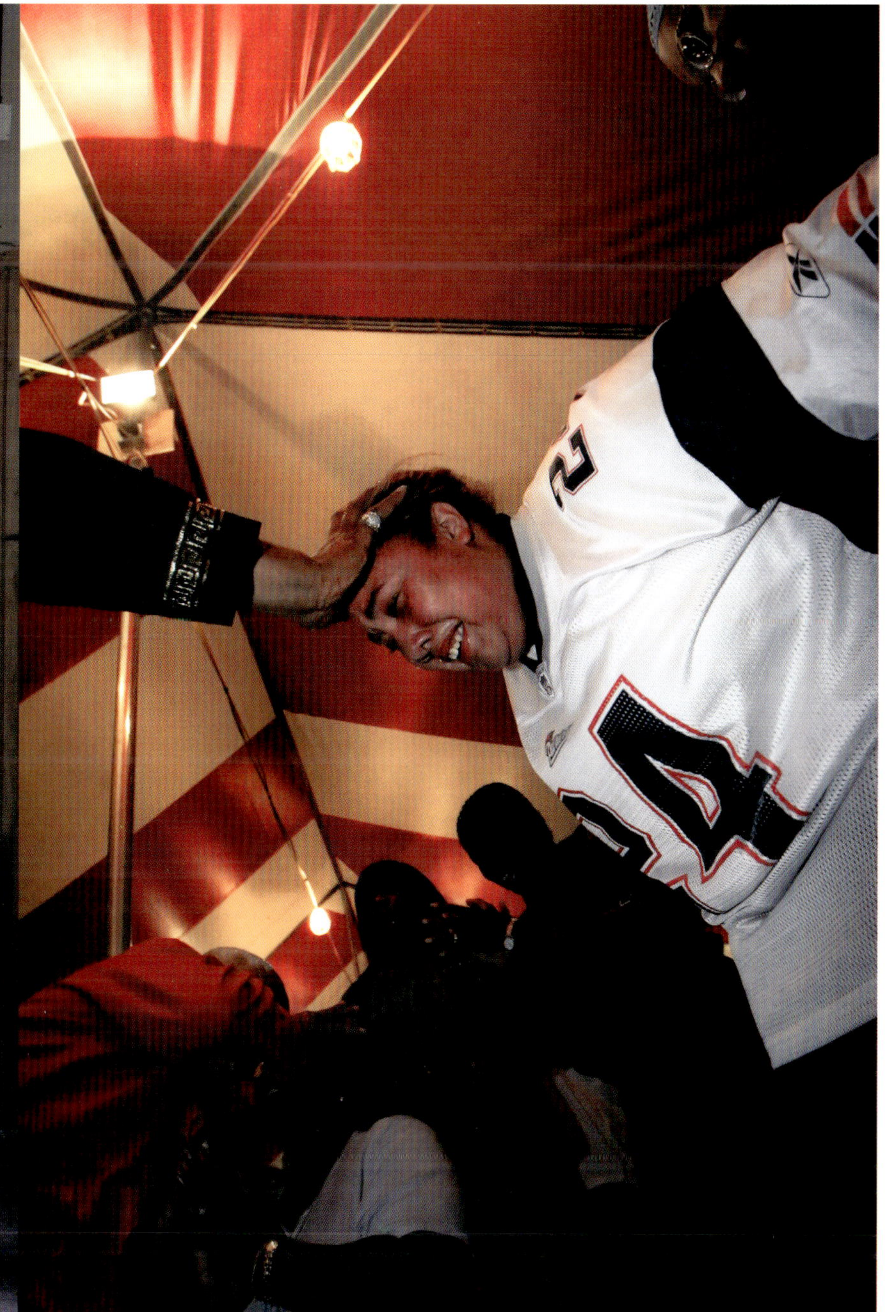

ON THE CORNER
Living Word of the Apostolic Faith
Church, June 18, 2006

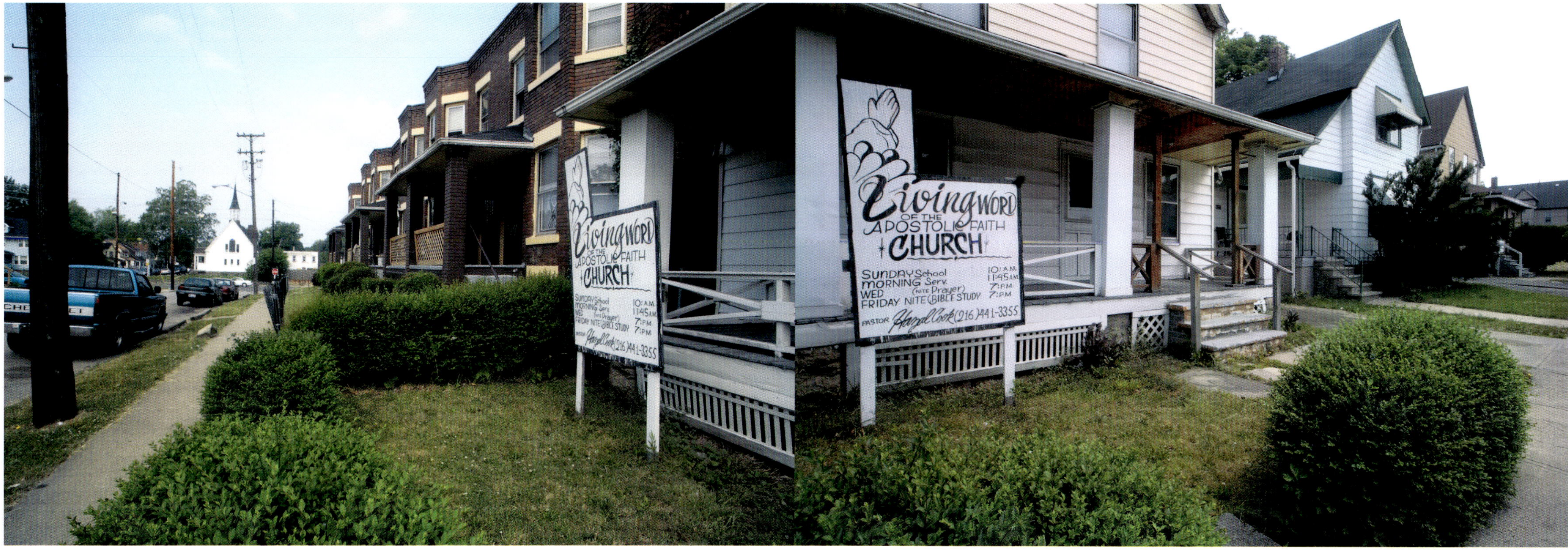
LivingWORD
OF THE
APOSTOLIC FAITH
CHURCH
SUNDAY School 10: A.M.
MORNING Serv. 11:45 A.M.
WED (NITE Prayer) 7: P.M.
FRIDAY NITE (BIBLE STUDY 7: P.M
PASTOR Hazel Cook (216) 441-3355

LIFE

Live Ministries/Church of Recovery, August 12, 2003 (left) and July 7, 2003 (right)

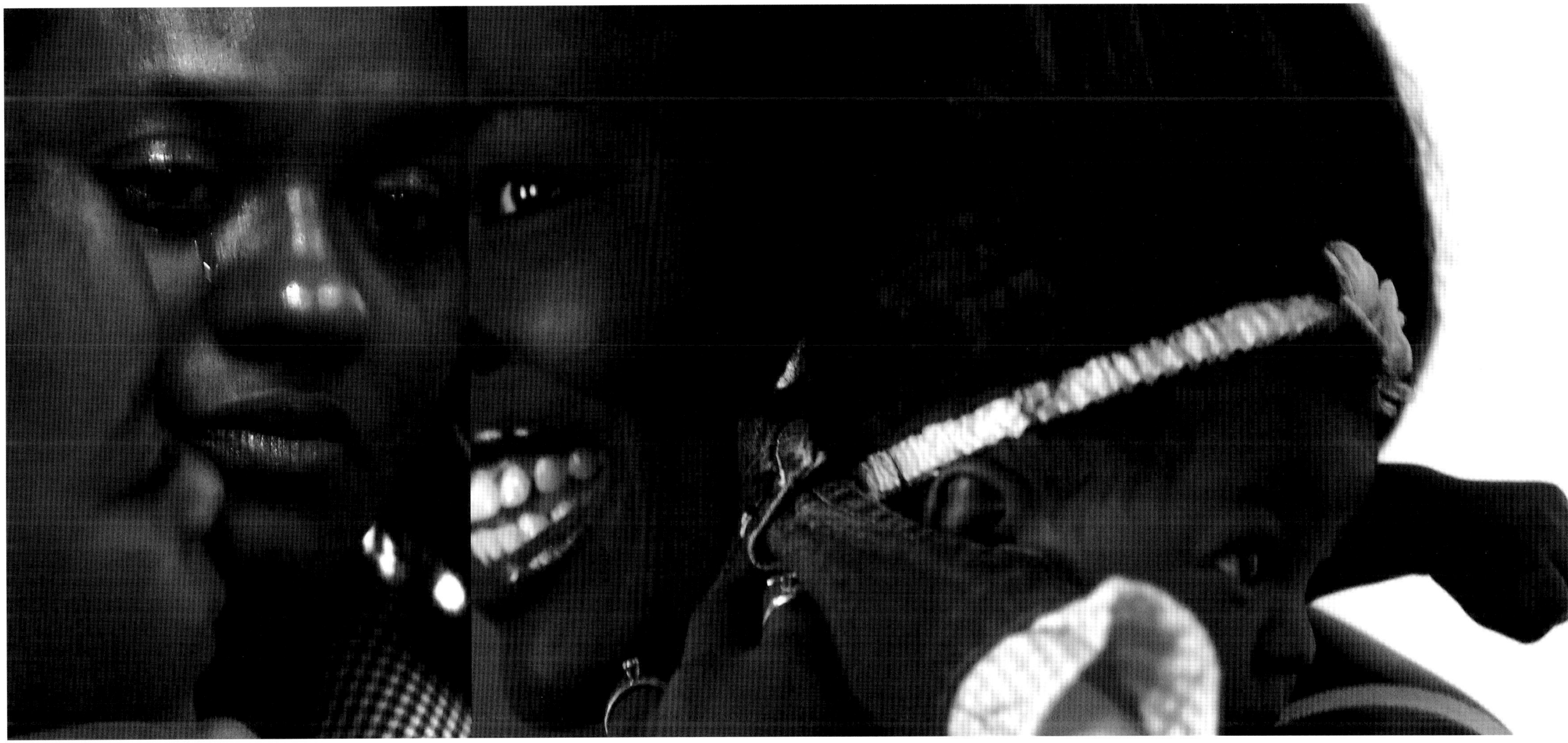

EASTER MORNING BAPTISM

Olivet Institutional Baptist Church,

April 11, 2004

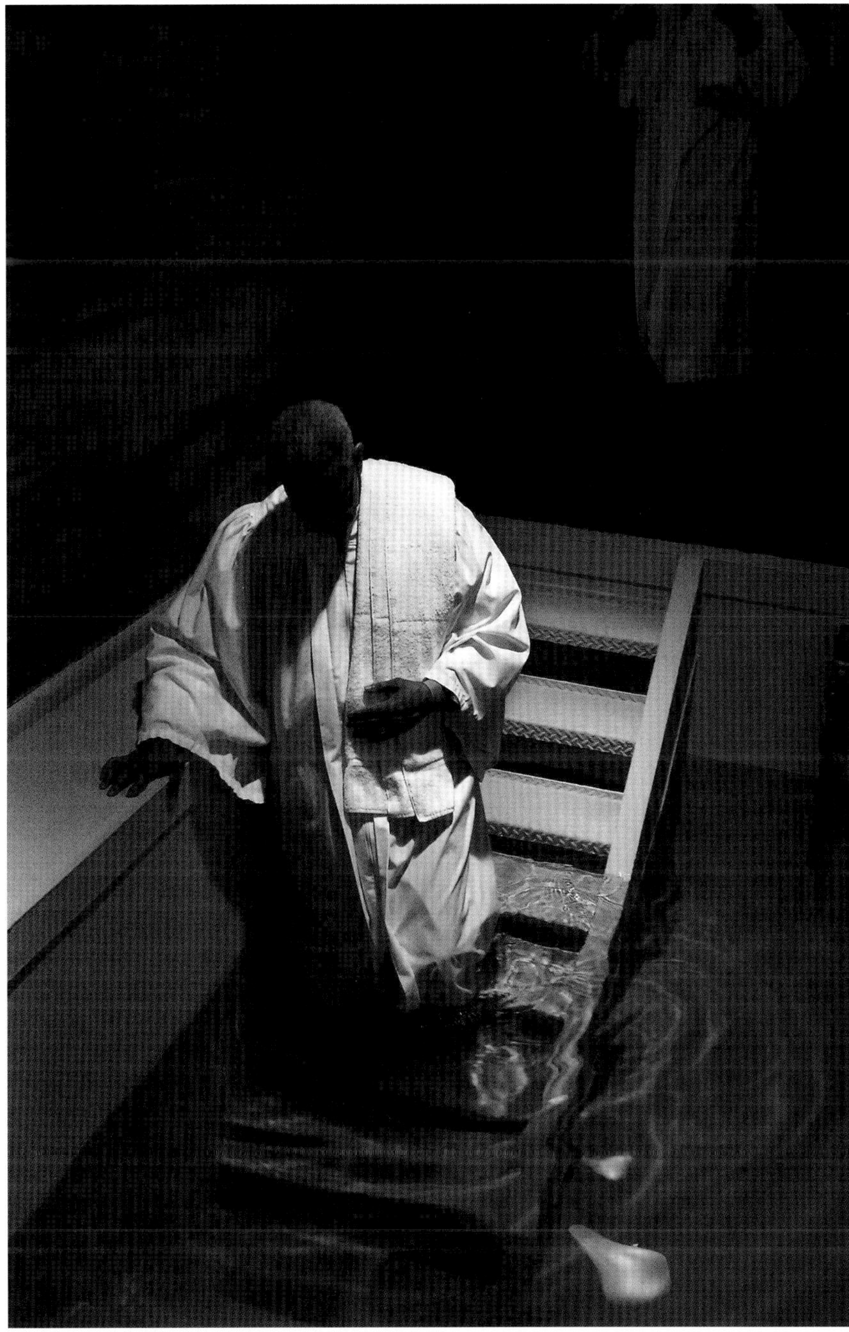

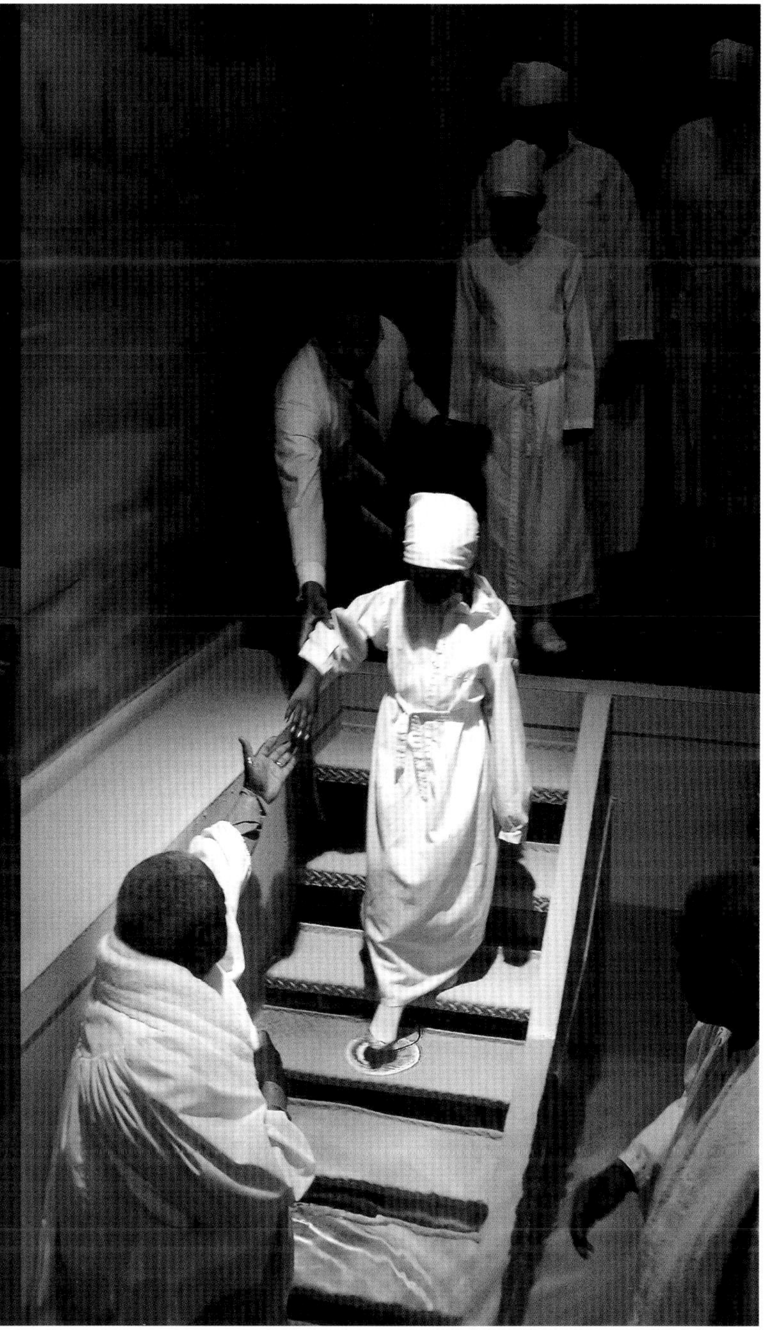

CHRISTMAS EVE

St. Adalbert Roman Catholic Church, December 24, 2006

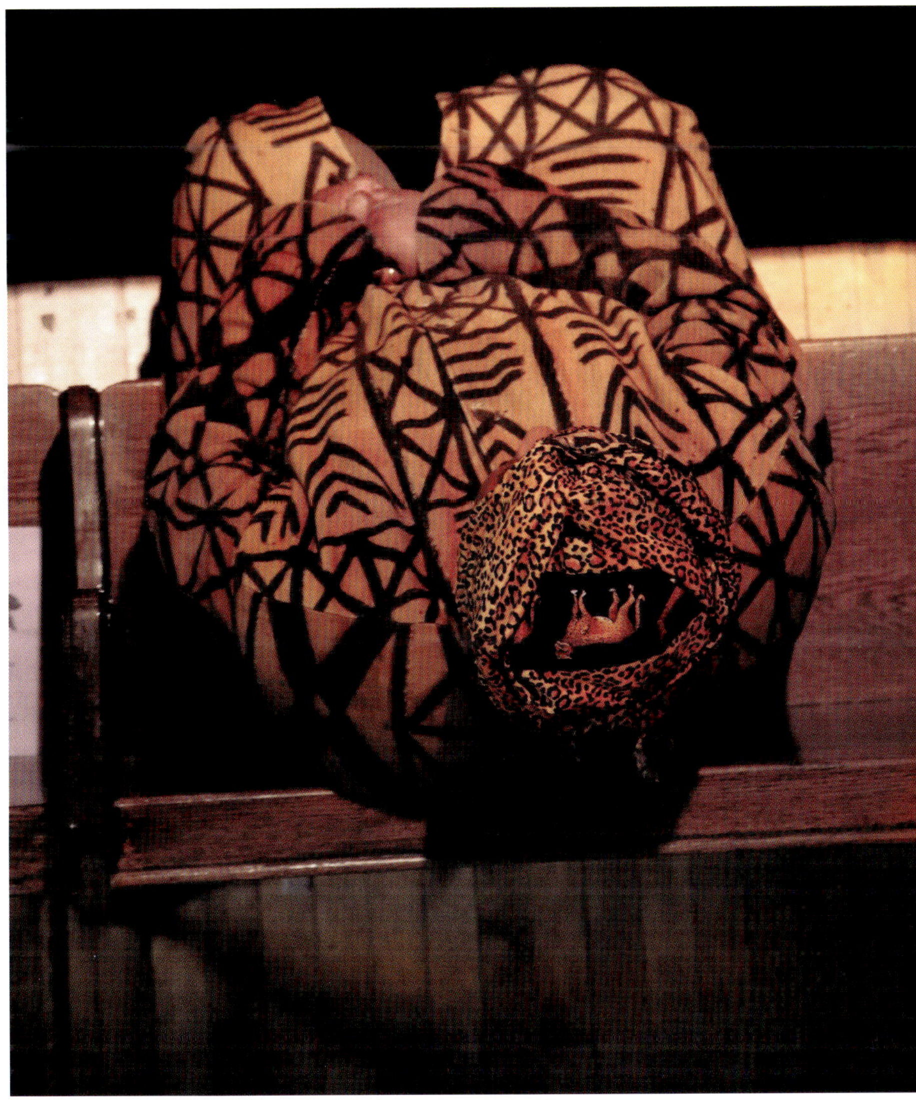

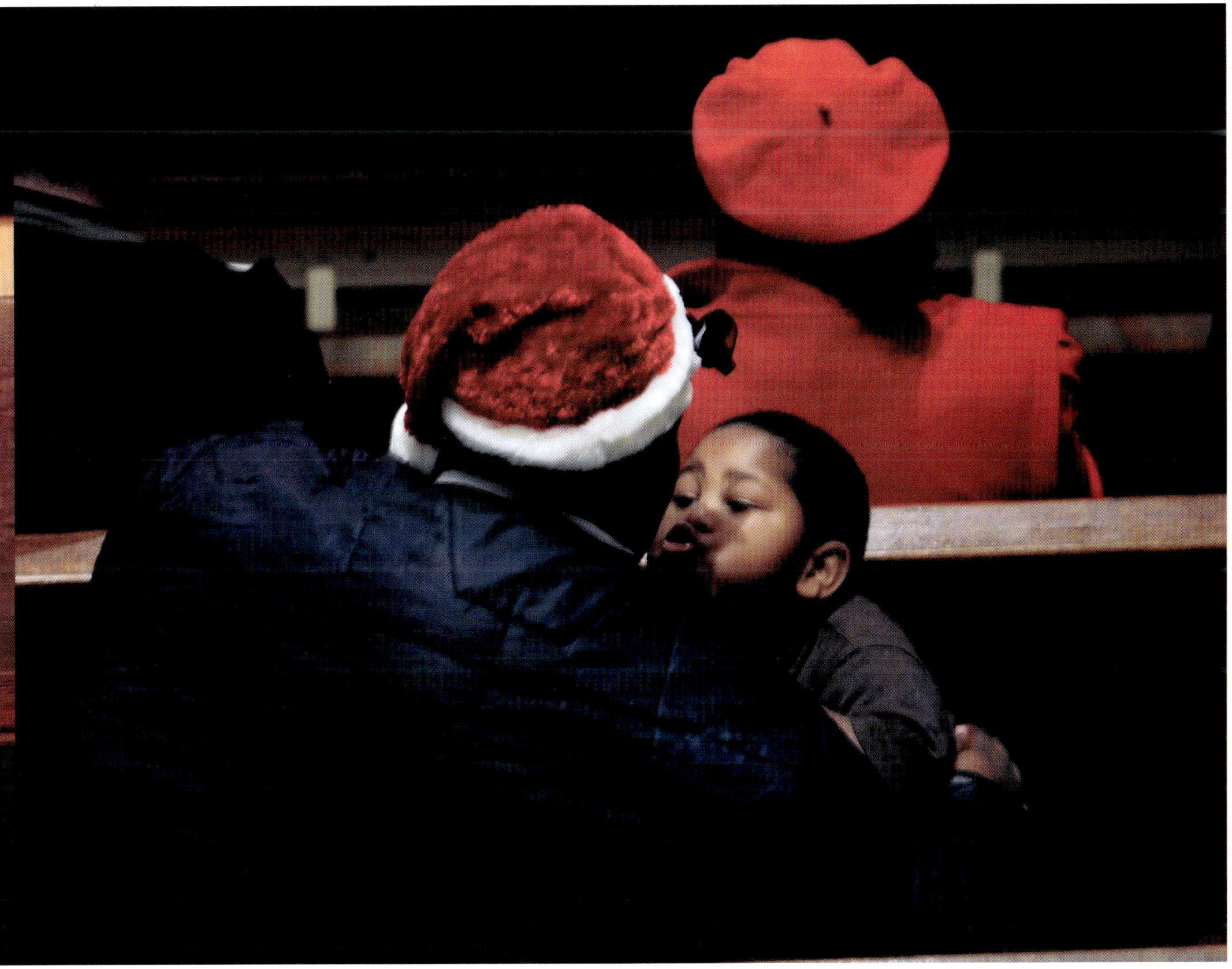

It's me, it's me, it's me, O Lord,
Standing in the need of prayer,
It's me, it's me, it's me, O Lord,
Standing in the need of prayer.

'Tain't my mother or my father,
But it's me, O Lord,
Standing in the need of prayer.
'Tain't my deacon or my leader,
But it's me, O Lord,
Standing in the need of prayer.

—Traditional

SADNESS AND JOY

Cleveland Church of Christ,
June 20, 2004

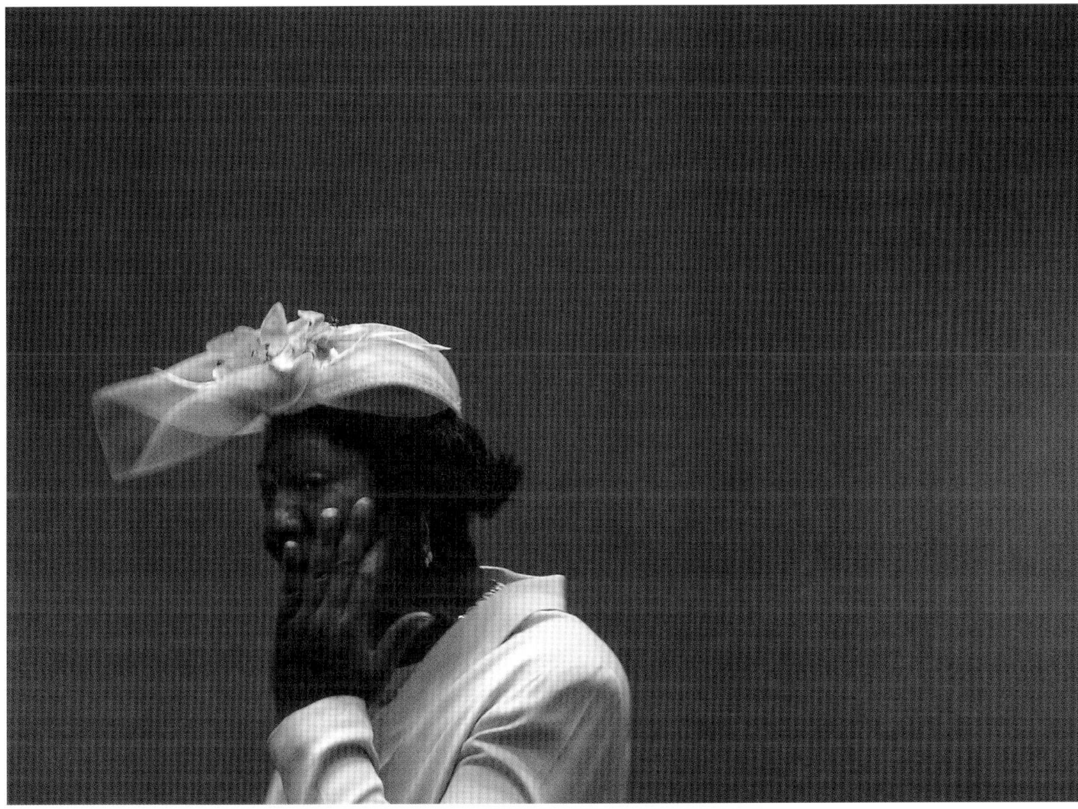

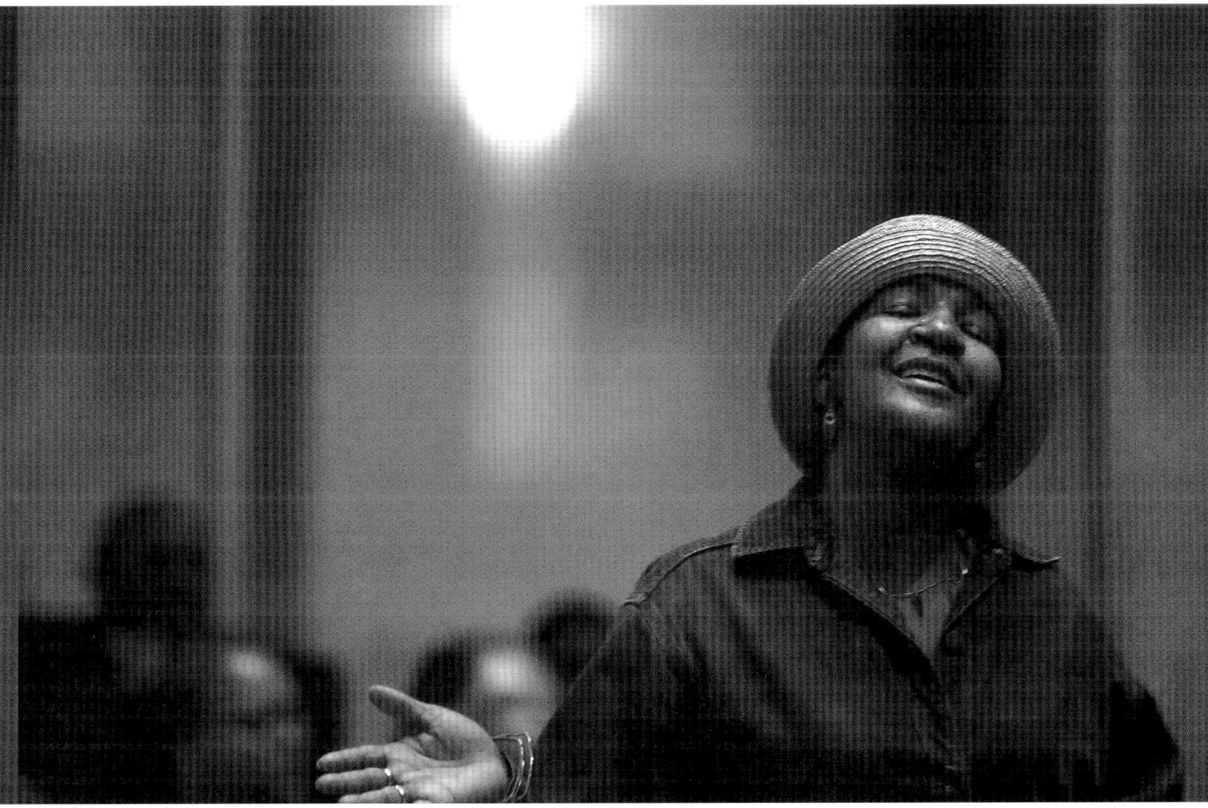

MAN IN PLAID SHIRT

Mt. Sinai Baptist Church, October
10, 2004

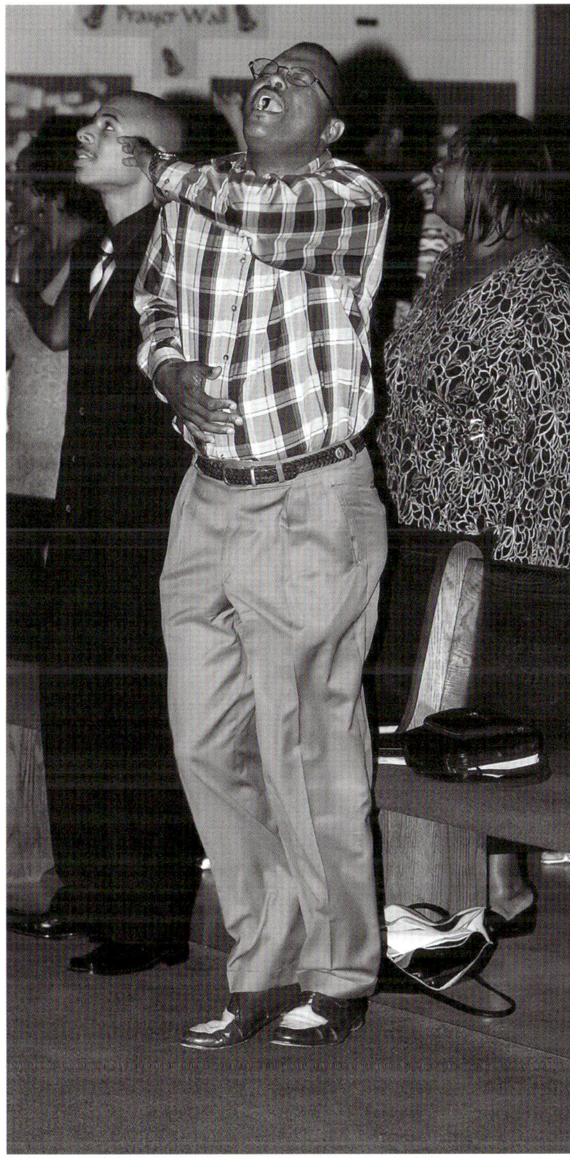
Prayer Wall

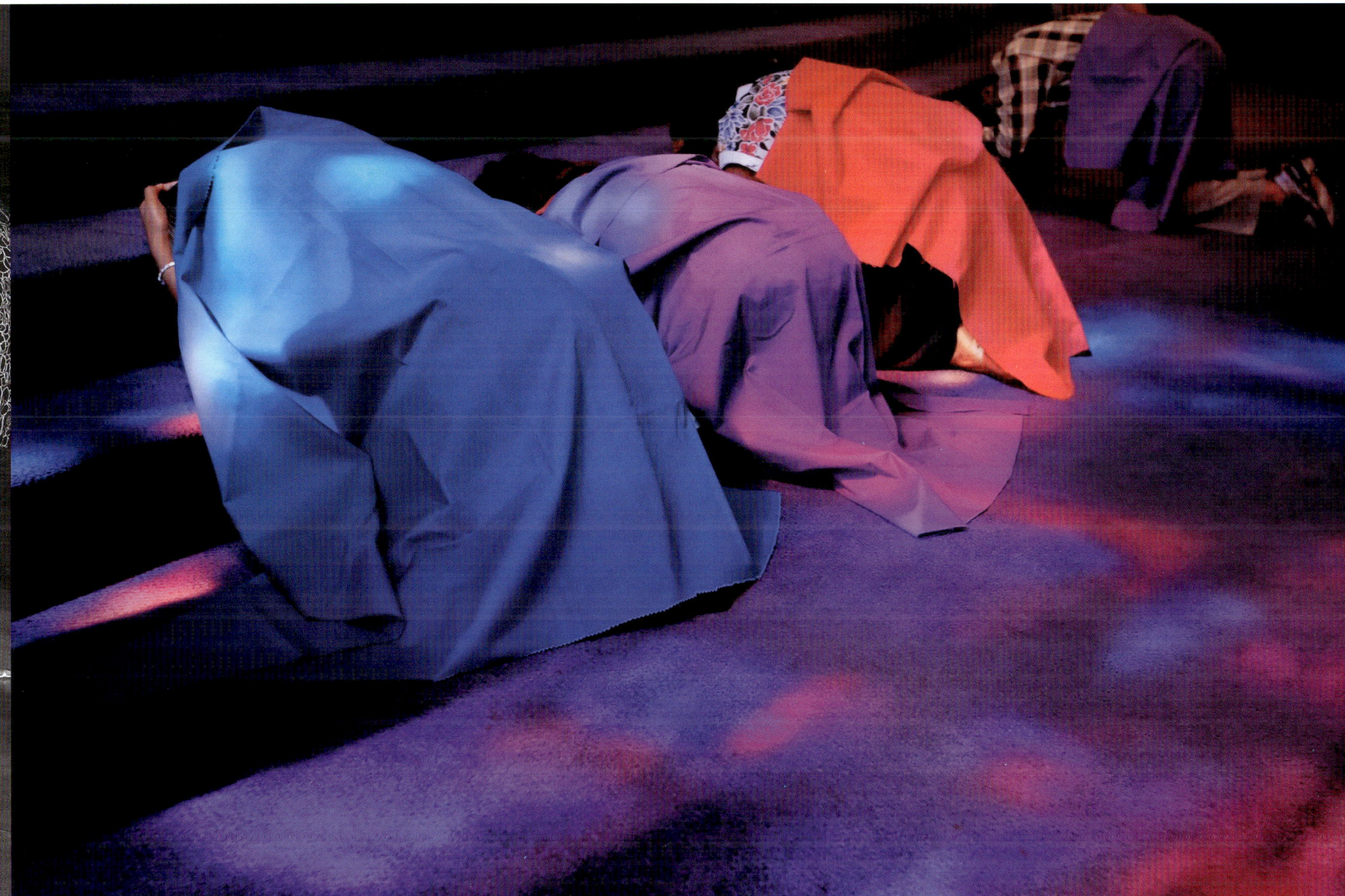

HANDS

(Left) Mt. Sinai Baptist Church, March 14, 2004. (Right) Windermere United Methodist Church, June 4, 2006

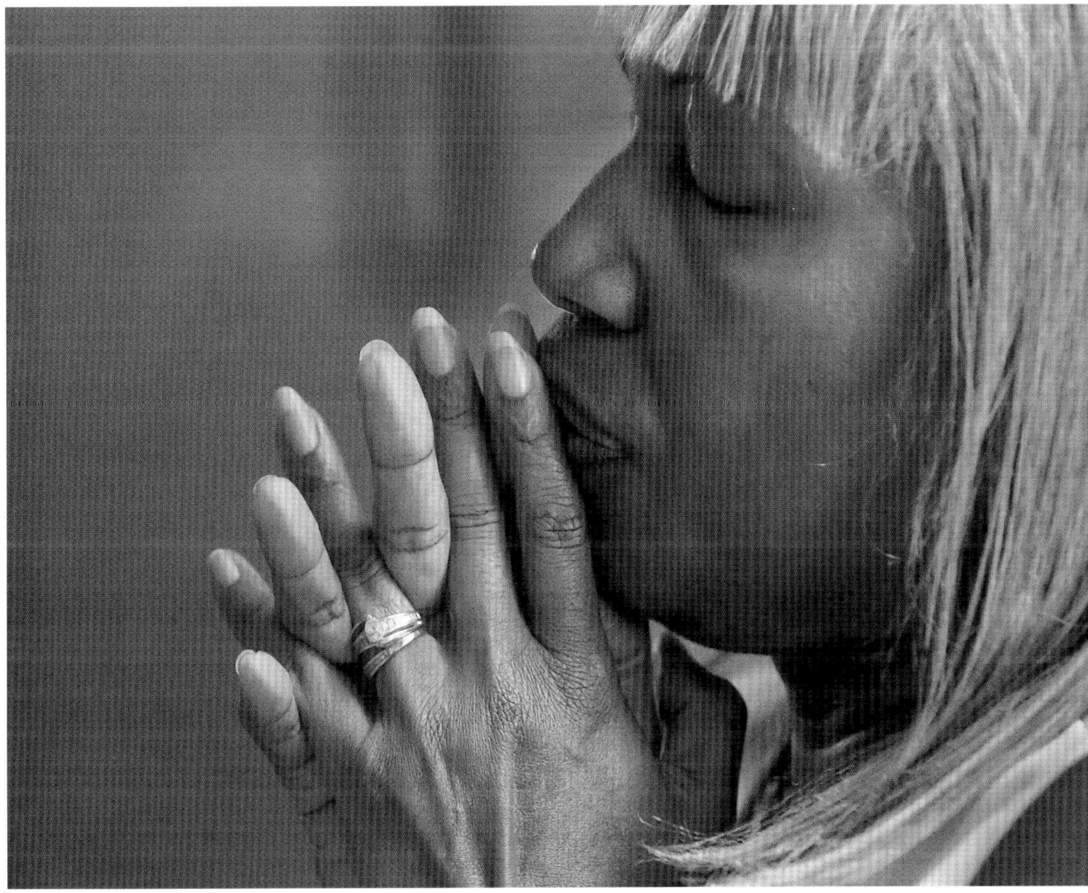

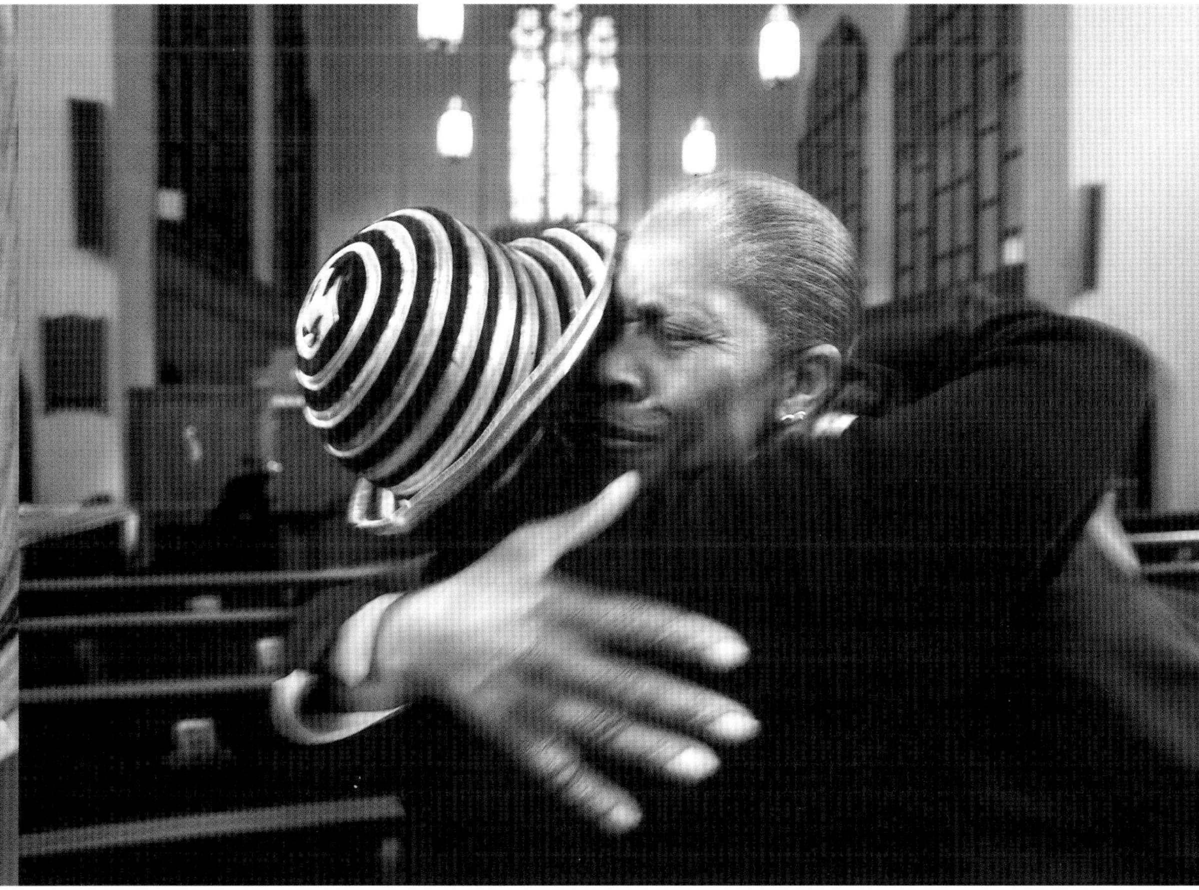

HEAVENLY FATHER

Living Word of the Apostolic Faith

Gospel Church, June 18, 2006

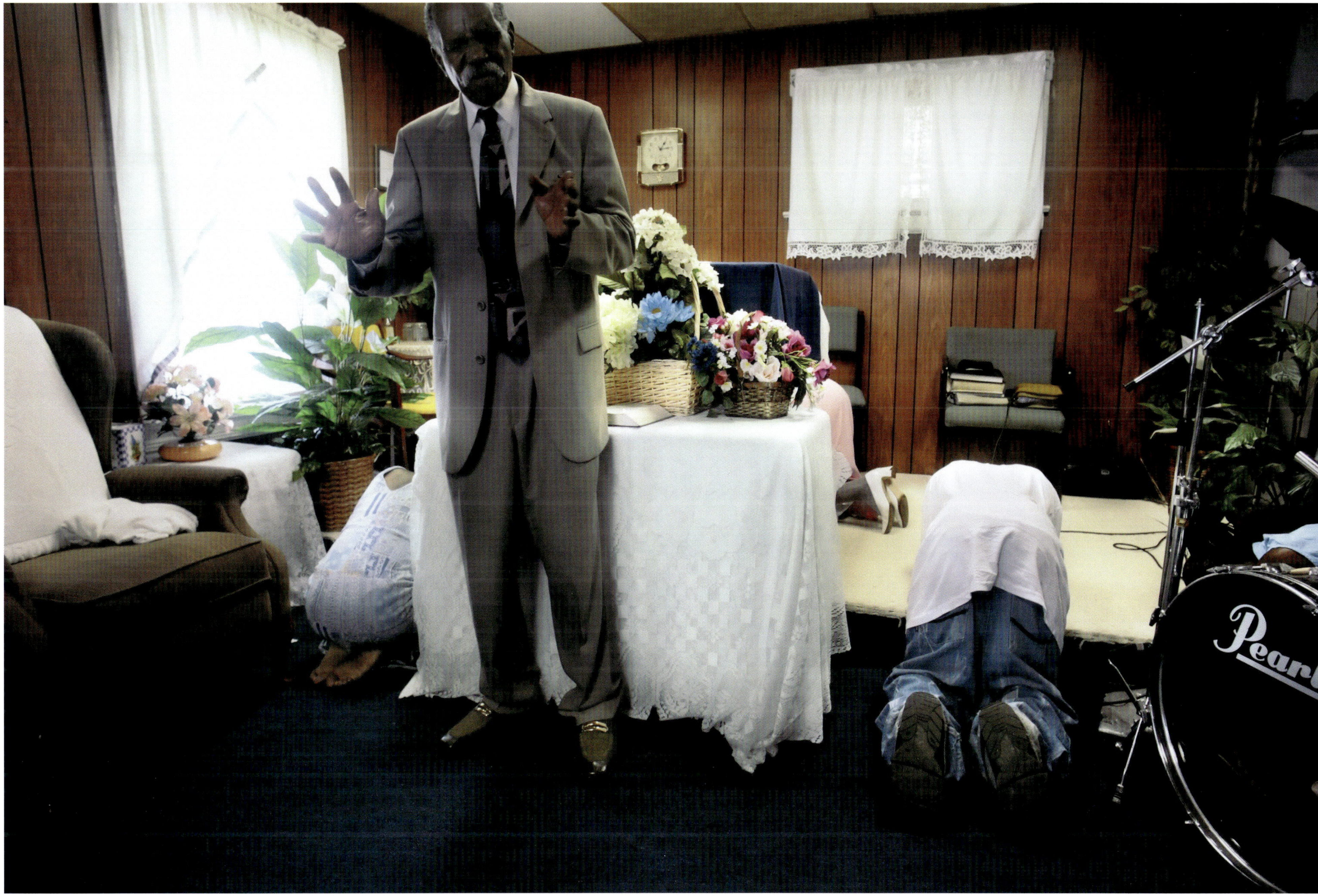
Pearl

GLASS

(Left) Pentecostal Church of Christ, February 8, 2004. (Right) Cory United Methodist Church reflected in window, September 20, 2006

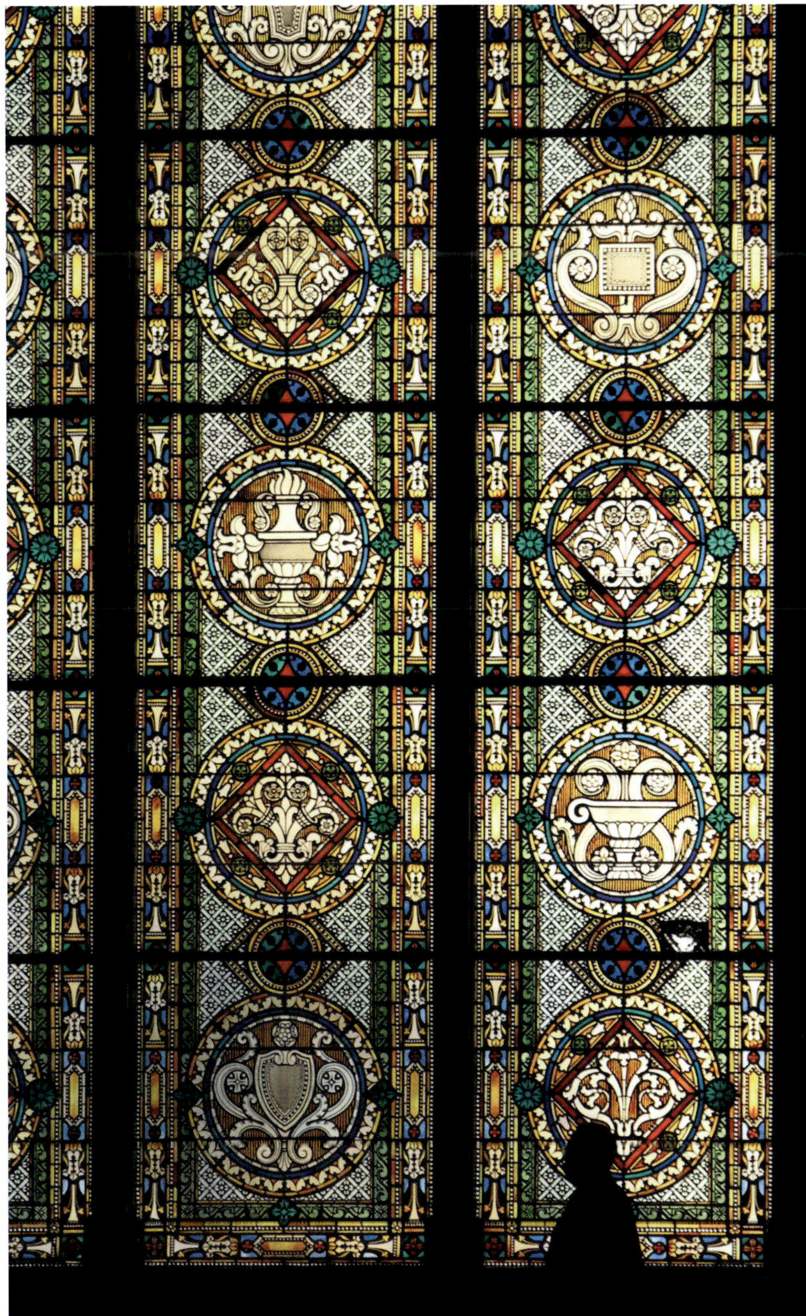

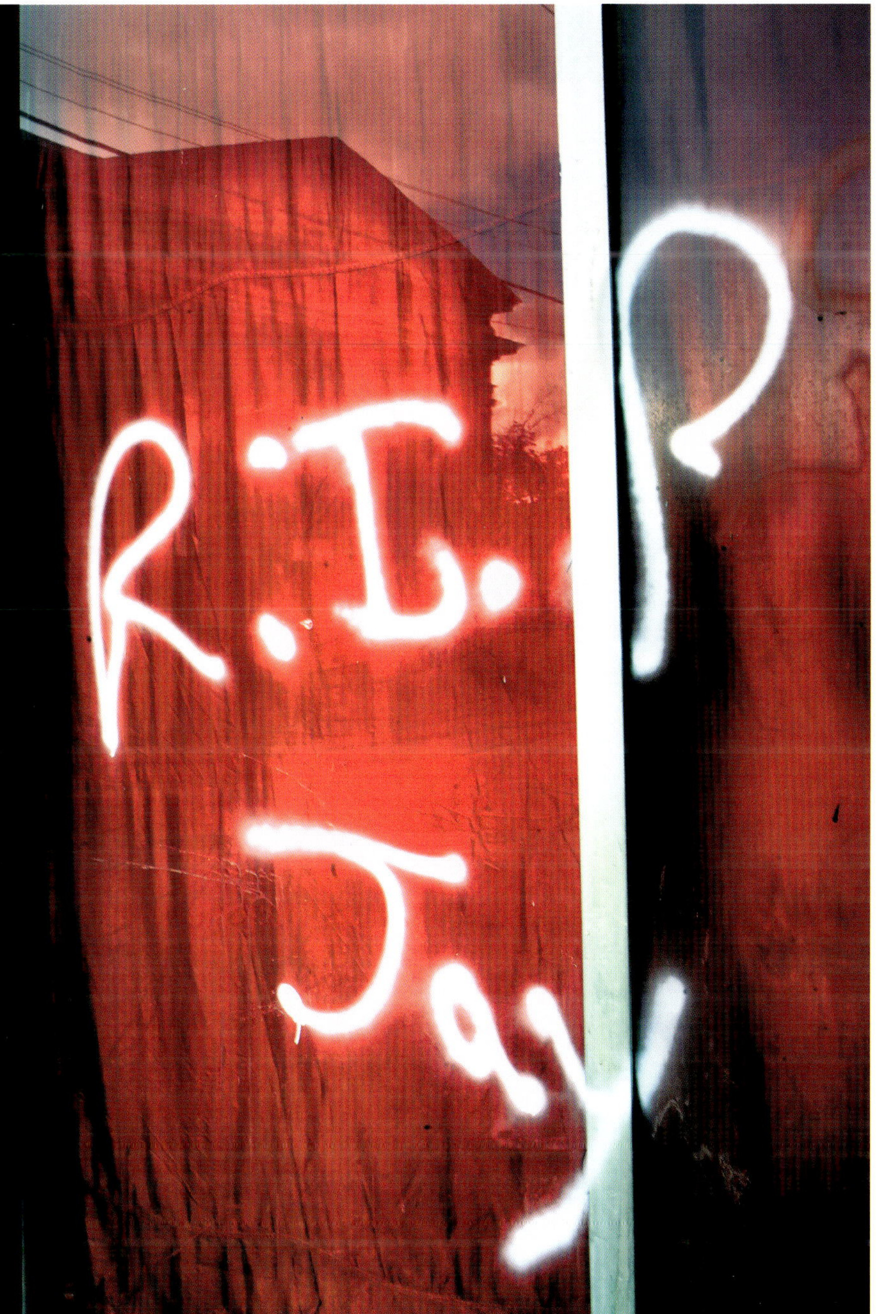
R.I.P
Jay

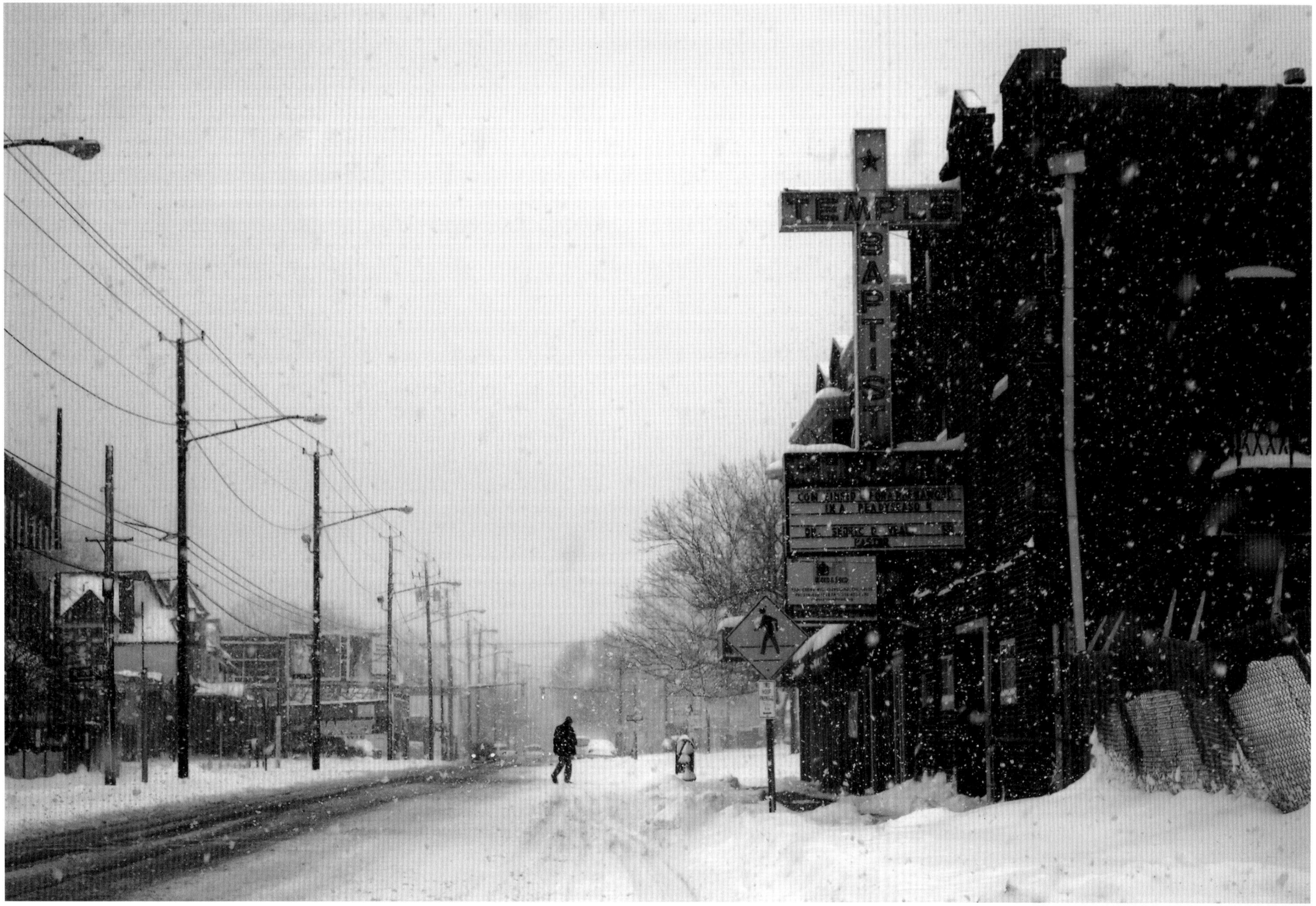
TEMPLE
BAPTIST

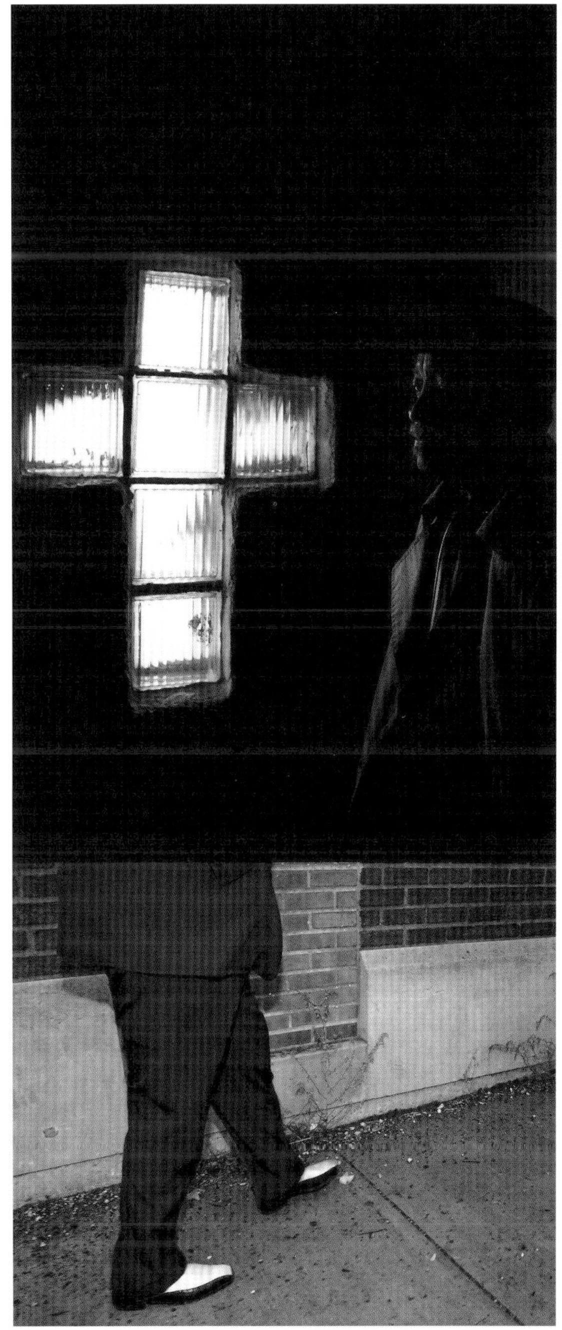

facing page

EASTER MORNING

A man heading to Temple Baptist Church along Cedar Avenue, April 8, 2007

this page

CROSSROADS

(Top) New Jerusalem Church of God in Christ, January 18, 2005. (Bottom) Going to a funeral, Mt. Sinai Baptist Church, October 25, 2003

CIRCLE OF LIFE

(Top) Mt. Sinai Baptist Church, February 5, 2006. (Bottom) Eaglewing Missionary Baptist Church, May 28, 2006

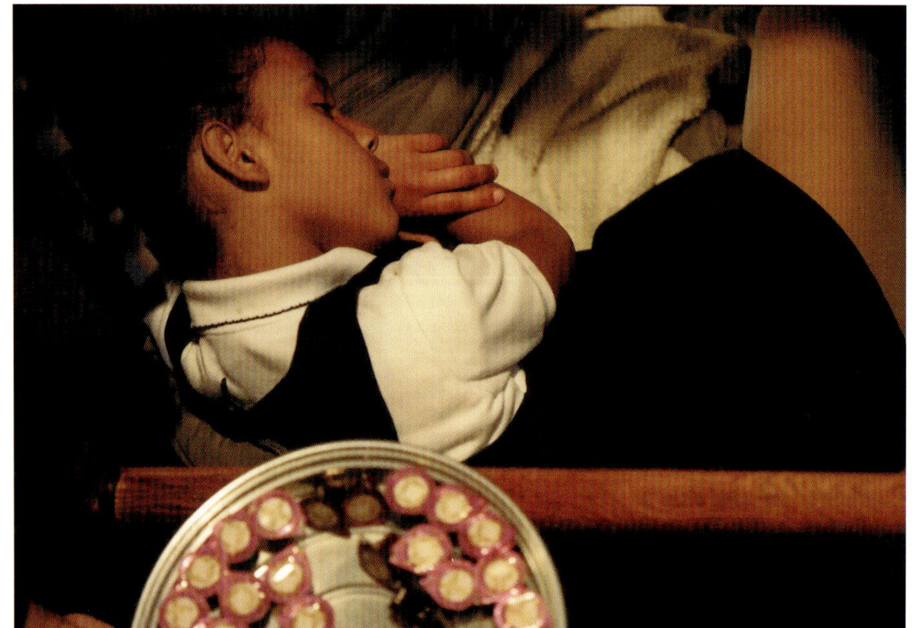

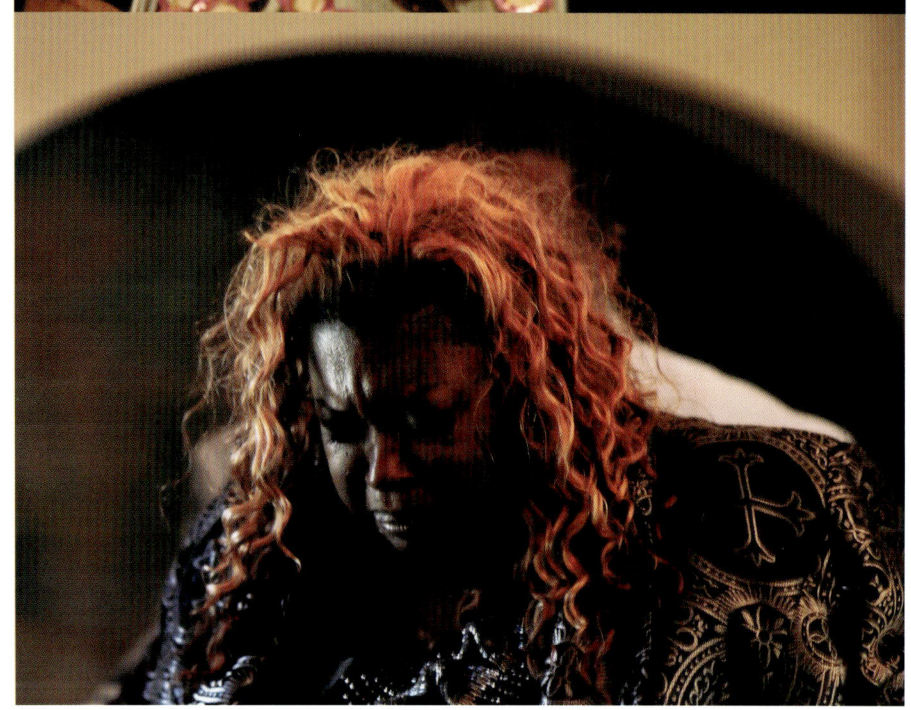

Jesus is on the mainline
Tell him what you want
Jesus is on the mainline
Tell him what you want
Jesus is on the mainline
Tell him what you want
Call him up and tell him what you want.

The line ain't never busy
Tell him what you want
The line ain't ever busy
Tell him what you want
The line ain't ever busy
Tell him what you want
Keep on calling him up
And telling him what you want.

—Traditional

H. TURNER THOMPSON

Antioch Baptist Church, July 25, 2006

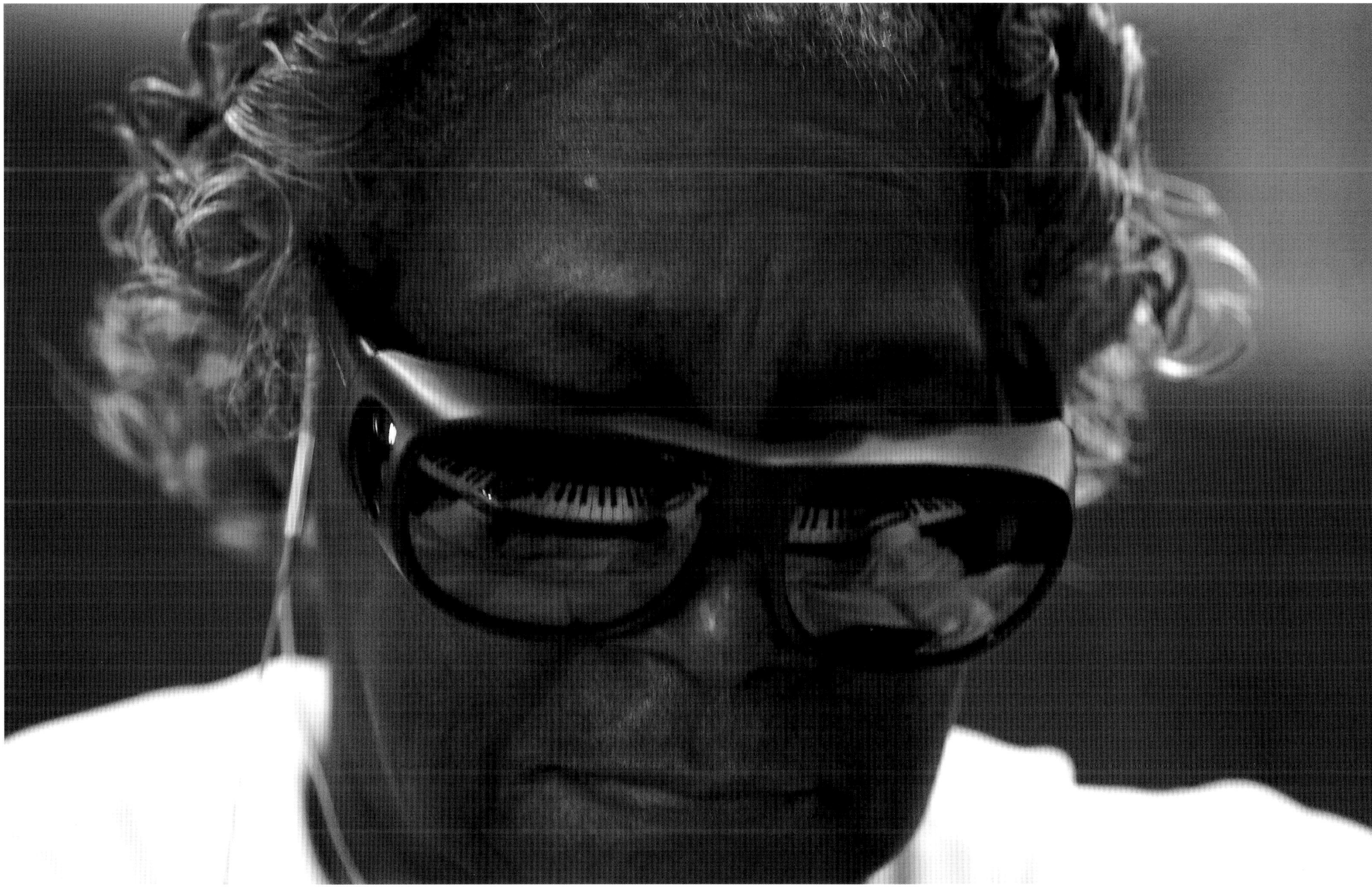

THE REVEREND C. J. MATTHEWS

Mt. Sinai Baptist Church, April 2, 2006

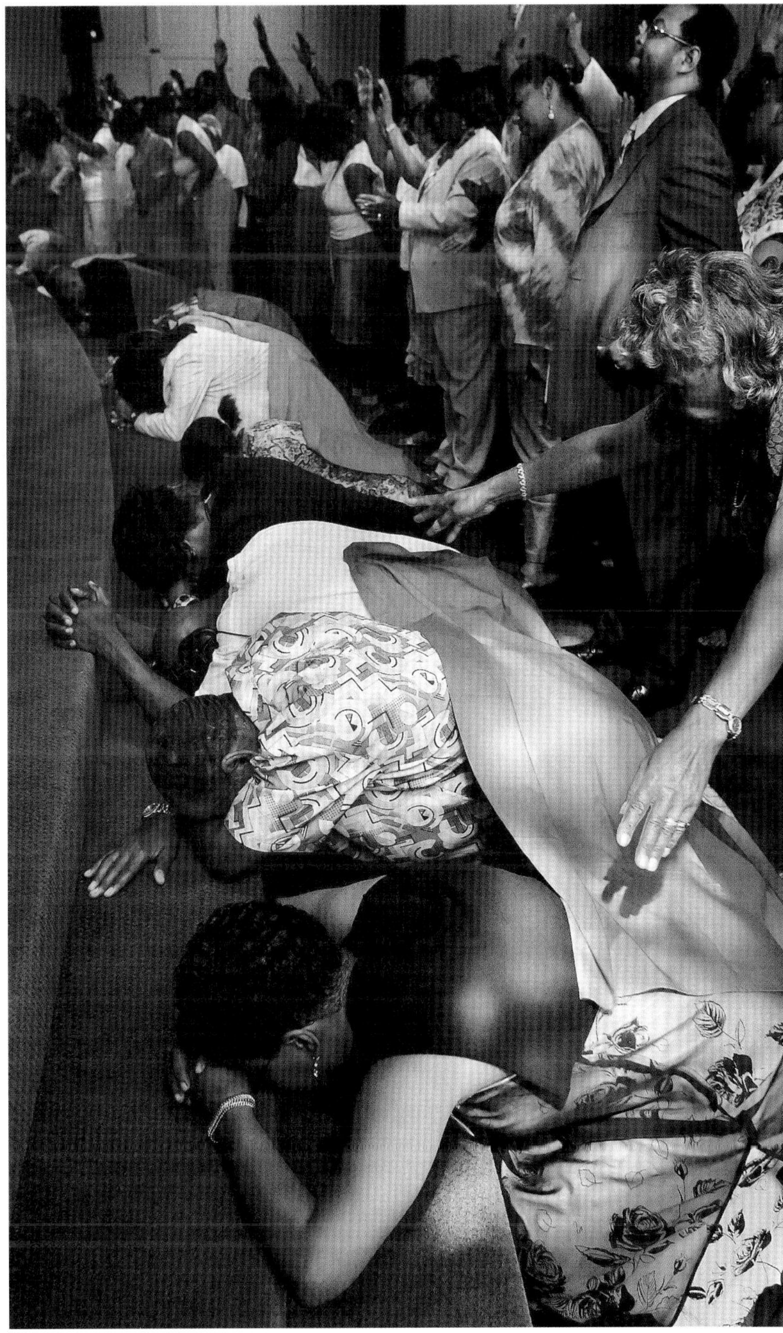

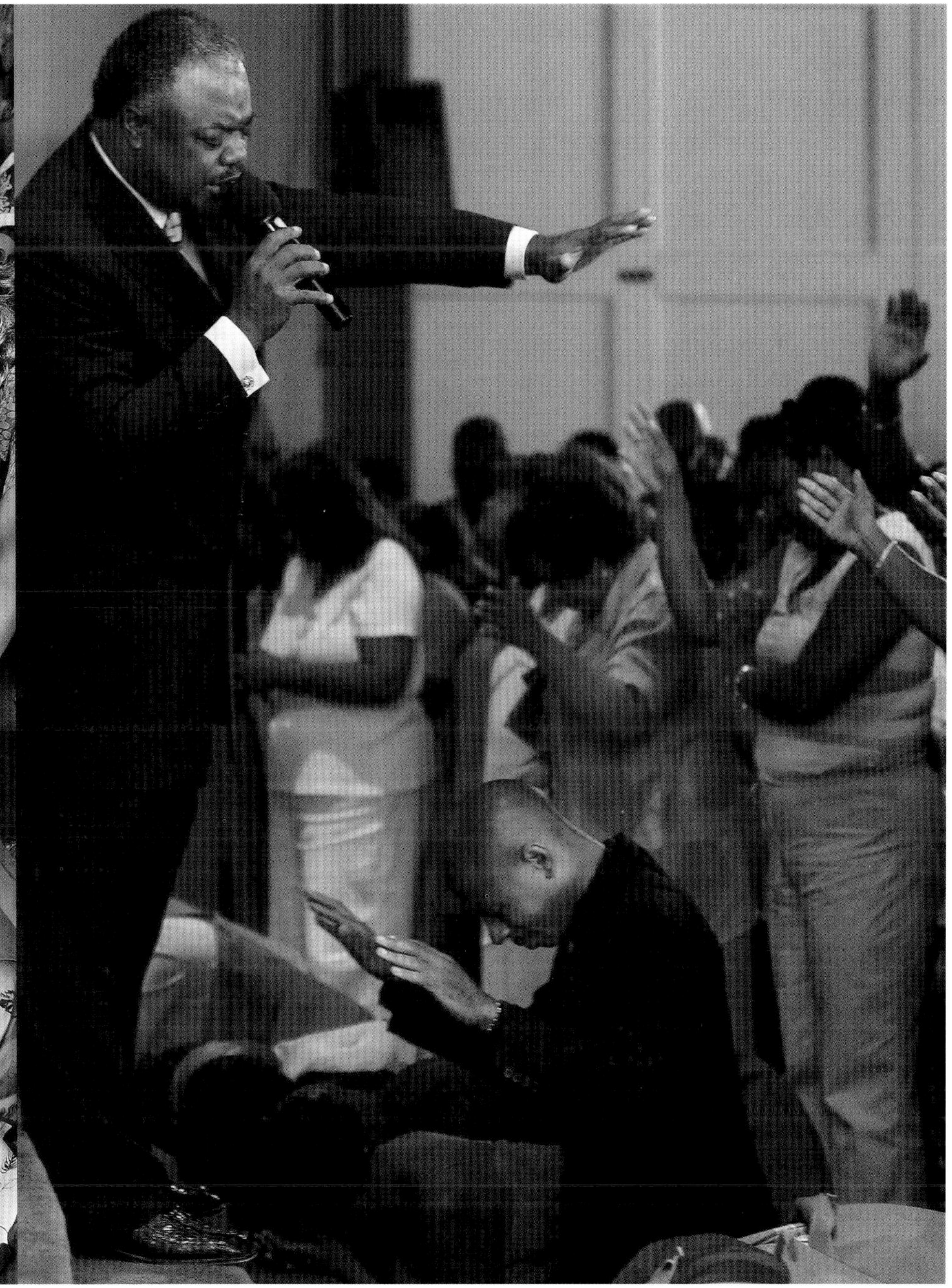

this page

CROSS

Mt. Haven Baptist Church,

November 9, 2003

facing page

RED TIES

Mt. Zion Church, August 6, 2006

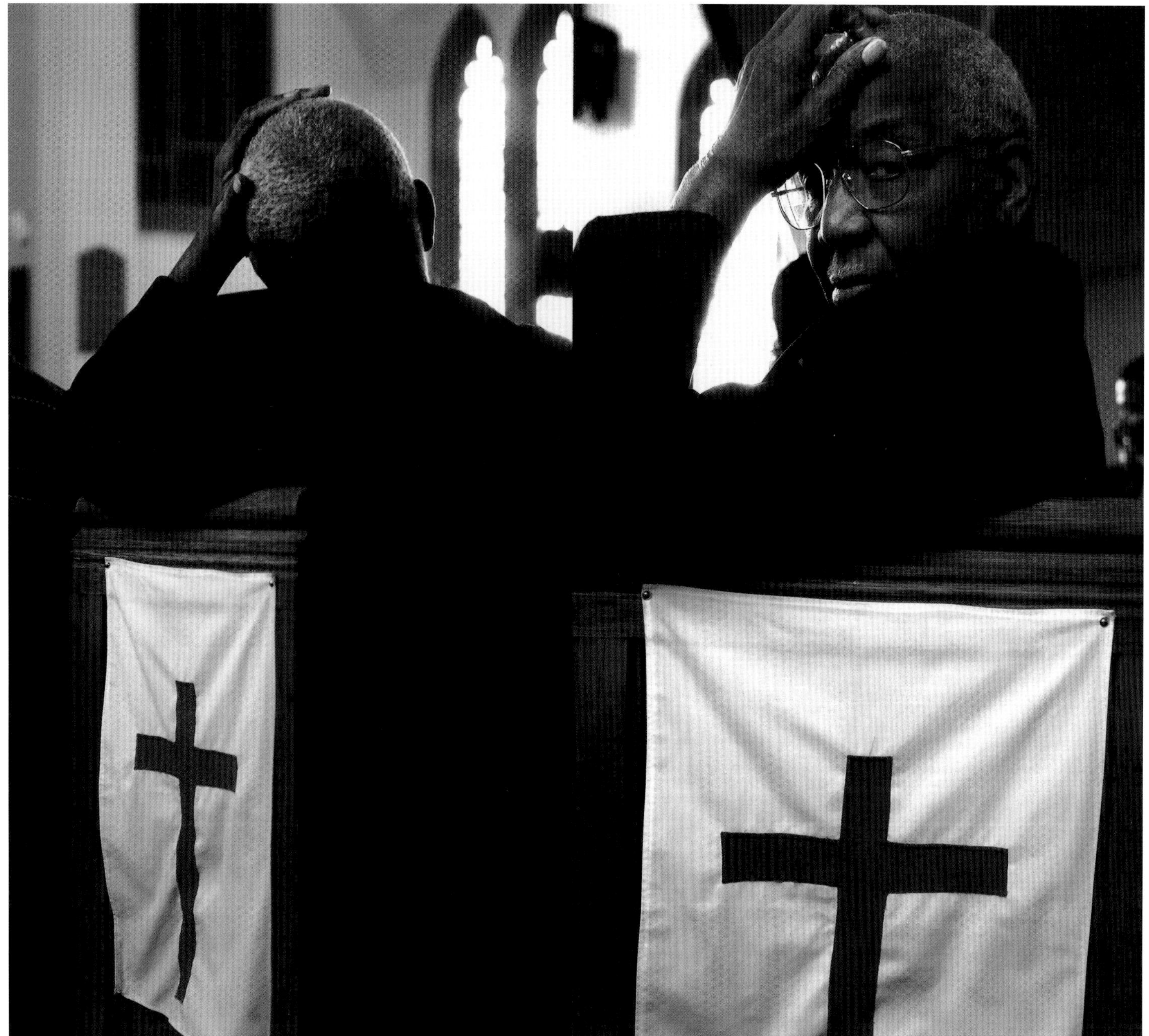

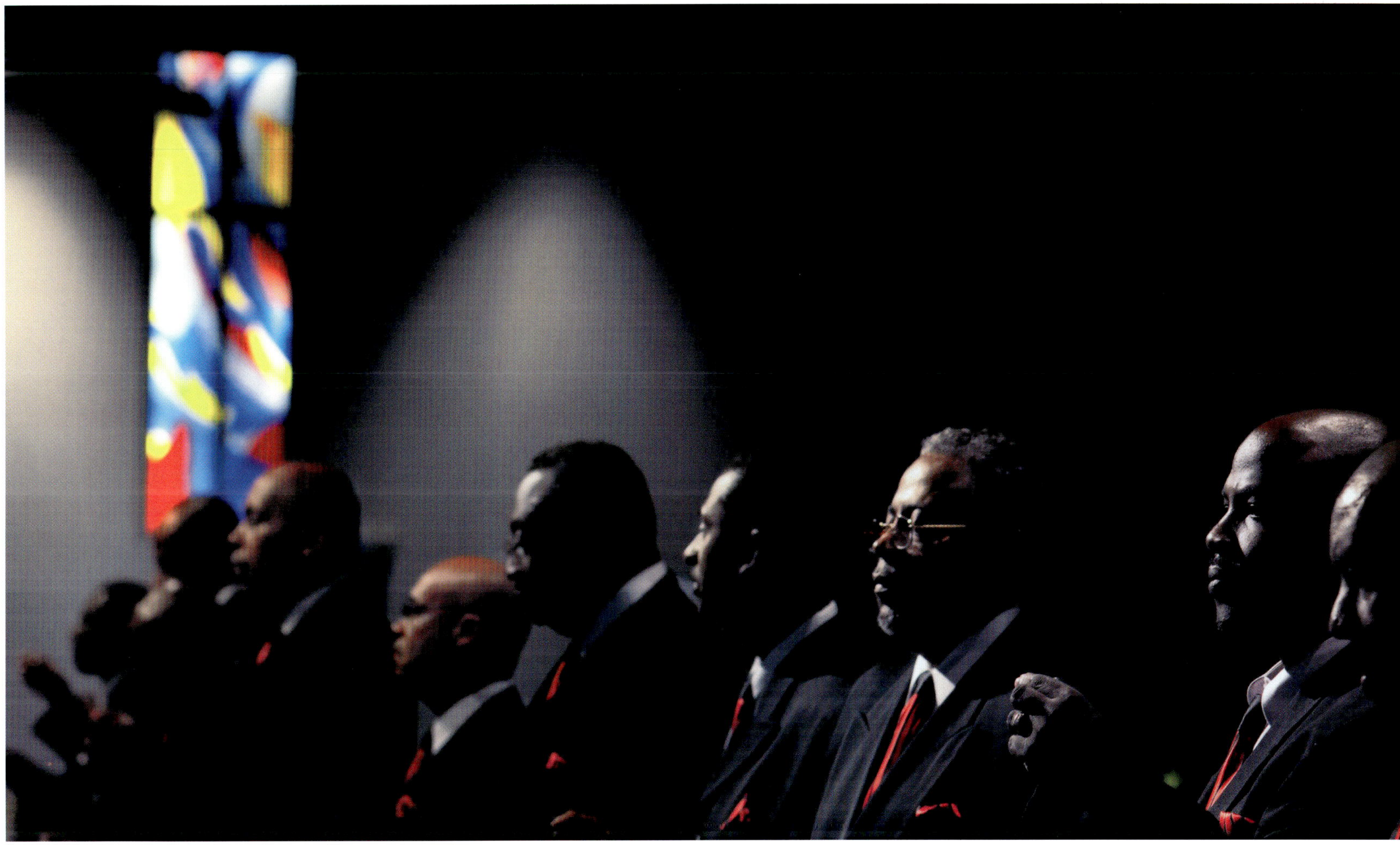
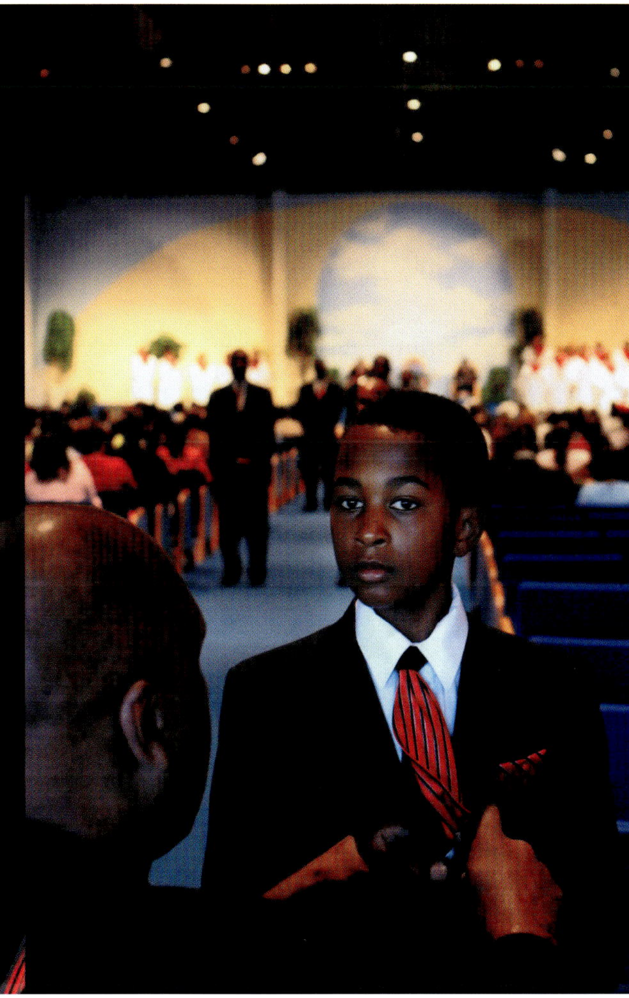

THE PASTOR AND TWO BROTHERS

(Left) Frank Smith, pastor of Live Ministries / Church of Recovery, July 13, 2003. (Right) Live Ministries / Church of Recovery, July 10, 2003

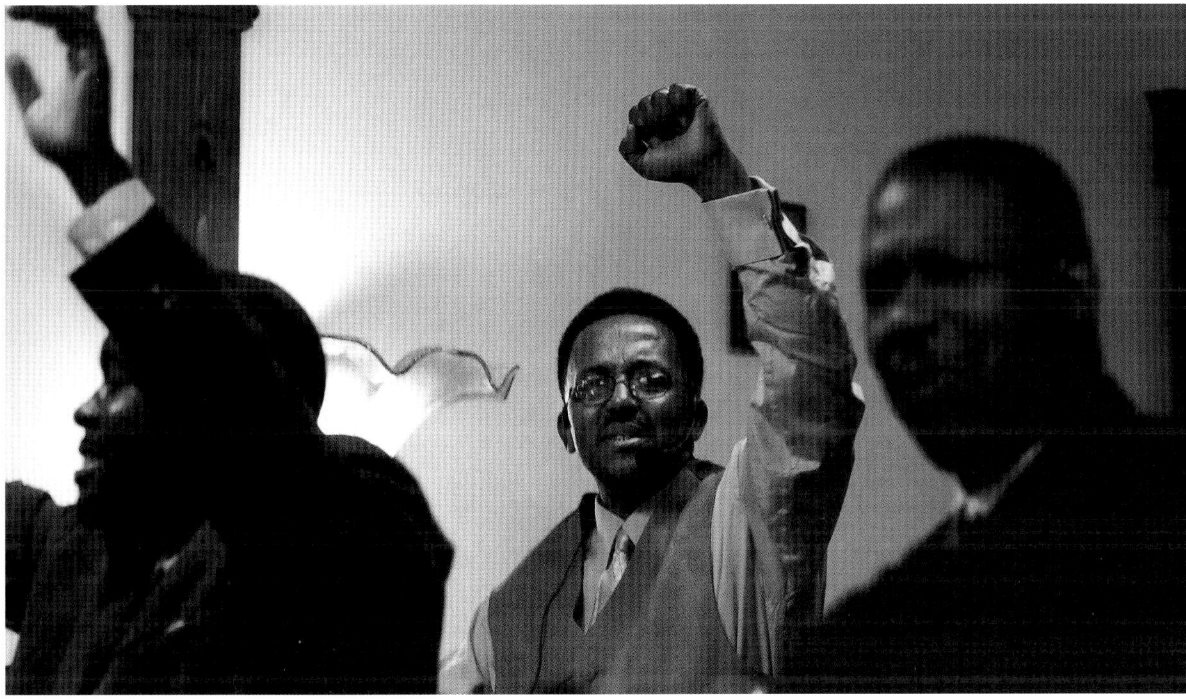

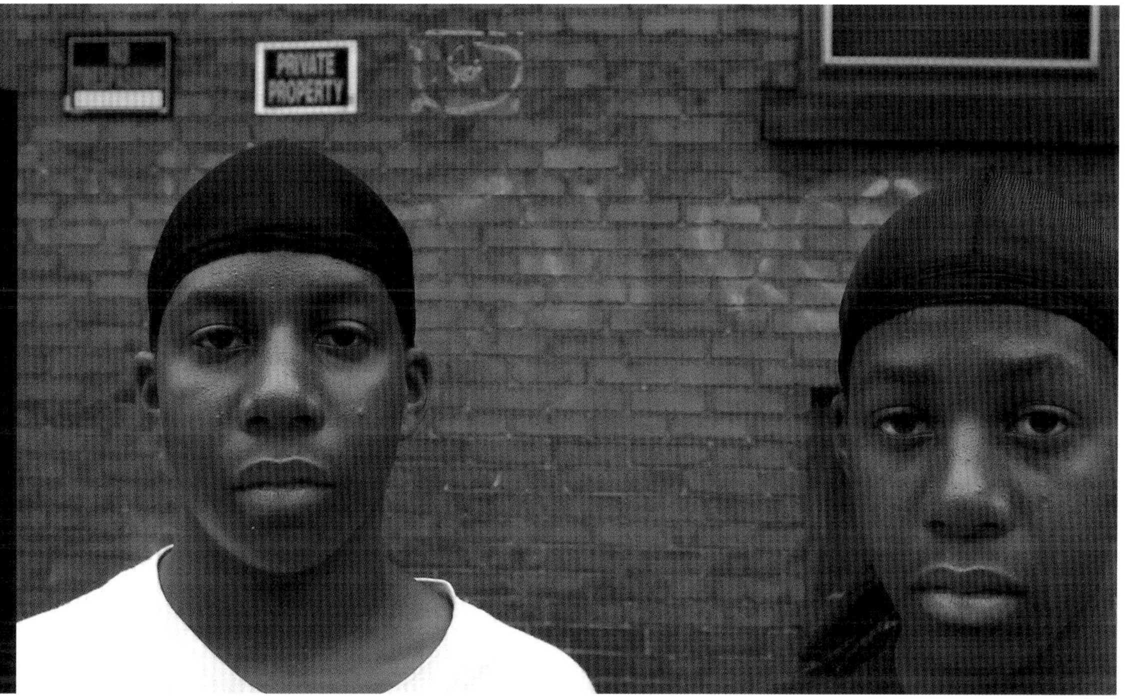
PRIVATE
PROPERTY

TWO FUNERALS

The funerals of young African American males killed by gang violence. (Left) Shiloh Baptist Church, January 25, 2005. (Right) Eaglewing Missionary Baptist Church, February 8, 2006

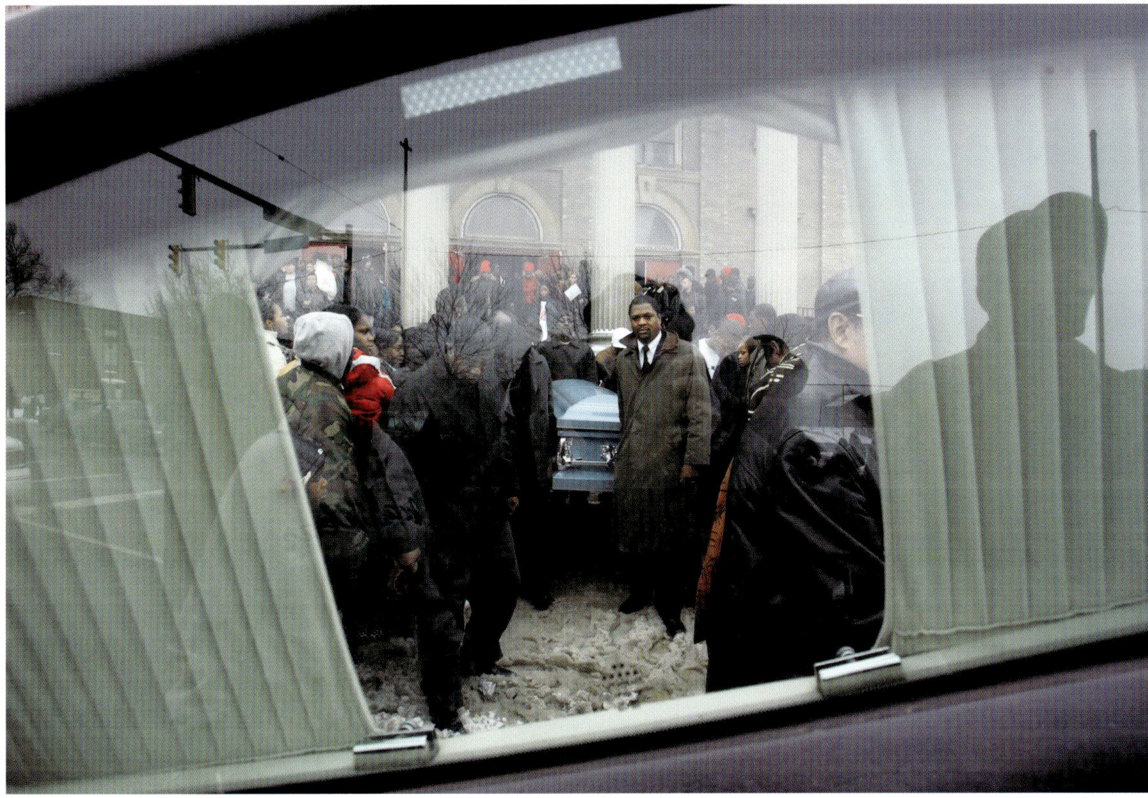

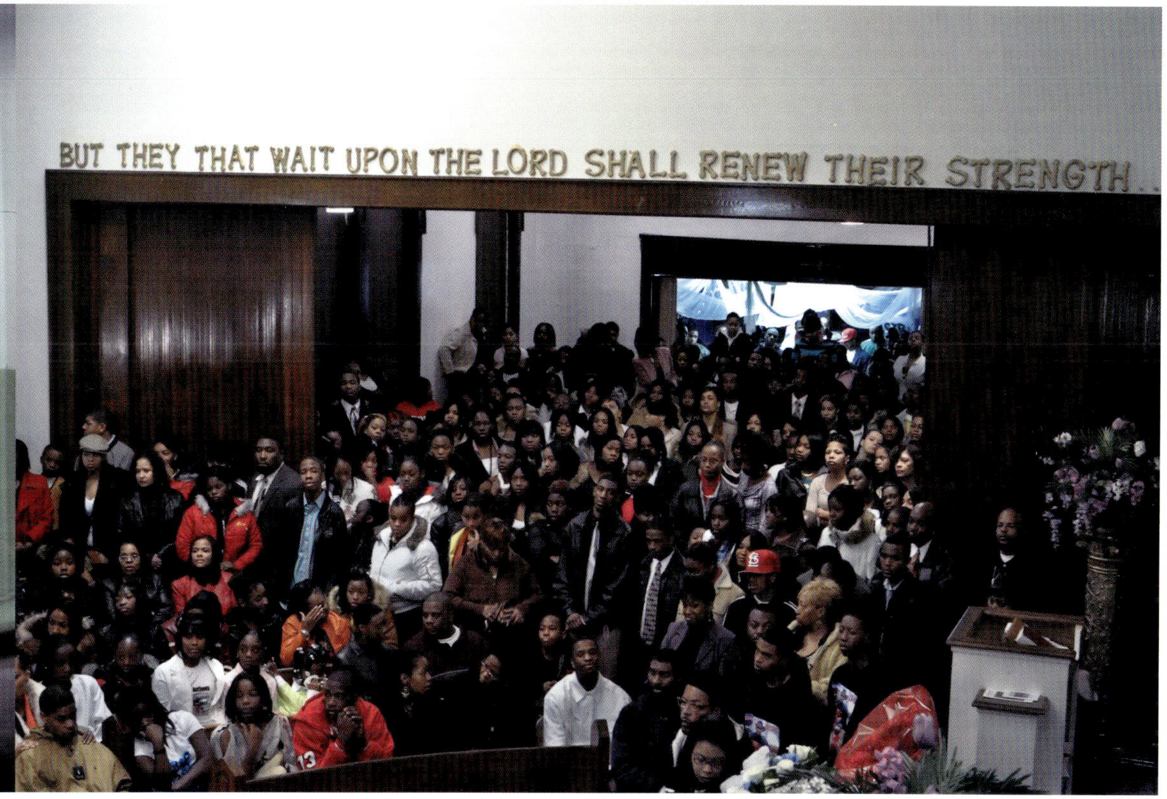
BUT THEY THAT WAIT UPON THE LORD SHALL RENEW THEIR STRENGTH . .

THE BIRD FLIES

(Left) Bethany Baptist Church, October 7, 2003. (Right) Live Ministries / Church of Recovery, August 6, 2003

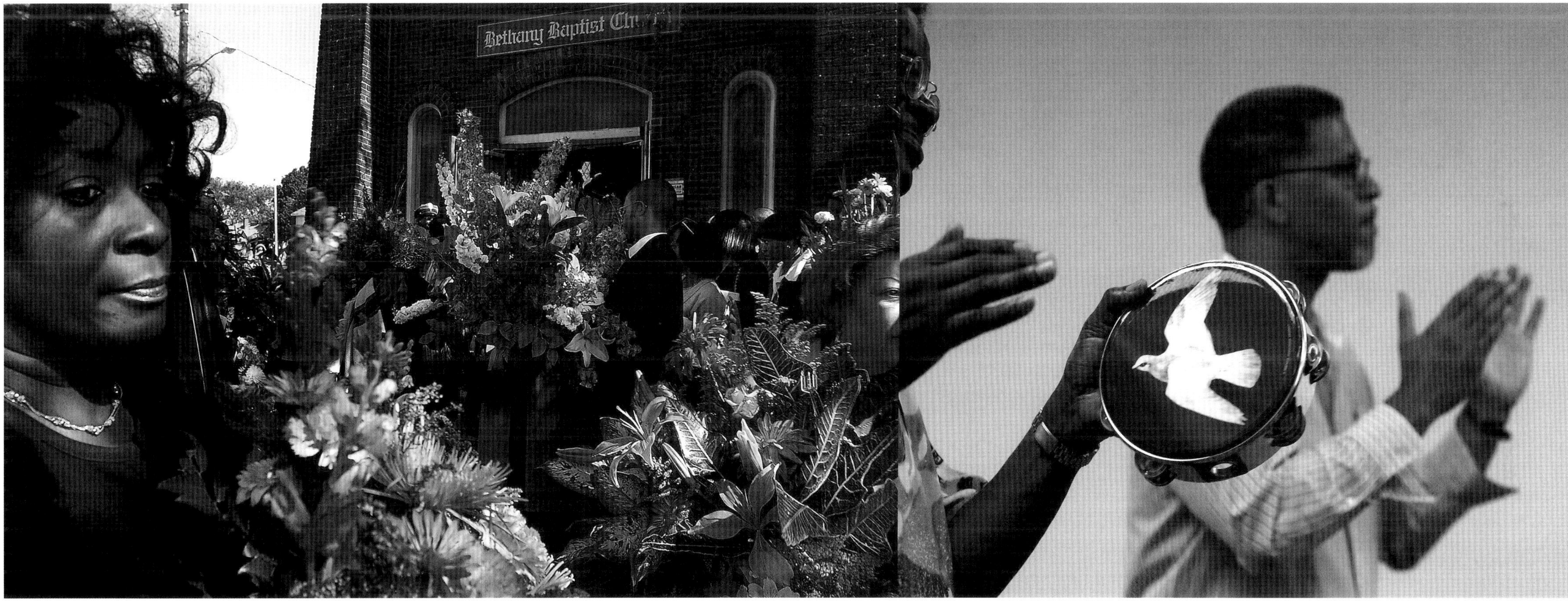
Bethany Baptist

I sing because I'm happy,
I sing because I'm free,
For His eye is on the sparrow,
And I know He watches me.
—Traditional

BACKGROUND, FOREGROUND

Mt. Haven Baptist Church,

November 9, 2003

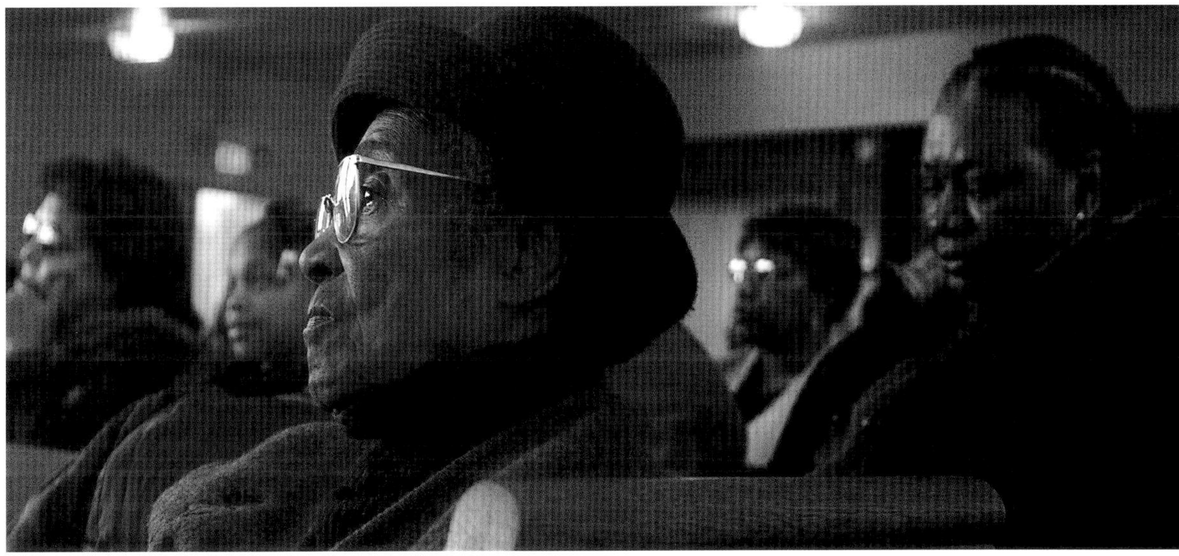

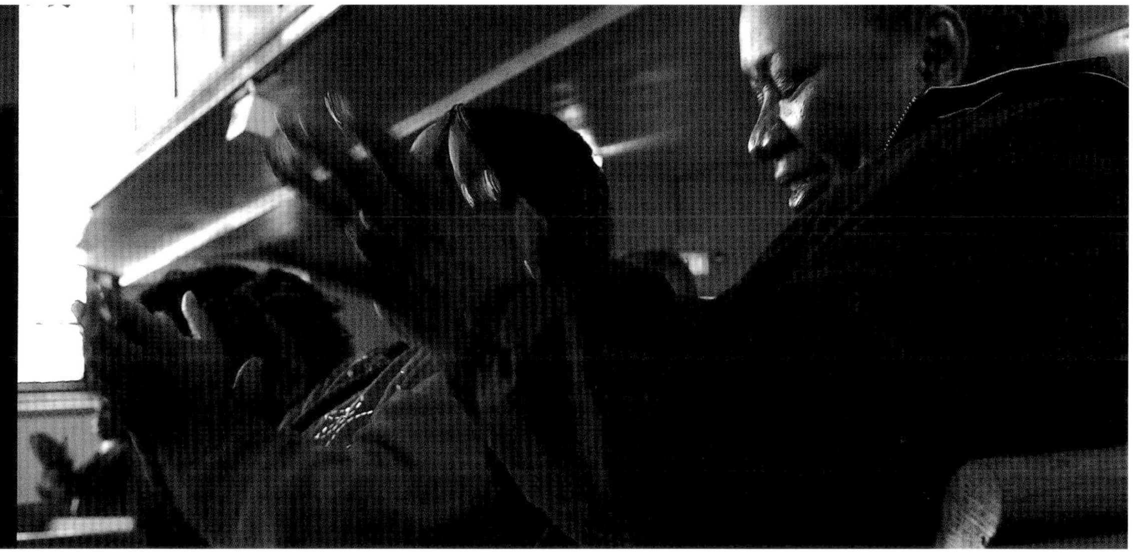

STILL SPRY

(Left) St. John AME Church, October 2, 2005. (Right) Greater New Canaan Baptist Church, August 6, 2003

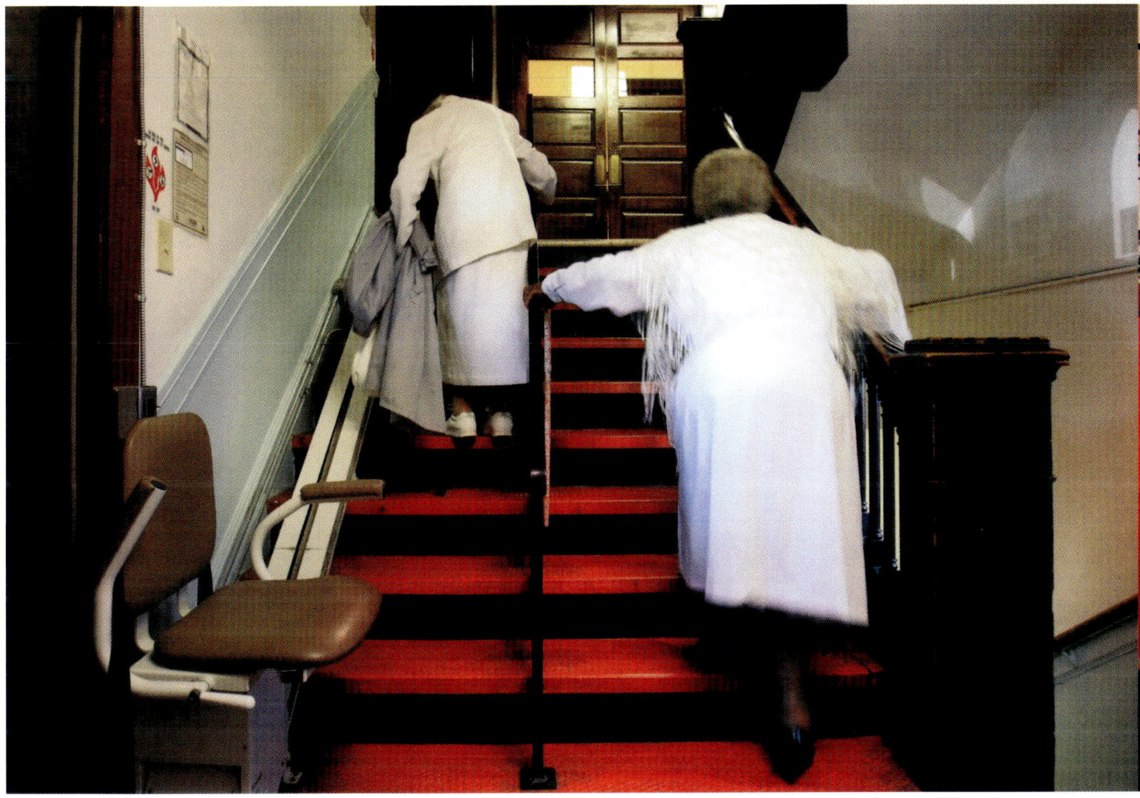

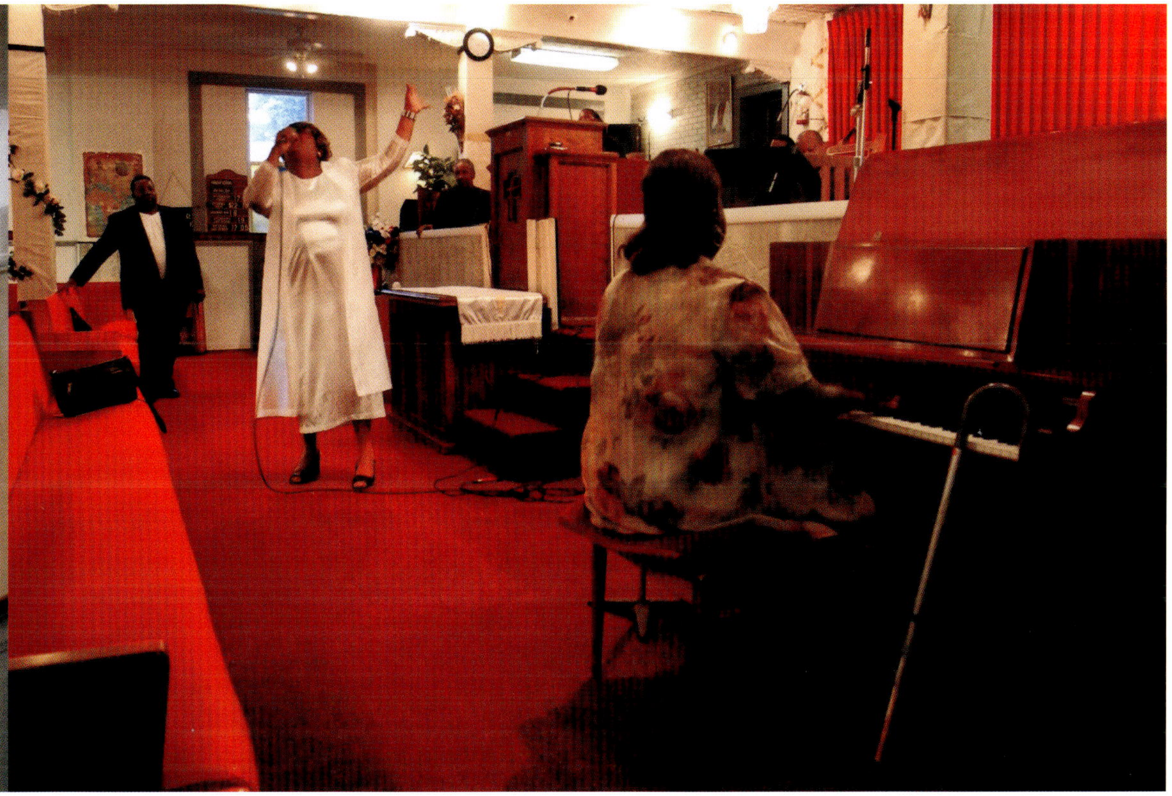

A PRAYER AND A SONG

(Left) A prayer rally at Quicken Loans Arena, Cleveland, February 13, 2006. (Right) Mt. Sinai Baptist Church, March 13, 2004

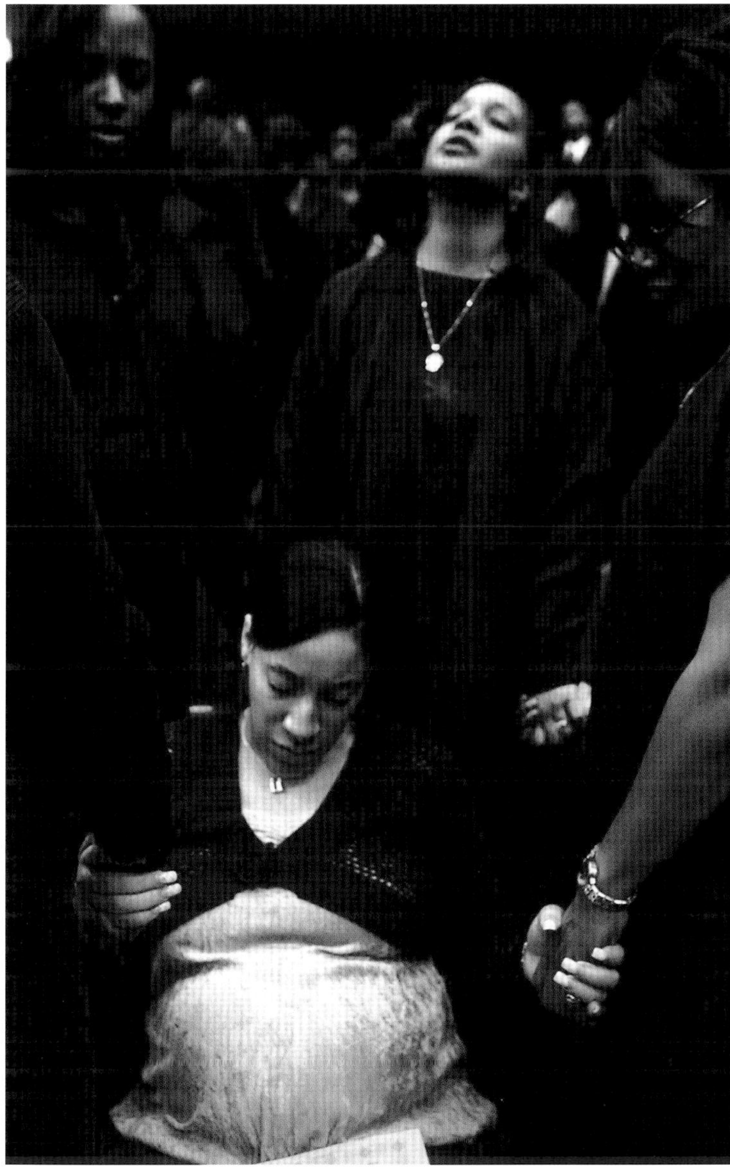

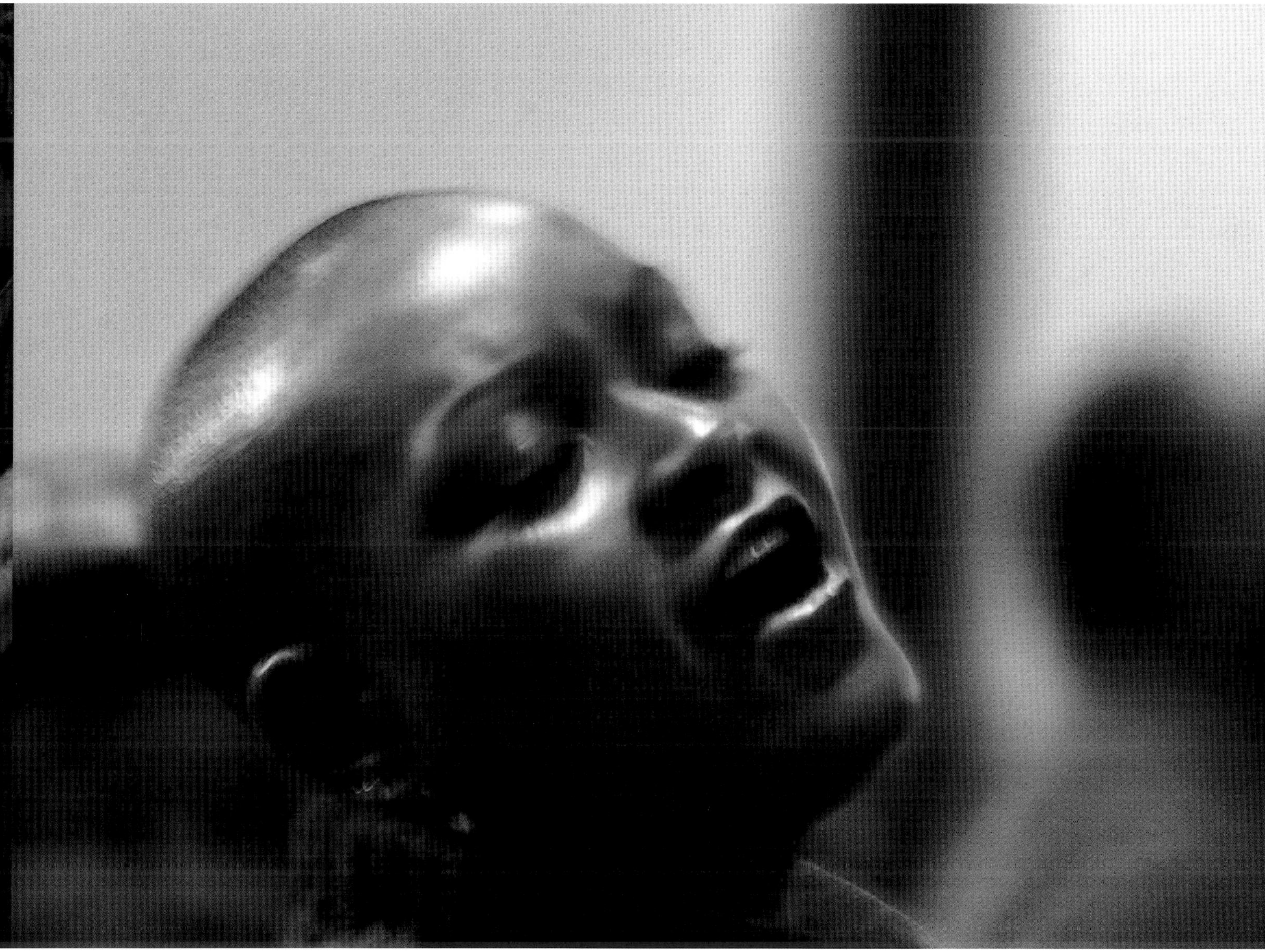

ROGUE SERVICE

The Harvest Baptist Church choir performs at the Cleveland Masonic Temple, June 6, 2004

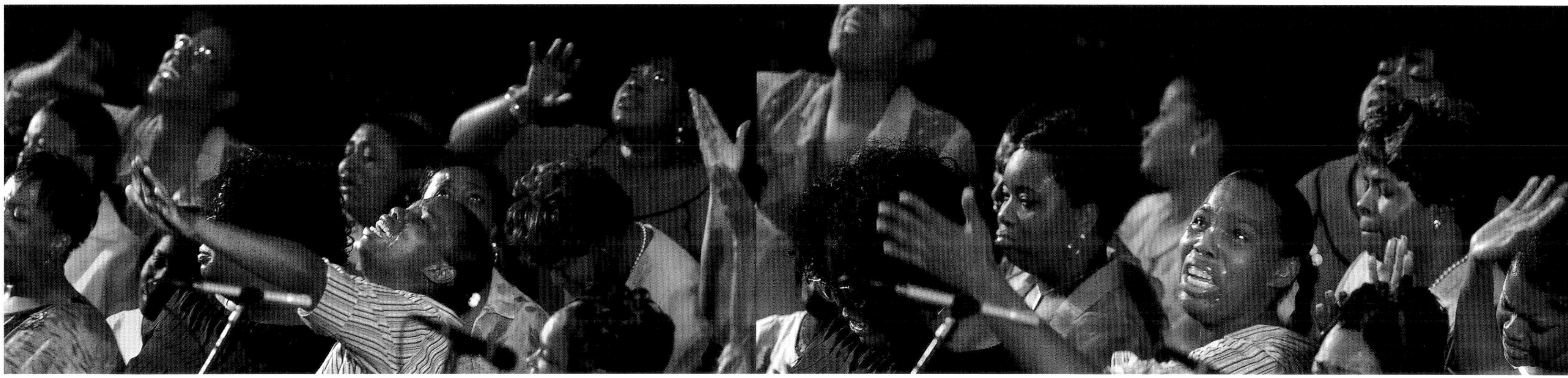

MATRONS AND USHERS

(Left) St. James AME Church, December 5, 2004. (Right) St. Paul AME Zion Church, January 18, 2004

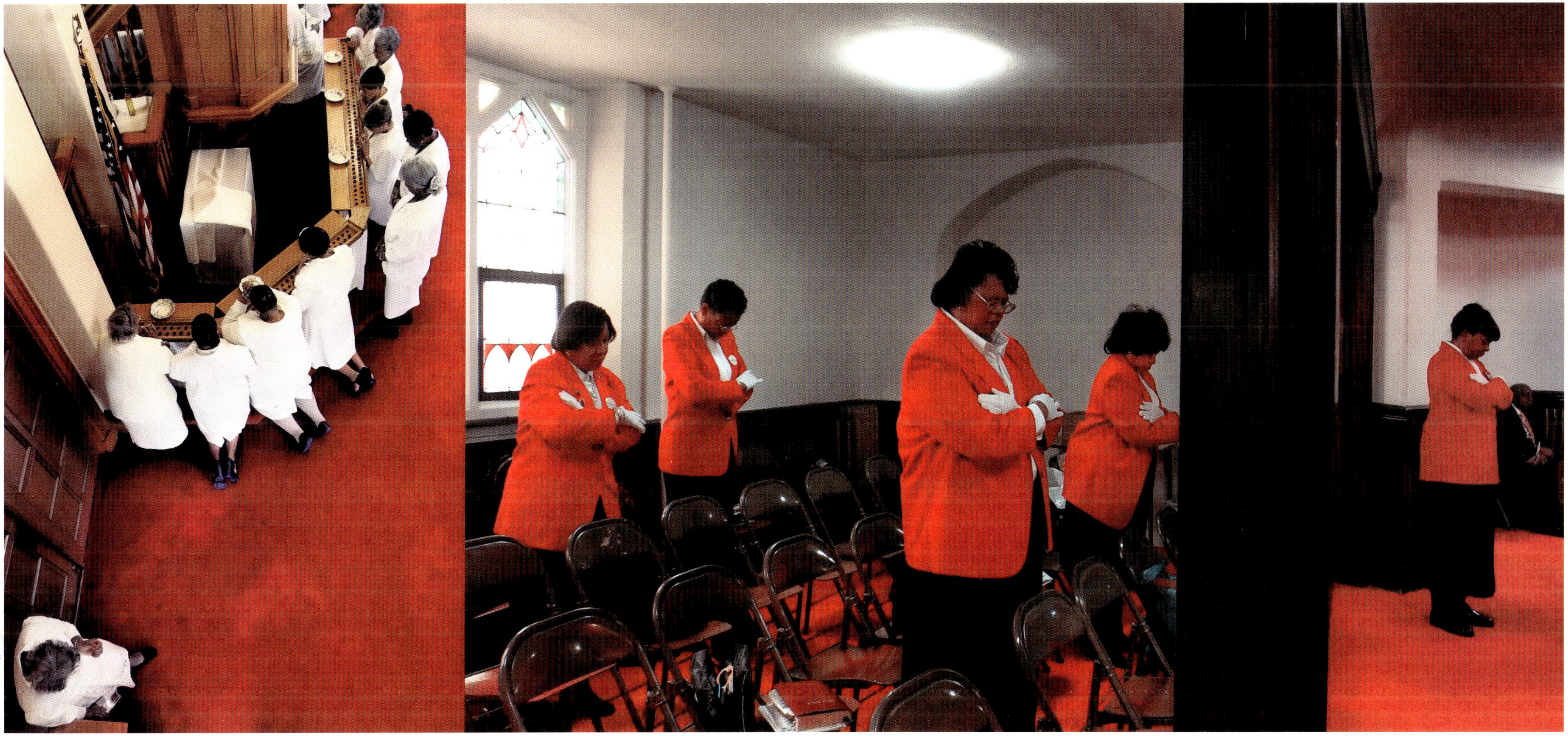

TO WORK

(Left) New Revelation Baptist Church, February 5, 2006. (Right) Windermere United Methodist Church, June 5, 2006

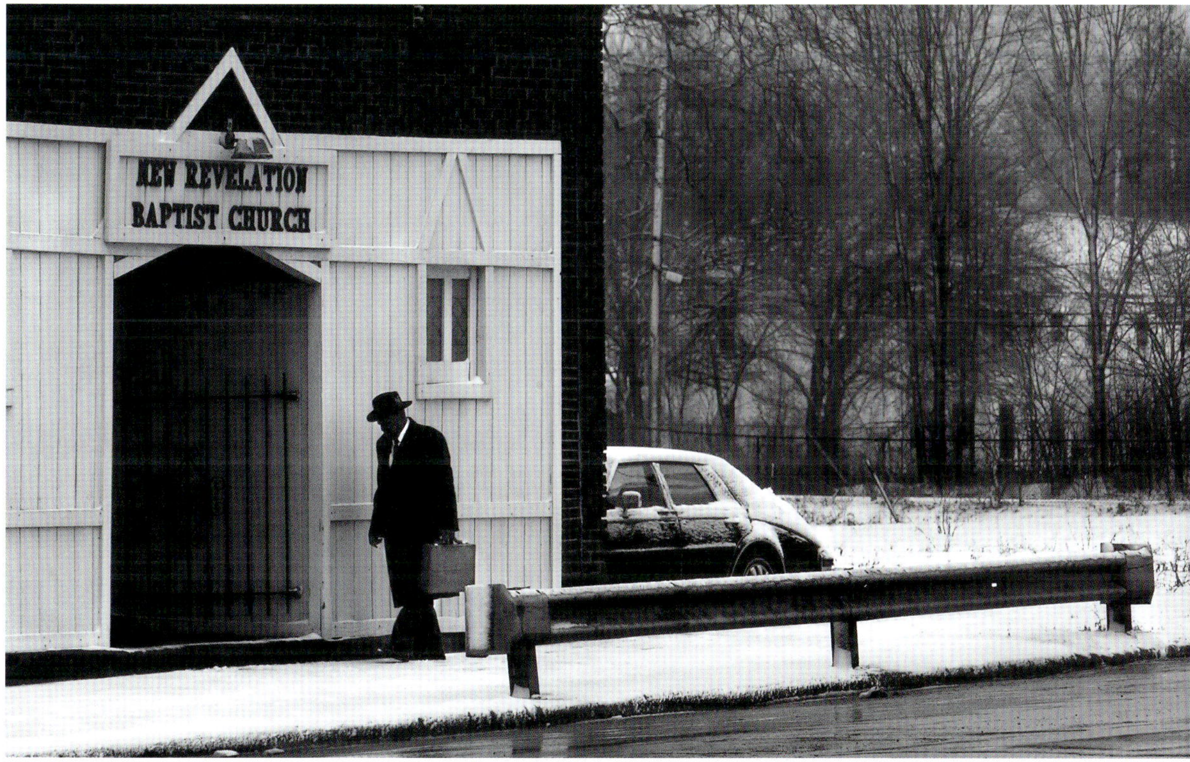
NEW REVELATION
BAPTIST CHURCH

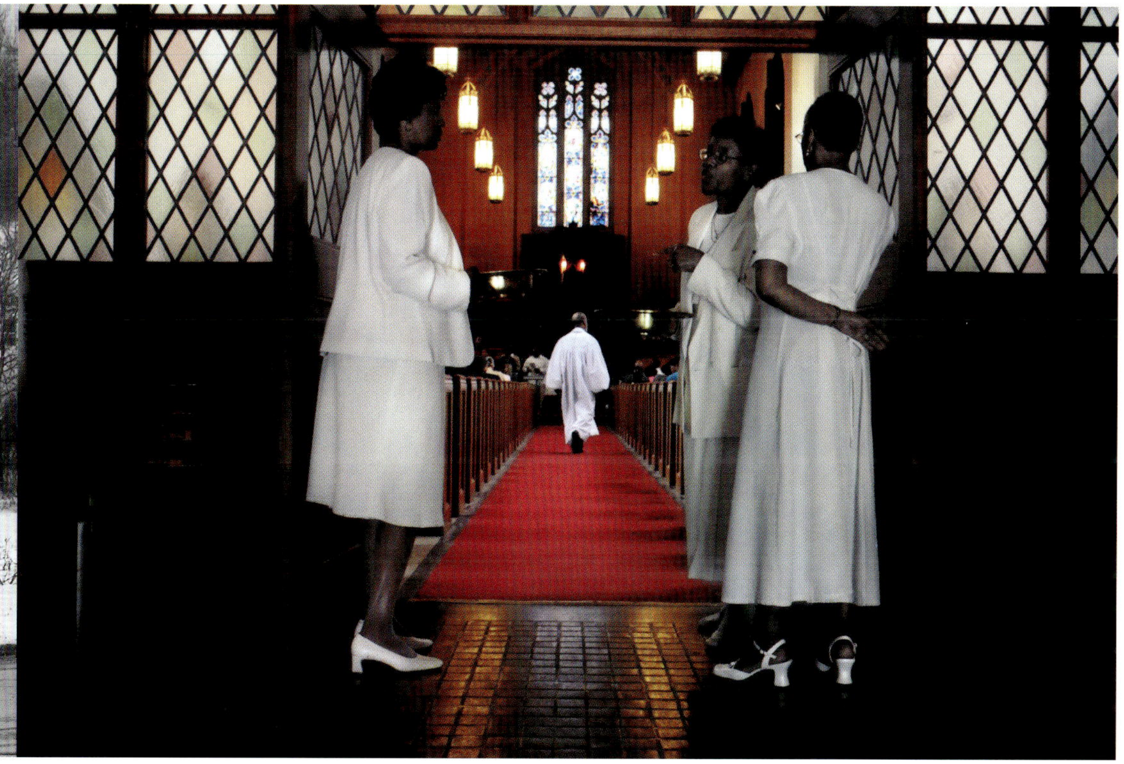

A PART OF THE CHURCH

(Left) St. James AME Church, October 3, 2004. (Right) St. Paul AME Zion Church, January 17, 2004

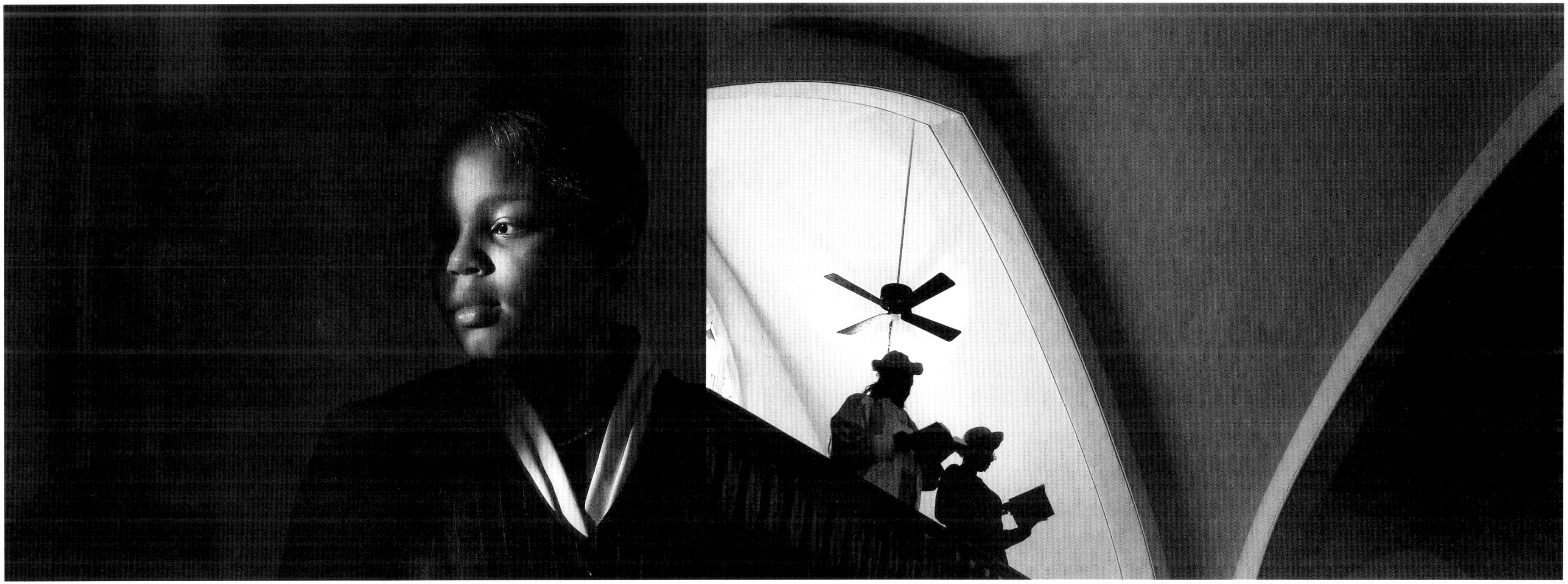

A MAN IN BLACK, A WOMAN IN WHITE

(Left) Mt. Zion Church, August 6, 2006. (Right) New Jerusalem Church of God in Christ, December 18, 2005

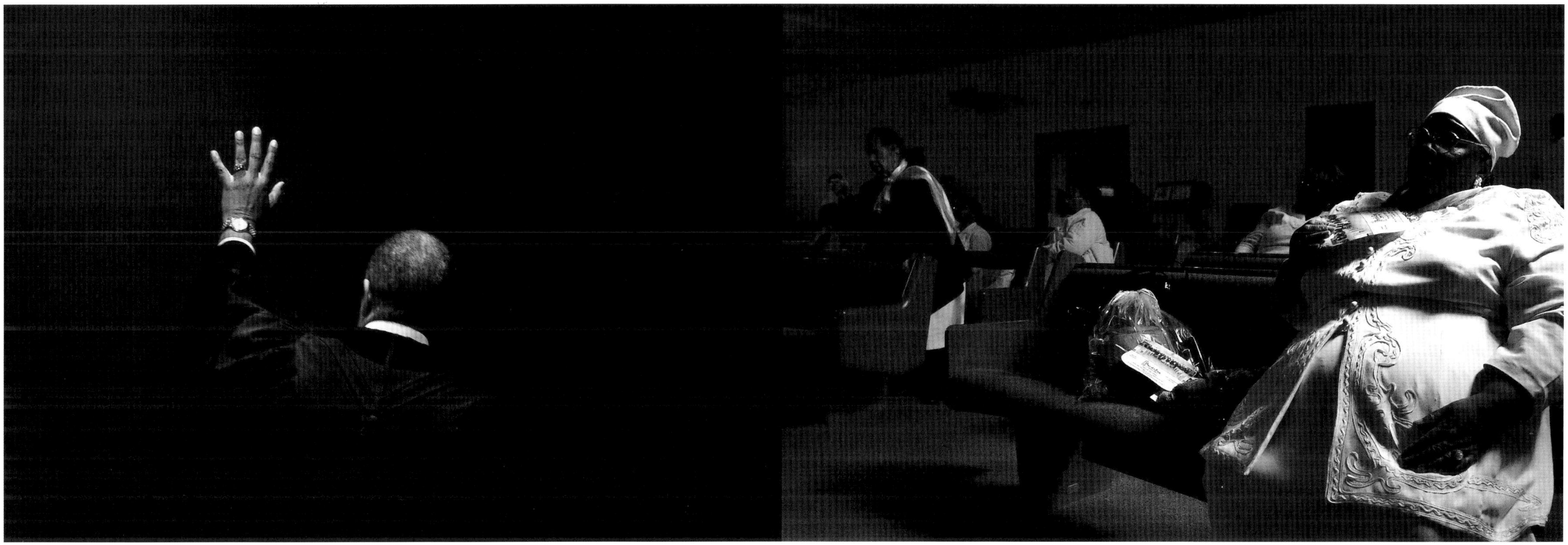

EAST 105TH STREET

(Left) Cory United Methodist Church (left) and The Greater Abyssinia Baptist Church (right), September 21, 2006. Along East 105th Street, within a two-mile stretch, there are more than fifty churches.

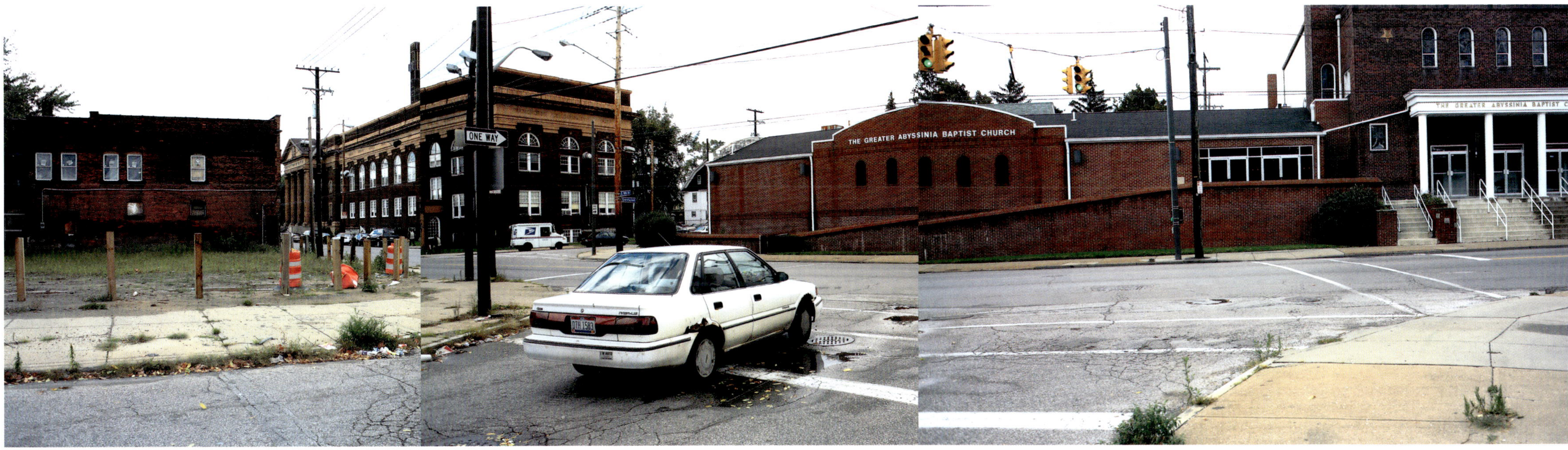
ONE WAY
THE GREATER ABYSSINIA BAPTIST CHURCH

TIME

(Left) St. James AME Church, December 6, 2004. (Right) The exterior wall of Live Ministries/ Church of Recovery, September 9, 2003

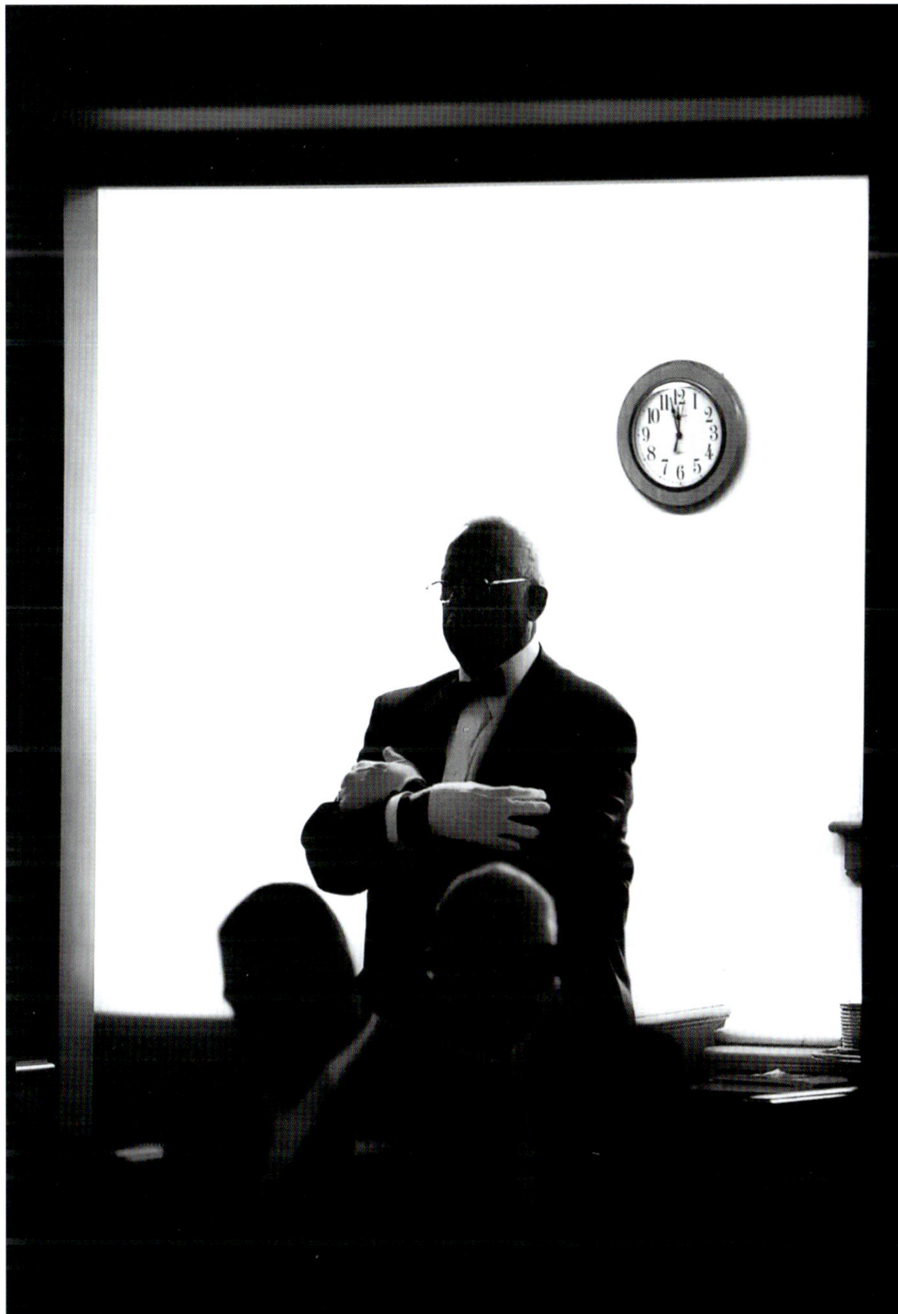

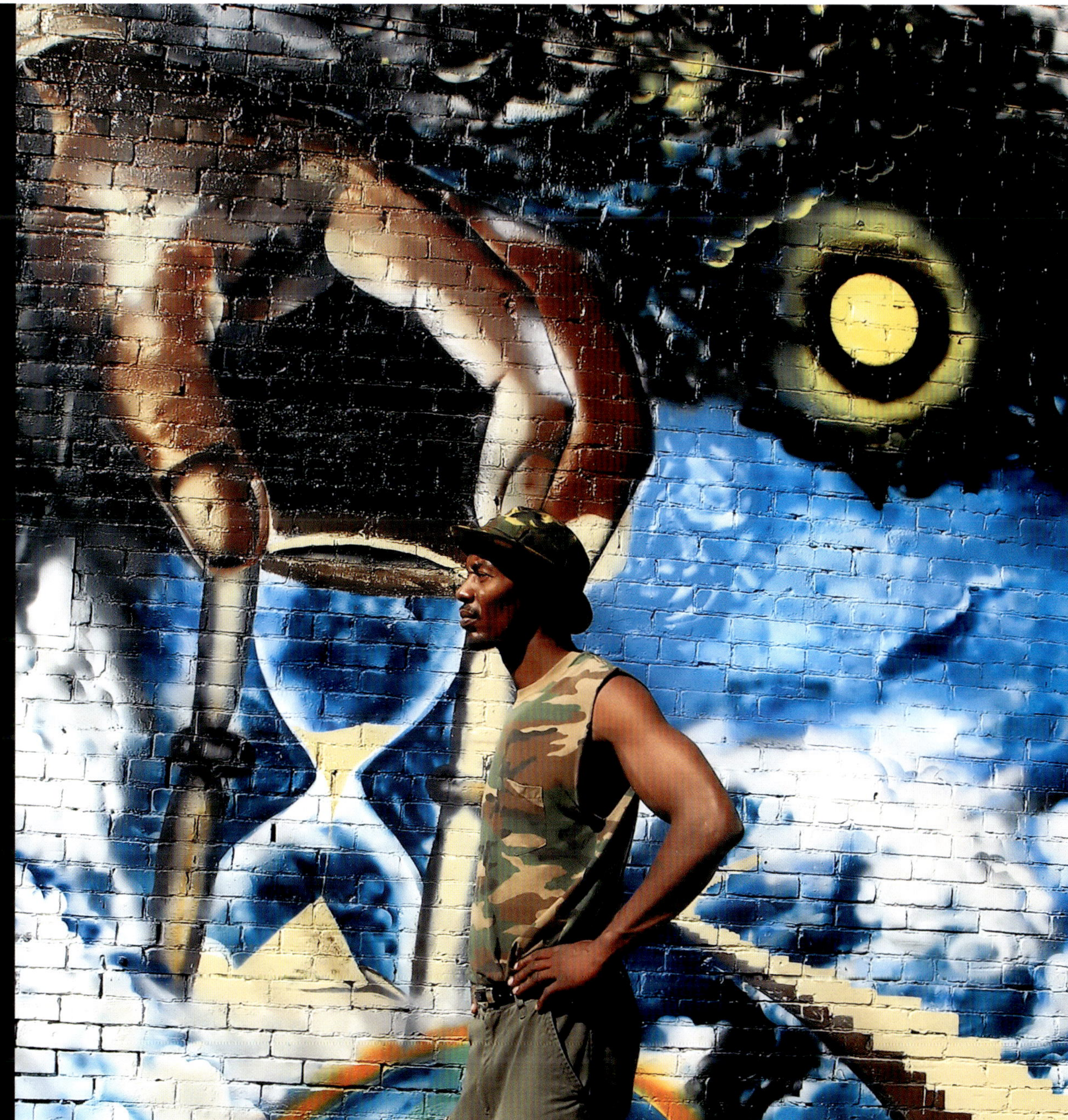

PROTECTION ONE

Upon This Rock Missionary Baptist Church, October 29, 2006

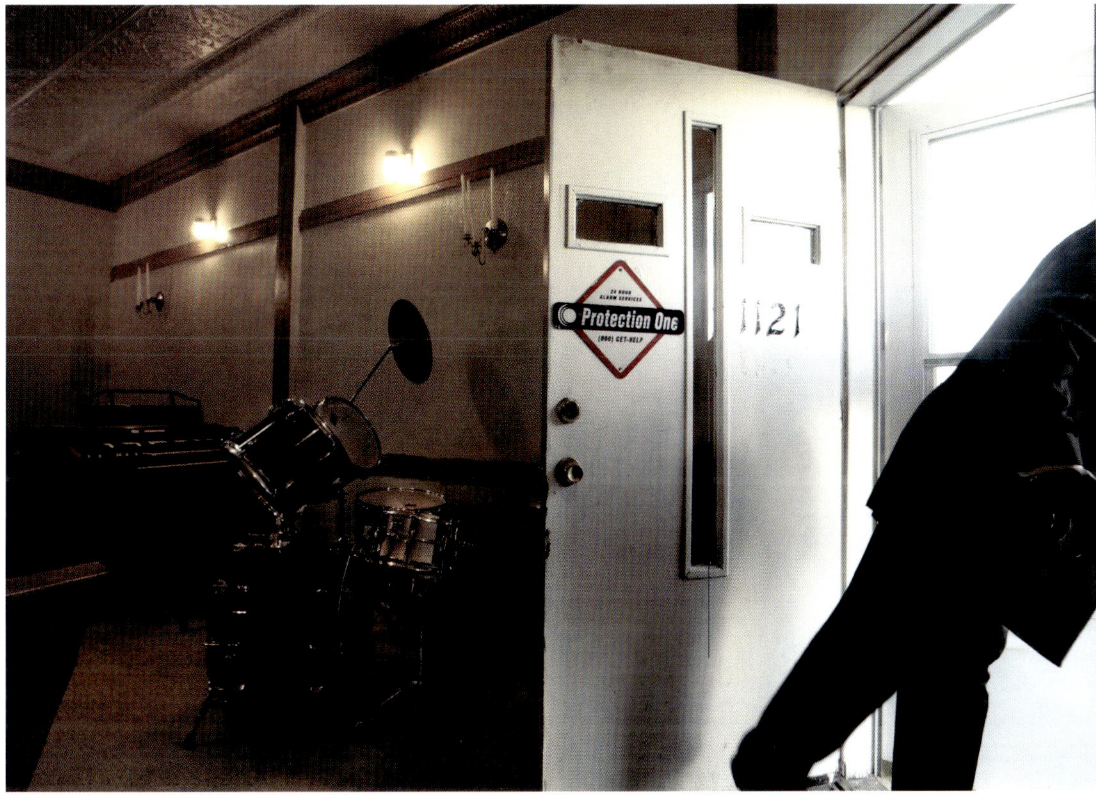
Protection One
1121

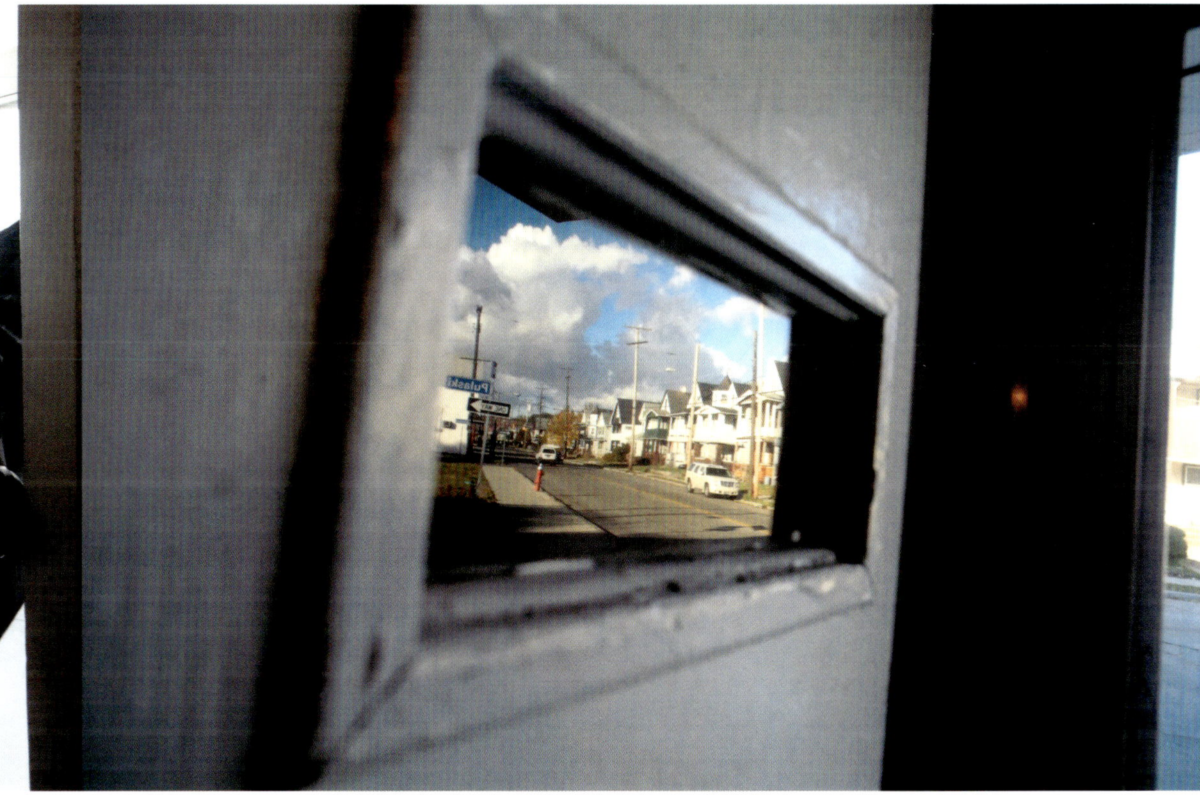

INTERSECTION

(Left) Pentecostal Church of Christ, February 8, 2004. (Right) Mt. Haven Baptist Church, November 9, 2003

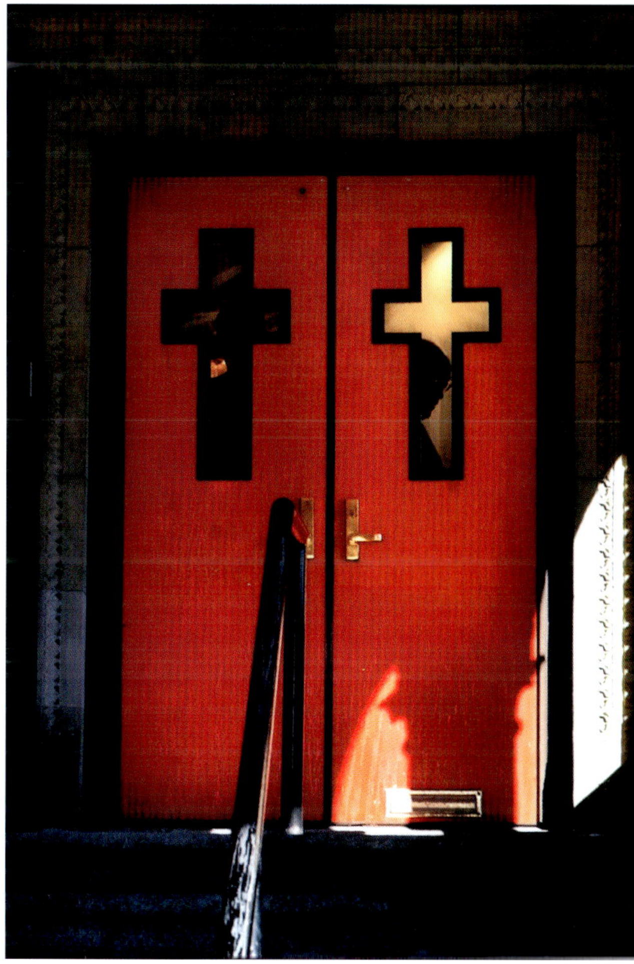

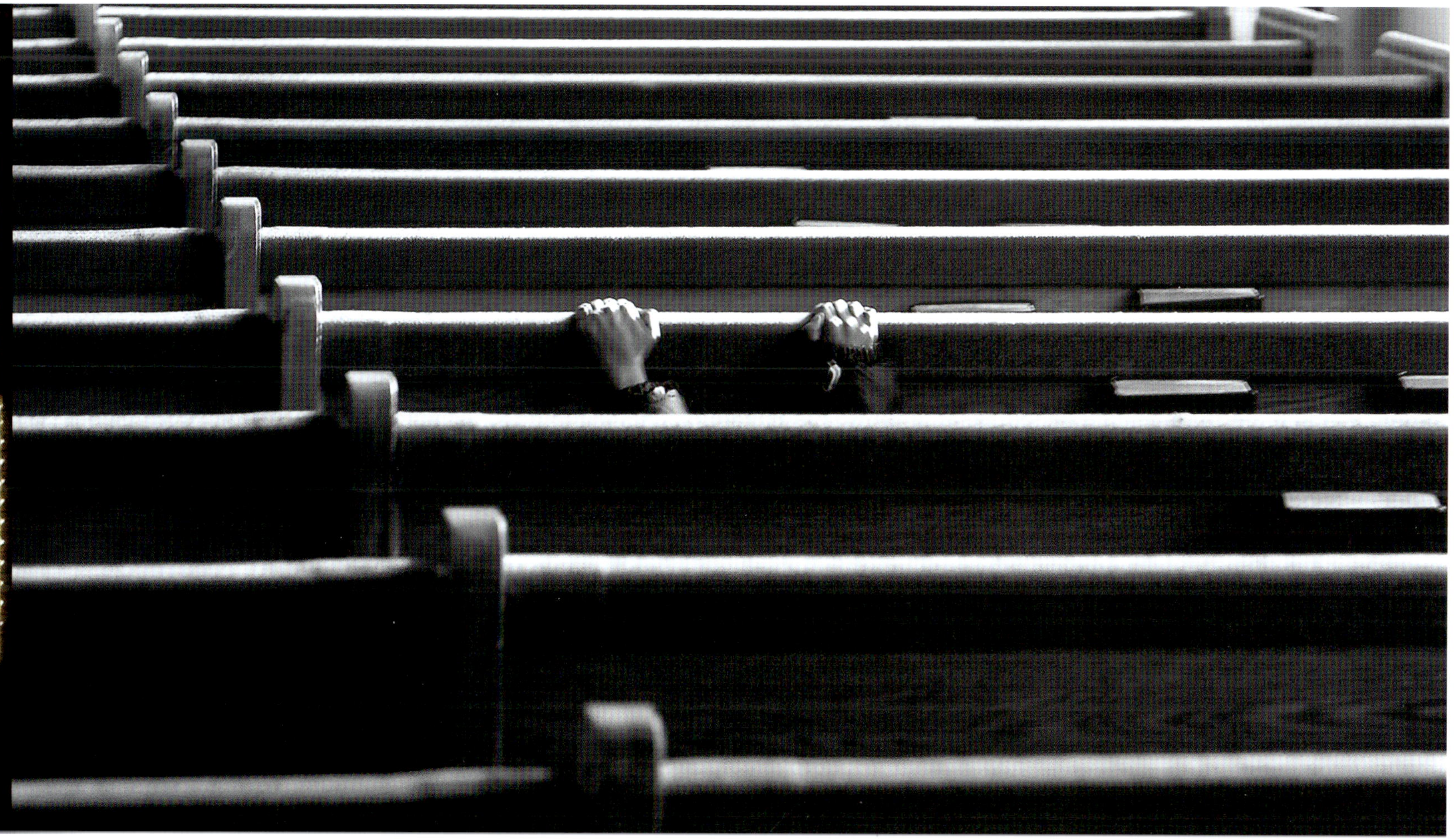

I'm going to tell you about the coming of the Savior,
Fare you well, fare you well!
I'm going to tell you about the coming of the Savior,
Fare you well, fare you well!

There's a better day a-coming,
Fare you well, fare you well!
Pray-er makers, pray no more,
Fare you well, fare you well!

Oh, preachers fold your Bibles,
Fare you well, fare you well!
For the last soul's converted,
Fare you well, fare you well!

In that great getting-up morning,
Fare you well, fare you well!
In that great getting-up morning,
Fare you well, fare you well!

—Traditional

AFTERWORD

Unseen Pillars of the Community

Norman Krumholz and Michael J. Tevesz

Despite their numbers, most of Cleveland's African American churches are all but invisible to the outside world. This is unfortunate given the impact of their good works within the city and its neighborhoods. Collectively, their efforts, neighborhood by neighborhood, offer the city and its residents realistic, practical, and effective hopes for the future. They are, in fact, largely unseen pillars of the community.

According to figures released by the U.S. Census Bureau in 2004, Cleveland is the poorest large city in America, with 31.3 percent of its people and 47 percent of its children living in poverty. Decent, low-cost rental housing has been disappearing from the housing market faster than new homes are being added. These trends have swollen the ranks of the homeless and caused a sharp rise in the number of poor families spending more than half of their incomes on rent. For example, about 70 percent of Cleveland's poor renters spend more than half their incomes on rent. During this period of duress, with very little fanfare or public notice, Cleveland's faith community has taken a dynamic approach to addressing housing, health, human service, and economic needs within Cleveland's neighborhoods and in the city as a whole.

The resources represented by Cleveland's African American houses of worship are enormous. They anchor their surroundings while at the same time act as magnets that attract congregants from the suburbs to the inner city. Moreover, they provide opportunities and services not otherwise available in their neighborhoods. These buildings and the people that worship in them are quiet, constant forces whose solid achievements are often overlooked.

There are many excellent examples of churches and neighborhood development groups working together. In the Fairfax neighborhood on Cleveland's East Side, the Fairfax Renaissance Development Corporation (FRDC) and nearby Emmanuel Baptist Church have sold and traded parcels of land to provide a site for FRDC's new headquarters building and shared parking for both groups. FRDC continues to work with pastors in the neighborhood to take advantage of other spiritual and development opportunities. In all, Cleveland's African American houses of worship exemplify the best of American civic vision: building community together for the common good.

The denominational affiliations, congregational ethnicity, and geographical distribution of these houses of worship reveal much about the beliefs and attitudes of the city's residents. Most congregations with a predominantly African American membership are found on the Cleveland's East Side, east of the Cuyahoga River. Scores of churches—predominantly Evangelical, AME, Baptist, Pentecostal—fill East Side neighborhoods along Carnegie, Cedar, Miles, and Harvard Avenues, for instance, and along major streets. In the Glenville neighborhood, more than fifty African American churches line East 105th St. and adjoining stretches of St. Clair and Superior Avenues. In contrast, Cleveland's West Side neighborhoods have neither the numbers nor concentration of African American congregations.

These ecclesial demographics tell an interesting story, one revealed through Mike Levy's superb photographs, about patterns of segregation and succession. These patterns go back more than 100 years to when most African Americans in Cleveland were segregated in the Central neighborhood on Cleveland's East Side. With the passage of civil rights laws, African Americans began to move out of Central and further east, while many people of European descent moved out of the city entirely, often selling their churches and synagogues to the newcomers. In Cleveland, it isn't a surprise to see Hebrew lettering on Tiffany windows in Baptist churches.

Most Americans have a vague realization that urban America is still a residentially segregated society, but few appreciate the depth of racial segregation or the degree to which it is maintained by institutional arrangements and individual actions. They believe that the civil rights, voting rights, and fair housing laws of the 1960s have fatally weakened segregation, and they view segregation as an unfortunate residual from a racist past, one that is fading rapidly as African Americans integrate just as other ethnic groups have done. However, the distribution of African American faith communities in Cleveland tells a different story, one that says segregation is not going away.

In 1968 the Kerner Commission, established to determine the causes of the racial riots of the late 1960s, reported bluntly that "segregation and poverty have created . . . a destructive environment totally unknown to most Americans" and that "white institutions created it, white institutions maintain it, and white society condones it." Nearly thirty years later, Harvard professors Gary Orfield and Susan Eaton made much the same point in 1996 when they wrote about school segregation: "Four decades after the Supreme Court's unanimous desegregation decision, Brown vs. Board of Education, the Supreme Court reversed itself in the 1990's, authorizing school district to return to segregated and unequal schools." Little has changed.[1]

The overall problems of American urban residential segregation are evident in the city of Cleveland, which has been and remains one of the most segregated housing markets in the United States. Since World War I, Cleveland's housing market has been characterized by "red-lining," restrictive covenants, racial steering, blockbusting, and physical violence designed to exclude and isolate African American homeseekers. The 2000 Census ranked forty-three large metropolitan areas for residential segregation on a scale of 0 to 100, with 0 being totally integrated and 100 being totally segregated. The Cleveland area scored 76.8 on the segregation scale, meaning that in 2000, 78.6 percent of all African Americans would have to move to achieve integration.[2]

Because of racial prejudice and segregation, African American ministers and other leaders, including those whose photographs grace this book, have struggled to define the best way to lead their people toward successful lives. Would the overall interest of their people best be served by a moderate strategy of accommodation and patience, or would it be better to urge vigorous political action and demands for immediate full equality? The issue is a difficult one, and the search for the right strategy has persisted for more than a hundred years.

Our government's—and society's—bland obliviousness to the plight of the poor in the last few years has placed more pressure on the racial fault line in the local and national communities. In addition, the quest for equality and empowerment is no longer described merely in terms of differences and tensions between "black" and "white." Immigration from Asia and the growing numbers of Hispanics in the United States means that the struggle for equality has significantly diversified. In addition, the ascent of growing numbers of African Americans into the middle class and the descent (or continuing presence) of white Americans into lower economic levels has broadened and perhaps even universalized this historic struggle into a multi-ethnic one between "rich" and "poor." Scholars have proposed that racial, ethnic, and economic turmoil may well be the coming theme of international history and that it will likely replace the long historical force of state nationalism.

African American religious leaders are at the forefront of this new interpretation. They understand the difficulties of their struggle; they have been leading their flocks since the first black church was founded in Cleveland in 1833. They have preached to their congregations in modest storefront churches as well as in larger surroundings, in architectural landmarks known for their middle- and upper-class congregations. The members of their congregations have sought them out for comfort, solace, hope, and empowerment. Indeed, many African Americans have overcome the obstacles of racial prejudice and have become members of the American middle class, even moving to the suburbs.

The photographs in this book, then, while focusing on the African American churches of Cleveland, reflect the universal themes of the struggle for empowerment, the need for comfort and guidance, and the need for mutual support common to all people. The religious leaders pictured here try to help lead their congregations and all of American society toward a transcendent plateau that will improve their lives.

Notes

1. Gary Orfield and Susan E. Eaton et al., *Dismantling Desegregation: The Great Reversal of Brown v. Board of Education* (Boston: New Press, 1997), 11.

2. Dennis W. Keating, forthcoming.

LIST OF CHURCHES

The following churches participated in this project, granting me permission to photograph their property and parishioners over the period 2003–7. They are listed here alphabetically.

Antioch Baptist Church
8869 Cedar Avenue, Cleveland

Bethany Baptist Church
East 105th & Hampden, Cleveland

Calvary Hill Missionary Baptist Church
E. 103rd Street, Cleveland

Cleveland Church of Christ,
Citadel of Hope Ministries
1035 E. 105th Street, Cleveland

Cory United Methodist Church
1117 East 105th Street, Cleveland

Eaglewing Missionary Baptist Church
1260 East 167th Street, Cleveland

Ebenezer Assembly of Christ
15209 Florida Avenue, Cleveland

Glenville Seventh-Day Adventist Church
737 E. 105th Street, Cleveland

The Greater Abyssinia Baptist Church
1161 E. 105th Street, Cleveland

Greater New Canaan Baptist Church
8324 Cedar Avenue, Cleveland

Harvest Baptist Church
3649 East 93rd Street, Cleveland

Holy Trinity Baptist Church
3808 E. 131st Street, Cleveland

Huey Harris Ministry

Live Ministries/Church of Recovery (Manna House)
8019 Cedar Avenue, Cleveland

Living Word of the Apostolic Faith Church
9320 Canton Avenue, Cleveland

Mt. Haven Baptist Church
3484 Martin Luther King Drive, Cleveland

Mt. Lebanon/Balm in Gilead Missionary Baptist Church
10820 Frank Avenue, Cleveland

Mt. Sinai Baptist Church
7510 Woodland Avenue, Cleveland

Mt. Zion Church
1 Mt. Zion Circle, Oakwood Village

New Jerusalem Church of God in Christ
952–956 E. 105th Street, Cleveland

New Revelation Baptist Church
8323 Wodland Avenue, Cleveland

Olivet Institutional Baptist Church
8712–14 Quincy Avenue, Cleveland

Pentecostal Church of Christ
10515 Chester Avenue, Cleveland

Shiloh Baptist Church
55 Scovill, Cleveland

St. Adalbert Roman Catholic Church
22345 E. 83rd Street, Cleveland

St. Andrews Episcopal Church
2171 E. 49th Street, Cleveland

St. James AME Church
8401 Cedar Avenue, Cleveland

St. John AME Church
2261 E. 40th Street, Cleveland

St. Paul AME Zion Church
2393 East 55th Street, Cleveland

Tent of Fire / God's House of Prayer and
Deliverance Holy Church
Woodland Avenue, Cleveland

Triedstone Baptist Church
3782 Community College Avenue, Cleveland

Windermere United Methodist Church
14035 Euclid Avenue, East Cleveland